The MURDER *of the* JEWS *in* LATVIA

1941–1945

BERNHARD PRESS

Translated from the German by Laimdota Mazzarins

NORTHWESTERN UNIVERSITY PRESS

Evanston, Illinois

Northwestern University Press
Evanston, Illinois 60208-4210

Printed in the United States of America

ISBN 0-8101-1728-2 (cloth)
ISBN 0-8101-1729-0 (paper)

Library of Congress Cataloging-in-Publication Data

Press, Bernhard.
[Judenmord in Lettland. English]
The murder of the Jews in Latvia, 1941–1945
p. cm.
Translation of Judenmord in Lettland.
Includes bibliographical references (p.) and index.
ISBN 0-8101-1728-2 (cloth)—ISBN 0-8101-1729-0 (pbk.)
1. Jews—Persecutions—Latvia—Råga. 2. Holocaust, Jewish (1939–1945)—Latvia—Råga—Personal narratives. 3. Press, Bernhard. 4. Råga (Latvia)—Ethnic relations. 5. Holocaust, Jewish (1939–1945)—Latvia. 6. Latvia—Ethnic relations. I. Title.

DS135.L32 R54713 2000
940.53′18′094796—dc21

00-20366

The paper used in this publication meets the minimum requirements of the American National Standard for Information Sciences—Permanence of Paper for Printed Library Materials, ANSI Z39.48-1984.

The Murder of the Jews in Latvia, 1941–1945

A human being is dead only when the memory of him has also died.

—Talmud

Contents

THE SURVIVORS

Preface to the English Edition

This book was conceived as a memorial to all of the Jews who perished on Latvian soil at the hands of murderers—German killers and their Latvian accomplices—during World War II. Originally written in German and now translated into English, it addresses itself to a wider audience, at the risk of not being properly understood, not only because of the sheer geographical distance of the country involved but also because of the monstrosity of events that may be hard to grasp.

In western Europe the emancipation of the Jews resulted in their attainment of the status of citizens in their own right in the nineteenth and twentieth centuries. But such was not the case in eastern Europe, where they remained second-rate citizens, although in fact the constitutions of those countries granted them all civic rights—but only on paper.

Such was also the case in Latvia, my native country, where since my early childhood I felt the glass wall of anti-Semitism separating us Jews from the Latvian majority of the population. In Latvia during the 1920s, that is, in the years after the founding of the Republic, anti-Semitism was nonaggressive. It mainly consisted of preventing us Jews from competing with Latvians on an equal basis in everyday life. A Jew was forever excluded from employment by the government, be it a job in the army, on the railway, in a state hospital, or in the police force.

In the 1930s, this dormant anti-Semitism was heated up by the rabid anti-Semitism spreading from Germany into the Baltic states, as well as by the accession to power of the dictator Karlis Ulmanis. Dormant anti-Semitism now erupted into overt hate. Jewish activities were gradually restricted and enterprises owned by Jews were "nationalized," that is, they passed into the hands of the government or into those of Latvian merchants.

When Hitler's armies crossed into the Baltic states in the course of their attack on the USSR in the summer of 1941, the final transformation of anti-Semitism took place. What had formerly been hatred and contempt changed into pogroms and massacres of us Jews, who had become fair game.

A large part of the population was immediately willing to collaborate with the German execution squads, while those Latvians who did not participate in the murder of their Jewish compatriots watched indifferently or with exultation as their friends and neighbors were driven to their graves. Surprisingly enough, that sector of a people which as a rule is its most advanced one, that is, the intelligentsia, proved to be its most regressive one in Latvia. Latvian intellectuals—parliamentarians, the clergy, university circles—remained mute in the face of murders committed before their very eyes. Students took part in shootings. All over the country, numerous journalists nourished their readers daily with anti-Semitic tales of a conspiracy of international Jewry that aspired to world domination.

Within half a year nearly the entire Jewish population of Latvia—about 75,000 souls—was slaughtered, and in the course of the war years another 100,000 Jews from all over Europe were deported to Latvia and murdered on Latvian soil. The Lithuanians acted in a similar, though not quite so atrocious, manner.

What made the Germans choose Latvia as a slaughterhouse and the Latvians as their fellow executioners is hard to tell. But history showed that their calculations were correct, though no digging into Latvian history, folklore, or relevant documents can reveal the roots of their bloodthirsty anti-Semitism.

What anguish and fear filled the hearts of innocent men, women, and children when they were marched off to the sites of their execution, we will never know.

For the historian, the story of the Holocaust remains forever an enumeration of official letters, commands to army and SS units, and statistics about the number of the dead in mass graves. For the survivors, it is the history of the utter destruction of their world and the deaths of their closest relatives, friends, and neighbors. And it brings with it questions that torment one for a lifetime: What did they feel when they looked into the eyes of death? Was their death quick and painless or long and agonizing? These are questions that cannot be answered.

It was G. Reitlinger who forty-five years ago wrote in his book *The Final Solution: Hitler's Attempt to Exterminate the Jews of Europe, 1939–1945* the following significant lines:

> The savagery of the Lithuanian and Latvian gangs who carried out the pogroms, coupled with the indifference of nearly the entire population towards the more scientific extermination practised by the Germans, must have given an unusual degree of satisfaction to Hitler and his circle. But to those who in pre-war days had attributed an almost Scandinavian respectability to the Baltic republics, the news of the massacres that leaked through was barely credible.[1]

The veracity of the events described in this book was confirmed to a certain extent by recent happenings in Latvia when the country, after breaking away from the USSR in 1990, regained its independence for the second time in this century. Almost within twenty-four hours, laws were passed to ensure that only persons of Latvian descent who could read and write Latvian could become Latvian citizens. The rest of the inhabitants were turned into an outlawed rabble without citizen status. Consequently, they had no civil rights and were also fired from their jobs. Because 50 percent of the inhabitants of Latvia were not native Latvians but came from various parts of the former USSR, half the population of Latvia had overnight become stateless and lacked valid identification papers. They were outlaws.

Yesterday's friends and neighbors were now regarded by Latvians as enemies who had occupied Latvia for fifty years and now had to pay the bill, deserving to be treated like underdogs. The Latvians were overwhelmed by unjustified hate, with intellectuals infecting each other with chauvinistic feelings. Attempts to soberly discuss these problems with them failed immediately, with the Latvians flying into a rage and declaring that all "migrants"—their name for all non-Latvians—on Latvian soil should clear out of their country at once. It made no difference to them that these so-called migrants had been living peacefully on Latvian soil for half a century, that many of them had been born there and regarded Latvia as their homeland. But for the lack of bloodshed, these events closely resembled those we had witnessed when Hitler's army invaded Latvia in 1941. Only this time we, the Jews, were not the victims.

History had repeated itself.

The Murder of the Jews in Latvia, 1941–1945

Preface

A person who dies continues to live in the memory of his or her relatives, friends, and acquaintances. But when the victims of the Holocaust died, the people nearest and dearest to them died with them; their entire social world was destroyed. Nobody remained in whose memory they could have gone on living. According to the saying in the Talmud that a human being is dead only when the memory of him has also died, most of the victims of the Holocaust are dead.

This book arose from my wish to at least recall a few names into the minds of its readers, so as to save the bearers of these names from the final death of being forgotten. The book is also intended to be an expression of the survivors' highest esteem for those who saved their lives, to whom they owe a debt of gratitude that can never be repaid.

We, the surviving Jews of Latvia, have not forgotten either the goodness shown to us or the evil done to us. It was our own fellow citizens who treacherously dealt us the first deathblow.

May this book remind its readers of Shakespeare's words: "The evil that men do lives after them."

The notes made by my father, Oskar Press, my own memories, and conversations with friends in Riga, Berlin, Stockholm, Brussels, and Israel are the basis of this book. In addition, as I wrote I drew support from the books written about the Riga ghetto by J. Katz, M. Kaufmann, G. Schneider, H. Sherman, and J. Wolff. The other sources I used have been listed in the bibliography. For their help and positive criticism, I thank my conversation partners I. Hait-Wolpert, M. Klaus-Goldberg, L. E., Ph. Israelson, C. Rudzitis, and all the others who helped me with their advice, without whom this book would never have been finished.

For the existence of this edition, I have to thank above all Professor Wolfgang Benz, who proposed the inclusion of this volume in the series Dokumente—Texte—Materialien (Documents—Texts—Reference Materials) published by the Center for Research on Anti-Semitism of the Technical University of Berlin. My sincere respect goes to him and to Dr. Juliane Wetzel, who edited the text.

Bernhard Press
Berlin, June 1995

THE DEAD

I

On the History of the Jews in Latvia

Before World War II Latvia, our homeland, with its capital city of Riga, was a widely known center of Jewish life and Jewish culture—of which nothing has remained except the blood-soaked earth and the memory. When we let our thoughts roam back into the past, and even today, more than half a century after the years of persecution and destruction, when we think back, full of pain, of all we have lost, the people nearest and dearest to us, our friends—in short, the whole world we lived in—are we not forced to ask whether we are indulging in illusion if it seems to us that the world of yesterday was warmer and more beautiful than the world of today? Is the reason we see the past in such a rosy light perhaps the fact that in those days we ourselves were young?

But no! Even those who at that time were members of the older generation agree that life in the Baltic states between the two world wars was indeed characterized by a special peace and serenity. There were many reasons for this. The Baltic states were agrarian countries with small but wealthy trading cities which had as yet been scarcely touched by industrialization; this gave life a rural-bourgeois and patriarchal character, while at the same time the intellectual culture of the upper class came into full bloom. Social problems did not have the same harshness here as in the countries of the West.

The Baltic states have a turbulent history. Baltic culture, overlaid with German culture since the twelfth century by merchants and missionaries, had developed its own German-Baltic texture over the centuries through the interweaving of its own way of life with those of neighboring peoples, primarily the Scandinavians, Poles, and Russians. Not only did Baltic culture reach a high point in its homeland—here stood the university founded in Dorpat (Tartu) in 1632 by King Gustav II Adolf of Sweden, which was closed in 1710 but reopened by Czar Alexander I in 1802—but its representatives also made an impact on world history. The Baltic states produced statesmen such as Duke Jacob of Kurzeme (Kurland), who founded colonies in Gambia in West Africa and on Tobago in the Lesser Antilles, and Duke E. J. Byron, who exerted considerable influence on the policies of the Russian court in the second half of the eighteenth century.

The Baltic states also produced world-class scientists such as K. E. von Baer, the founder of modern embryology, the surgeon Ernst von Bergmann, and the Nobel laureate Wilhelm Ostwald, the father of organic chemistry. Johann Gottlob von Herder also worked in Riga at the beginning of his career. Here the Latvian J. Rainis created immortal masterpieces of poetry, which, because they were written in Latvian, are unfortunately not accessible to a wider circle of readers. The Baltic-German publicist G. Merkel contributed substantially, through his pamphlet "The Latvians" (1796), to the abolition of serfdom in the Baltic states (in 1817 and 1819), which subsequently led to the emancipation of all the serfs throughout Russia in 1861.

Intellectual life in the Baltic states under Czarist Russia and later in the free democratic republics after World War I created a milieu in which people could develop in a multitude of ways. Before World War II Riga had only slightly more than 300,000 inhabitants, but before World War I, when the Baltic states were still part of Russia, it had a population of half a million, making it Russia's fifth-largest city, after Petersburg, Moscow, Kiev, and Warsaw.

Jews are first mentioned in a document in Livland in 1536. Their emancipation began in Russia under Czar Nicholas I, almost one hundred years later than in Western Europe; this was a consequence of the backwardness of Czarist Russia. The Russian Jews had an upper class that grew rapidly in the nineteenth and twentieth centuries; this was due not only to their thirst for knowledge after centuries of living without rights, but also to the restrictions imposed on them. For example, they could live and acquire land only in a certain area, the so-called pale of settlement.

Later on, there were restrictions that prevented the normal development of the Jews in Latvia as well. For this reason, in Czarist Russia and the Latvian Republic, only a very few Jews held positions where they received a state salary. Only after the USSR's annexation of the Republic of Latvia in 1940 did Jews as a group gain access to positions in the civil service for the first time (for a more detailed account see chapter 2). The pendulum swung back after World War II, when a state-controlled anti-Semitism began to spread throughout the USSR and Jews were gradually forced out of their positions. Under these circumstances, the extent to which an individual Jew was able to develop his or her abilities depended to a large extent on the political situation of the Jews in the different historical periods.

The culture of the Jewish upper class changed in character in the course of the nineteenth and twentieth centuries. Initially it was primarily a religious-philosophical and to some extent also a musical culture, but soon, following the German-Baltic and Russian cultures, it became an internationally oriented bourgeois one, only to transform itself, with the flowering of Zionist ideals, into a national or religious-national culture.

After the foundation of the democratic Republic of Latvia, Riga, where 47 percent of Latvian Jews lived, became the political, cultural, and social center of the Latvian Jews. The aforementioned restrictions on the Jews' choice of profession in Czarist Russia, the lack of access to educational institutions and state enterprises in the newly founded Latvia, and anti-Semitism, which was covert in some periods and overt in others, led to uneven development within the upper class itself. Thus, for example, before the outbreak of World War I almost all the dentists and 20 percent of the doctors in Riga were Jews. The nearly complete absence of Jews in the Latvian civil service led to the circumstance that there were numerous highly educated Jewish academics but only a very few who held a high academic rank.

For the aforementioned reason there were practically no farmers among the Jews; however, there were numerous craftspeople, shoemakers, plumbers, and tailors. There were many merchants with small businesses and a limited number of affluent merchants with large businesses. Many academics had studied in Dorpat (Tartu), others at Russian universities, some in Germany, Austria, Italy, or Switzerland. The *numerus clausus*, or restricted entry, to the Faculty of Medicine of the University of Latvia also caused many to study abroad. The number of excellent musicians was great, but only a very few of them had positions in which they received a state salary.

Most of the Jews of Latvia were religious; they observed the Sabbath more or less strictly and celebrated their festivals—a right explicitly guaranteed to them by the constitution of the Republic. Since the end of the nineteenth century, the greatest influence was exerted by three exceptional personalities: Joseph Rozin and Meir Simha Ha Kohen, both of whom worked in Daugavpils (Dünaburg or Dvinsk), and Abraham Isaak Kook (Kuk).

Joseph Rozin was born in Rogatshov in the Gomel district and attracted public attention even as a child; at the age of thirteen he knew the Talmud by heart. In later years he was able to quote from memory the Babylonian and the Jerusalem Talmud, as well as the entire Tannaic and Amoraic literature. In fact he was able to put on paper his famous interpretations of the Talmud, which often diverged from the traditional ones, and other writings without ever having to refer to the relevant works. Known as the "Rabbi of Rogatshov," he was a man of great wisdom and an uncontested authority on religious questions for the entire Jewish world. Of imposing appearance and seemingly limitless learning, he was nonetheless a modest man who was loved and admired by his Hasidic community in Daugavpils, which he had looked after since 1889. He died in 1936. His wife was still living when the Germans occupied the city in 1941. A Russian helped her and Rabbi Fuchs of Daugavpils to escape the massacre of the Jews and brought her to Braslava on the Polish border. There both of them later died.

Meir Simha Ha Kohen, born in 1843 in Daugavpils, was the rabbi of that city for forty years. His treatises on Maimonides earned him worldwide renown. Over the years he became an outstanding expert and commentator on the Talmud. His works threw new light on the interpretation of this work and testified to the depth of his thought and his penetrating logic. His wisdom and goodness had already made him famous by the end of the last century, and in 1906 the leaders of the Jewish community of Jerusalem offered him the post of rabbi there. Meir Simha declined this offer after the Daugavpils community wrote a letter to the Jerusalem community that revealed how attached its members were to him and what he meant to them. They wrote that

> not only would this, God forbid, destroy us, but it would destroy the entire Diaspora. After all, he is the authority who can give an answer to every person who wants to know something about God's word.

During World War I, as German troops were about to occupy Daugavpils, nearly the entire Jewish population of the city fled to Russia. But some Jewish citizens remained behind, which caused Rabbi Meir Simha to stay as well, because he believed he could not abandon members of his community. He died in 1926.

Abraham Isaac Kook (Kuk) was a man who had an extremely unusual worldview for a rabbi schooled in the nineteenth century. Born in Griva, near Daugavpils, he was already the rabbi of Zaumele at the age of twenty-five. In 1895 he became the rabbi of Bauska and in 1904 the rabbi of Jaffa. During World War I he was the rabbi of a community in London, and after the end of the war he became the chief rabbi of Jerusalem. Rabbi Kook was a supporter of Zionism, which led to antagonism between him and the rabbinate. He felt that the irreligion of the younger generation showed that religious thought had lagged behind the scientific thought of our age and called for a renewal of Jewish religious experience. He conceived of a yeshiva, or school of the Talmud, which would also study the Bible and would not exclude worldly problems from its curriculum. In 1924 he succeeded in founding a school of this sort. Rabbi Kook died in 1935 and was borne to his grave in Jerusalem accompanied by an enormous crowd.

At the beginning of the twentieth century, new movements arose in the life of the Jews of Russia, and thus also on the territory of the future Latvia—socialism, nationalism, and Zionism. They were led by men who were the first to take up the struggle for Jewish rights in Czarist Russia and who later exerted great influence on the Jewish population of the Republic of Latvia. Among the spiritual leaders of the Jews of Latvia were Mordechai Dubin, Rabbi Mordechai Nurock, the jurists Professor Paul Mintz and Professor Mattatyahu Laserson, the lawyers O. Grusenberg and M. Schatz-Anin, and Noah Meisel.

These were men who had risen to leading positions on their own merits rather than thanks to external circumstances such as personal wealth or membership in a political party. Their influence was due solely to the fact that they had been actively committed for years and decades to the Jewish cause. Inspired by the wish to see the Jews become a people with the same rights as the other peoples of the world, they struggled for the religious and political rights and cultural development of their people. Their involvement in the Jewish cause was thoroughly selfless. Recognition of this selflessness and the greatness of these men was the reason why people rallied around them.

Mordechai Dubin was the head of the Jewish community of Riga and leader of the Agudat Israel, an Orthodox movement that actively supported the national aspirations of the Jews. For years he was their representative in the Latvian parliament, an adroit politician and at the same time a very clever, energetic, and helpful human being. He was on good terms with influential Latvian circles, including even the dictator Ulmanis, and he used his connections to benefit the community. It was thanks to him that during the Nazi regime before World War II many of the refugees from Germany and Austria found refuge in Latvia, and thanks to his efforts many of them even received entry visas into the United States.

Toward the end of the 1920s, when the rabbi of Lubavitch, J. I. Schneerson, leader of the religious Jews of the USSR and head of a branch of Hasidism known as the Habad, was arrested in the USSR, leading Jewish figures throughout the world made efforts to get him released. Here too Mordechai Dubin played an outstanding role. It was thanks to his efforts that the rabbi did in fact receive an exit visa from the USSR. Rabbi Schneerson lived until 1934 in Riga and founded new Habad centers there and throughout the rest of the world; later on he resettled in Poland.

Mordechai Dubin was arrested in 1940 by the Soviet authorities, deported, and released in 1942. After the war he returned to Riga, where the local press attacked him violently, of course on orders from above. Thereupon he was once again arrested and deported in 1948. He died in 1956 in a concentration camp near Moscow.[1]

During the war Dubin's son and his secretary Golovchin were initially in the Riga ghetto. In 1944 both of them were deported to Germany and in the spring of 1945 they were working in the Polte factory near Magdeburg. Golovchin died there. M. Kaufmann, the author of the book *Die Vernichtung der Juden Lettlands* (*The Destruction of the Jews of Latvia*), saw young Dubin for the last time as the prisoners were on their march from the Magdeburg camp to the camp in Sachsenhausen.

Rabbi Nurock was the leader of the religious Zionists, a man who had rendered outstanding service in Czarist Russia to the Jews of the Baltic states. Thanks to his energetic activity, the Czarist government passed a decree permitting a larger number of Jews to settle in Kurzeme (Kurland) and Riga than had previously been planned, even though this region lay outside the pale of Jewish settlement. Rabbi Nurock was one of the founders of the Jewish World Congress and was active in the religious Zionist Mizrachi movement. In 1941 he was arrested by the Russians and deported. His wife and two sons stayed behind in Riga and died there during the war. In 1945 Rabbi Nurock emigrated to Palestine, where he later became a member of the Knesset. In 1952 he became postmaster general of Israel.

Professor Paul Mintz, born in Daugavpils, was a member of the first Latvian government and became a professor of criminology at the University of Latvia. The Latvian Penal Code was formulated under his direction. Moreover, he rendered outstanding service on behalf of the rights of the Jews of Latvia and their national autonomy. He was chairman of the Jewish National Party, founded the Society to Promote the Culture of the Jews of Russia, and was also a member of the Jewish Agency. In 1941 he was, like so many other Jews, arrested by the KGB (then still known as the NKWD) and deported to Siberia; he died in the winter of 1941–42 in the Tajshet concentration camp.

The jurist, historian, and Zionist professor Mattatyahu Laserson played a considerable role in the political life of the Jews of Latvia. He was a Member of Parliament for the Socialist Zionist Party and taught law at the Jewish Commercial College. After the Ulmanis coup of 1934 he was imprisoned for a time and subsequently emigrated to Palestine. From there he later went to the United States, where he became an instructor at Columbia University. At the same time, he headed the legal division of the Institute for Jewish Issues.

Another eminent jurist, probably the best-known Jewish lawyer of the century, O. Grusenberg, lived in Riga from 1926 to 1932. In Russia he had successfully defended the famous writers V. Korolenko and M. Gorky and the politician P. Milyukov against political persecution by the Czarist government. But he celebrated his greatest triumph in 1913 in the so-called Beiliss trial, which attracted the attention of the entire world, when he attained the release of the Jew Beiliss, who had been accused of ritual murder. Highly esteemed because of his intellect, education, and experience, Grusenberg assumed a central position among the lawyers in Riga. He took part in the political life of the Jewish community, was active in the Zionist movement, and helped found the expanded Jewish Agency, becoming a member of its executive board. After 1936 he resettled in France.

The lawyer and publicist M. Schatz-Anin, who was born in Jaunjelgava (Friedrichstadt) and settled in Riga, was one of the founders of the United Jewish Workers' Party. He was a member of the illegal Communist Party of Latvia, and after the annexation of the Republic by the USSR he was appointed professor at the University of Latvia.

The Jewish Workers' Party, the Bund, was represented in the Latvian parliament by Dr. Noah Meisel, who worked in the Department of Health. The party had a relatively small degree of influence on Jewish public life. Like so many other leading Jewish and non-Jewish politicians, Dr. Meisel was arrested by the Soviet regime in 1940 and deported to the far north of Russia, where he died in 1956.

At the beginning of the 1920s the waves of the Zionist movement lapped higher and higher in Latvia. This was perceived by no less a personality than V. Jabotinsky, the highly gifted journalist, publicist, and active, fiery defender of Zionist ideas, who gave a lecture to this effect on December 17, 1923, in Riga. In 1925 he was to found a new Zionist party, the Zionist Revisionist Party.

A special position was occupied in Riga by the world-renowned historian Professor Simon Dubnow. Born in White Russia, he had lived and worked in Russia until 1922 and then gone to Berlin, where he lived until 1933. The Nazis' seizure of power caused him to emigrate to Latvia, where he settled in Riga. Professor Dubnow had already made a name for himself in Czarist Russia through his numerous works on the history of the Jews and of Hasidism. Between 1916 and 1920 he published a history of the Jews of Russia and Poland in three volumes. Between 1925 and 1929 his history of the Jewish people appeared in ten volumes, and in 1941 he added one more volume in order to update his work to include the current state of affairs.

From 1930 to 1932 he compiled his studies of Hasidism, pursued over many years, into a history of this sect. Dubnow, who had devoted his entire life to the study of Jewish history, had his own ideas about the peculiar nature of the Jews' historical development. For example, he believed that the Jews had already reached the highest stage of development a people can attain, namely that of a spiritual people. Concerning the future of the Jews, he believed the Jews had to strive for national and cultural autonomy in the states in which they lived, and that these autonomous communities, this network, should be subject to a general Jewish council. His worldview prevented him from being either a Zionist or an anti-Zionist, although in the last years of his life he rather leaned toward Zionism. He did not see Jewish history as an unceasing tragedy; instead, he was of the opinion that the "extraterritoriality" of the Jews was a challenge that proved their great strength as a spiritual nation.

Professor Dubnow had always been a central figure in Jewish intellectual life, and he continued to be one in Riga. He was revered because of his immense historical knowledge, and men of the most varied political views often asked him for his interpretation of the turbulent events of the prewar years. On this subject he made the following remarks:

> Future historians will have a very difficult task, for who knows how much historical material will be destroyed through the annihilation of the largest Jewish centers. Perhaps this will be the most tragic part of Jewish history after the destruction of the Second Temple. It is possible that the number of victims will be so great that for a long time we will no longer be able to think clearly; nonetheless, we should avoid panicking. A historian who reads the pages of Jewish history will realize the following fact: that the deepest meaning of our history is hope, which over and over becomes a reality, because tyrants will always drown in their own blood. I am convinced that Germany will be destroyed, just as strongly as I am convinced that snow melts in the springtime. Perhaps the Jewish communities in Europe will be destroyed for years, but we still have a powerful Jewish community in the United States of North America, in the Latin American and in the English-speaking countries. Possibly Palestine will experience a great crisis in the coming years, but I hope that the settlements there will grow and flourish. We need Palestine, even the

> non-Zionists need it, for our continued existence. In the English-speaking countries we must commit ourselves to the English language, but we must not neglect Yiddish. American Judaism will have to grow spiritually in order to understand the great task that fate has laid upon it.[2]

Funding from the state and local authorities was not by itself sufficient to develop the cultural life of the minorities of Latvia; moreover, after the coup of May 15, 1934, and the subsequent liquidation of the minorities' cultural autonomy, this funding was withdrawn entirely. For the Jews, up to this time the state had in any case only supported primary and secondary schools with Hebrew or Yiddish as the language of instruction, not those with Russian or German. Thus the Jews, like the other minorities, had always been forced to finance their own schools and cultural life, as well as their social-assistance organizations and medical institutions, from private sources and with donations from foreign organizations such as the American Jewish Joint Distribution Committee. The foundation of the schools was the result of the initiative of the Jewish community and individual idealists who saw their life's purpose in the promotion of their people's intellectual development.

Because of the varied origins of the Jews of Latvia, the mother tongue of some was German, of others Russian, and of many others, especially in the eastern part of the country, Yiddish. Jews whose mother tongue was Latvian were growing up in rural areas and small towns. Most Jews spoke the three national languages: Latvian, German, and Russian. As a rule the members of the upper class also spoke one or two foreign languages as well. Many Jews who intended to emigrate to Palestine wanted their children to learn Ivrit, or modern Hebrew. Consequently there were Jewish schools with German, Russian, Yiddish, or Ivrit as the language of instruction. The director of the Gymnasium, or college-preparatory school, that had Yiddish as its language of instruction, I. Bärs—who had represented the interests of the Jewish Workers' Party as a Bund delegate to the Constitutive Assembly when the Republic of Latvia was founded—was removed from office after the coup of 1934 on the grounds of "political unreliability." His son, the renowned mathematician L. Bärs, lives today in the United States.

The secondary school that had Ivrit as its language of instruction was founded by the Association for the Promotion of Science and Art, whose chairman was the physician Dr. H. Wassermann. In 1941 Wasserman was deported by the KGB, and in 1947, just after returning from exile, he was deported a second time.

The engineer J. Landau was the founder and director of the school that had Russian as its language of instruction; he also represented Jewish interests at the Ministry of Education in the department for minorities. The Yeshiva, or Jewish religious academy, was headed by Chief Rabbi M. M. Sack, who was killed in the Riga ghetto during the war.

Although the Jews of Riga spoke German almost without exception, there was no Jewish newspaper in German. This was because most of the German-speaking Jews were readers of the *Rigasche Rundschau* (*Riga Panorama*), which had been published by Germans since the previous century. A Jewish daily newspaper in German, the *Europa-Ost* (*Europe East*) started to be published only after National Socialist tendencies had become increasingly evident in the German press. The owners of the large and influential Russian newspapers *Sevodnya* (*Today*) and *Sevodnya Vetsherom* (*This Evening*) were J. Brahms and the surgeon B. Pollack; their editor in chief was M. Milrud. These newspapers had a large Russian and Jewish circle of readers. They had a highly qualified staff and correspondents throughout the country and abroad, including the well-known journalist Henri Gris, and they published articles by prominent Jewish and Russian publicists. *Frimorgn* (*Early Morning*) was a Yiddish newspaper of smaller size, but it also had a considerable number of readers. Its publisher was the socially oriented politician and publicist J. Z. W. Latzky-Bartholdy, who also published a second daily newspaper in Yiddish, *Das Folk* (*The People*). One of the newspapers also had a satirical supplement, *Der Letz* (*The Jester*). One of the few Jewish writers of Latvia, Mark Rasumny, wrote in Yiddish and made a name for himself as a poet and prose writer. His works were published in the USSR even after World War II.

Physicians occupied a prominent position in the Jewish upper class. This was due not only to their education but primarily to the fact that they simply outnumbered the academics in other fields, the architects, pharmacists, and lawyers. Thus there were "medical clans" in which all the male family members were doctors, some of them already in the second generation and a few even in the third generation. The Jewish doctors' level of knowledge and their ethical commitment to their profession and patients were high. So it was no wonder that the patients of Jewish doctors included many Germans and Latvians. Most Jewish doctors were internists and gathered around the highly respected Dr. V. Kretzer, whereas Professor W. Mintz, who had been one of the leading surgeons of Russia before World War I, was the definitive authority for the younger generation of Jewish surgeons.

Both Dr. Kretzer and Professor Mintz worked at the Jewish Hospital, Bikkur Cholim, which had a very good reputation in the city. For many years the hospital director was Dr. I. Joffe, a man of outstanding intelligence and an efficient organizer. He died of lung cancer in the ghetto in the fall of 1941.

His son, M. Joffe, was a heart specialist. In 1940, after the Republic of Latvia was annexed by the USSR, he became the deputy director of the City Health Department; later on he became the deputy people's commissar (minister) of health, a position he held both before and after World War II. Typically, in the USSR too, M. Joffe, as a Jew, could be only a deputy minister, not a minister.

Many excellent surgeons were produced by the school of Professor Mintz; after World War II some of them became instructors at the Medical Institute of Riga and played a significant role in the medical life of the Republic. They included the surgeons Professor M. Dubinski, Professor L. Hnoch, and Professor H. Schneider, as well as Assistant Professor V. Goldberg, a urologist. Dr. Kretzer also had many brilliant students; one of them, Professor S. Cherfass, taught for many years at the Medical Institute of Riga. Another equally outstanding student, Dr. H. Fonarev, lives today in Israel.

For the city's gynecologists the central institution was the Women's Hospital, or Linas Hazedek. It was headed by the experienced and highly esteemed gynecologist Dr. B. Herzfeld. During the 1930s the gynecologist Dr. Siegbert Joseph, formerly of the Moabit Hospital in Berlin, also worked there after fleeing to Latvia from Germany. Dr. Herzfeld died of a heart attack shortly before the war. His wife was killed in the Riga ghetto, while her younger son, who had been with her in the ghetto, managed to survive. The older son fled to Russia when the war broke out, and upon his return after the war he became one of the most successful and respected surgeons in the Latvian Republic.

Jewish doctors also distinguished themselves in the field of psychiatry. For example, one of the best-known psychiatric clinics of Czarist Russia, located in Atgasen near Riga, was founded in 1898 by Dr. M. Schönfeld. The hospital's archives still include the medical history of the highly talented Russian painter M. Vrubel, who was a patient at the clinic at the turn of the century. After World War I the clinic was directed by Dr. A. Schönfeld, the founder's son.

Bikkur Cholim and Linas Hazedek were financed by the foundations of the Jewish merchants and the funds granted to them by the American Jewish Joint Distribution Committee. As in Jewish communities throughout the world, in Riga too the poor received assistance from the Chevra Kaddisha and the Malbische Arumim, which received voluntary donations from the community.

The Jewish doctors, like their German, Russian, and Latvian colleagues, met one another at their associations, where they attended lectures on the latest advances in medicine and reports on interesting cases and on specialized training courses abroad that had been attended by one or another of them. But the interests of many doctors were by no means limited to their medical specialties. For example, at the end of the nineteenth century Dr. I. Brennsohn published a two-volume biographical lexicon on the physicians of Livland and Kurland which became a standard reference work on the history of medicine in the Baltic states. I. Joffe, already mentioned as the director of Bikkur Cholim, conducted archival research on the history of the Jews of Kurzeme.

A renowned Jewish personality was Professor M. Centnerszwer, a student of W. Ostwald and P. Walden, who occupied the chair of chemistry at the University of Latvia. However, he kept a distance from the Jewish life of the city. His later life will be dealt with further on.

Music was played in a great variety of circles; there were collectors of books, porcelain, and paintings; and there were aesthetes who were attracted to philosophy, literature, and linguistics. Typically, the name of the oldest Jewish student fraternity in the Baltic states, Limuwia, founded in Dorpat at the turn of the century, was an abbreviation for Literarisch-Musikalisch-Wissenschaftlicher Verein (Literary-Musical-Scientific Association).

Riga was a city with a long musical tradition, and there were many musically gifted Jews there, as well as in the rest of Latvia. In Czarist Russia, two Jewish singers from Riga were well known; later on they became internationally famous. One was the baritone Joseph Schwarz, who sang at the Riga Opera before World War I and became one of the stars of the Berlin State Opera. He died in Berlin in 1926 and was buried in the Jewish cemetery in Berlin-Weißensee. His mausoleum bears the inscription, "Lord, you are my refuge for ever and ever." These words took on a literal meaning for many Jews, because the mausoleum served many of them as a refuge during the period of Nazi terror. The second singer was the world-famous tenor Hermann Jadlowker, who was born in Riga, studied in Vienna, and sang at the Berlin Royal Court Opera as a Royal Chamber Singer for many years until 1919. Later on he sang at the Metropolitan Opera in New York. In the late 1920s he returned to Riga; there he became a cantor and gave voice lessons at the Conservatory. He emigrated to Palestine before the start of World War II and died in Tel Aviv in 1953.

Another native of Riga was the composer and music historian S. Rosowski, a student of Rimsky-Korsakov, Glazunov, and Liadov. In 1920 he founded the Jewish Conservatory in Riga. He emigrated to Palestine in 1925 and later taught at the Institute for Cantors of the Jewish Theological Seminary in New York. His work on the vocal performance of the Bible, *The Cantillation of the Bible,* made him very well known.

The renowned conductor and composer G. Fitelberg was born in Daugavpils and initially worked in Petersburg; after World War I he became the conductor of the Polish Symphony Orchestra and rendered outstanding service to musical life in Poland.

A relatively small number of Jewish musicians held state-paid positions in the Republic of Latvia. One of these was Professor A. Metz, a student of L. Auer, the founder of the Russian Violin School. Professor Metz was head of the violin department at the Riga Conservatory. The highly talented violinist S. Raschina, a favorite of Riga concertgoers, was a graduate of his school; the war and the ghetto put an end to her promising career. The aforementioned cardiologist Dr. M.

Joffe had had in addition to his medical education an excellent musical one; he was a good cellist and played for years in the Symphony Orchestra of Riga. Next to him in the orchestra sat his cousin P. Berkowitz, who was also a physician but had preferred the career of a musician to that of a medical doctor. P. Berkowitz also played occasionally in trios and quartets and sometimes performed as a soloist. A few years before World War II he gave a series of successful concerts in Kaliningrad (Königsberg). From the late 1920s on, he lived in Kaunas (Kauen or Kovno), where he had a position in the Symphony Orchestra. During the German occupation he escaped imprisonment by acquiring false papers, learned to do bookkeeping, and managed to make a living as an accountant. After the war he was appointed to a professorship, and during the last twenty years of his life he was dean of the Lithuanian Conservatory in Vilnius (Vilna).

Another one of the few Jewish musicians with a state salary was the violinist J. Jungmann, a student of Professor Metz. He had also studied at the State Academy of Music in Berlin and while there had won the Fritz Kreisler prize twice.

R. Stender, also a student of Professor Metz, was unable to get an appointment in Riga and moved to Lithuania, where he became the concertmaster, conductor of the ballet, and instructor at the Conservatory in Kaunas. He was killed in the Kaunas ghetto. L. Arnoff-Aronsohn, a promising cellist and a student of Piatigorsky, had no permanent position and had to struggle along by giving private lessons. He survived the Riga ghetto and moved later to the United States, where he was employed in the Dallas Symphony Orchestra and was also a professor at the College of Music. Before the war Arnoff-Aronsohn had a small six- or seven-year-old pupil named Chasan who showed a quite extraordinary talent for composition. For this reason his teachers used to call him "the little Mozart." He was killed in the ghetto.

There were outstanding pianists in Riga, but none of them had permanent employment in the democratic Republic of Latvia. Only after Latvia became a Soviet republic did the pianists Maria Salmanovich, L. Schalit, and S. Tager receive positions in the Riga Conservatory. Salmanovich and Tager were both killed in the ghetto. Schalit survived the Riga ghetto and the Stutthof concentration camp, where he, like so many others, was severely abused.

The pianist M. Schur, who occasionally gave concerts with Jungmann and Arnoff-Aronsohn, earned his living as a concert critic, and at the end of the 1930s he emigrated to Sweden. The excellent pianists E. Thal and H. Godes were also unable to find permanent employment in Latvia. Thal struggled along as a sales representative for foreign firms. Both ended up in the ghetto, where Thal lost his life. Godes survived and lives today in the United States. The married couple V. Babin and V. Vronskaya, who performed on two grand pianos, enjoyed great popularity among concertgoers in Riga. Babin was a student of A. Schnabel. They emigrated to England in the late 1930s and later moved to the United States. There he was director of the Aspen Institute in Colorado from 1951 to 1955 and then director of the Institute of Music in Cleveland until his death in 1972.

Jewish singers also found it difficult to make a living. Among them was the baritone J. Joffe, who had begun to make a name for himself in the final years before World War I but had no state-paid position. But he had sung a few times in operas shortly before the war broke out, when Latvia was already a Soviet republic. During the war he fled from the ghetto and lived in hiding with a Latvian family. According to reports, he sang loudly on Christmas Eve or New Year's Eve 1943. His voice attracted the neighbors' attention, and they reported it to the police, whereupon the police searched the house, found Joffe, and arrested him. He died in the Riga Central Jail.

The tenor Schelkan, who was the husband of the aforementioned violinist S. Raschina, and the tenor L. Sachodnik were both given appointments in the opera after the annexation of Latvia. Schelkan survived the ghetto and the concentration camp and managed to get to the United States, where he got a position as a cantor. Sachodnik fled to Russia when the war started and within a short time became very popular there.

M. Alexandrovich, a lyric tenor, did not receive an appointment in Latvia and earned his living as a cantor in Kaunas. He too fled to Russia after the war broke out and had a brilliant career there. Nor did the outstanding singer and teacher R. Ratner have a state-paid position in the Republic of Latvia. She was killed in the Riga ghetto.

A number of world-famous Jewish musicians from abroad spent time in Riga, some of them for several years. One of the most famous was Leo Blech, who after emigrating from Germany became conductor of the National Opera in Riga and gave guest concerts in Moscow which were extraordinarily successful. After the Germans occupied Riga in the summer of 1941 he received permission to emigrate to Sweden with his family. Another famous Jewish conductor, who also led the opera orchestra for a long time in the 1920s, was E. Cooper. Otto Klemperer spent some time in Riga as a guest conductor.

Riga had a very good Jewish theater which frequently traveled abroad to give guest performances. In this troupe, the actor Eines made a name for himself. Several highly gifted Jewish actors such as E. Buntchuk and Astarow were constant performers for many years at the Russian theater. S. Mickoels(-Vovsi), probably the best-known Jewish actor of the USSR, who was already famous before the war, was born in Daugavpils. During the war he was the head of the Jewish Anti-Fascist Committee in the USSR and made passionate appeals to the Jews of the West to support the USSR's war efforts. He was murdered by the KGB in Minsk on January 13, 1948. A. Raikin, also a native of Riga, was another very popular Soviet actor.

Professor M. Vovsi of Moscow, one of the leading internists in the USSR, was a close relative of the aforementioned actor S. Mickoels-Vovsi and was born in Kraslava, near Daugavpils. He was the personal physician of the top Soviet party leaders, and in 1953 he was arrested and accused, together with a group of professors, of having planned to murder leading members of the government, including Stalin. Stalin's death saved their lives. Professor S. Reinberg, author of standard Soviet works in the field of radiology, was born in Riga. The physiologist L. Stern, one of the most outstanding women in medicine in the USSR, was originally from Liepaja (Libau). Although a winner of the Stalin Prize, she was sent to Siberia in 1948 and was not rehabilitated, with the restoration of her full rights, until after Stalin's death in 1954.

There were a relatively small number of Jews in the visual arts in Riga. They included the Ritov brothers, who were respected painters and graphic artists. M. Jo (Joffe) was also a painter and graphic artist, and an excellent designer and interior decorator as well. In 1941 he was sent to Siberia by the KGB, but during the war he managed to get to Moscow, where he worked as an illustrator in a publishing house for Jewish literature. He returned to Riga after the war. In 1951 he was once again arrested and deported. He did not see his homeland again until after Stalin's death.

Jewish young people sought recreation and diversion not only at the theater or at concerts. Those who enjoyed sports joined the Makkabi, Ha-Koah, and B'rit Trumpeldor (Betar) sport clubs; the latter was revisionist in its ideology. In the early 1930s the Jewish sailors of Riga founded the Baltic Yacht Club. The revisionists also owned a sailing vessel, the Theodor Herzl, which served as a training ship for the instruction of Jewish sailors.

In the early 1920s, after World War I and its struggle for its independence from the USSR and Germany, Latvia was impoverished. Its agriculture was backward and its industry underdeveloped. Twenty years later, by the end of the 1930s, before it was engulfed by the USSR, Latvia had become a flourishing agricultural nation with well-developed light industry. Jewish intelligence and hard work had made a not inconsiderable contribution to the nation's prosperity. For example, soon after the foundation of the Latvian state, the banker Friedmann played a significant role in designing the national currency and establishing the state savings and loan bank, which developed later into the State Bank.

With the help of Jewish merchants (J. Mühlmann, A. Schmuljan, A. Sobolevich), the timber industry and the timber export trade developed. Jewish firms were involved in the import of gasoline, coal, and wheat, and thanks to them the country's flax, linen, and textile industries revived (L. and J. Hoff, R. Feldhuhn). Jews were also involved in the confectionery industry, and the popular Elite chocolate factory that exists today in Israel is nothing other than a new incarnation of the Laima chocolate factory in Riga, which its owner, the industrialist I. Fromchenko, sold before the war and rebuilt in Israel.

But there was one thing for which the young republic's prosperity was not sufficient, and that was housing construction. Between the two world wars, when Riga was the capital of the Republic of Latvia, scarcely any new residential buildings were built in the city. Almost all the buildings dated back to the time of the czars. During this period, most of the architects in Riga were Germans, but a few Jewish architects also made a name for themselves, in particular P. Mandelstamm. He designed a number of residential buildings in the old and new parts of Riga, as well as the headquarters of the Jewish Club at the corner of Dzirnavas Street (Mühlenstraße) and A. Upitis Street, which he built together with E. von Trompovski.

Few people know that many of the outstanding Jewish figures in the world were born in Latvia. These include Yeshaya Leibowitz, who was born in 1903 in Riga and has since 1935 been a professor at the University of Jerusalem, where he was active as a biochemist as well as a neurophysiologist. Also born in Riga was Alexander Lipschütz (1883), famous for his pioneering work in the field of experimental oncology. He taught first at the University of Dorpat (Tartu) and then, from 1926 on, at the University of Concepcion (Chile). He revisited his hometown in 1962 on the way to Moscow for the World Cancer Congress. Another native of Latvia was the philosopher and politician Sir Isaiah Berlin (born in 1909), who made a name for himself not only as a scientist but also as the teacher of many generations of students in England and the United States.

Over the years, people's cultural expectations increased. People wanted to live in cultivated homes surrounded by beautiful furniture, good paintings, and valuable books. The local publishing trade, which produced primarily Latvian books, experienced a considerable upswing, so that Latvia's book production eventually took second place in Europe, just behind Denmark. Large bookstores offered the latest Western literature as well as numerous works of local, primarily Latvian, writers.[3] The theaters—Latvian, German, Russian, and Jewish—played to standing-room-only audiences. Moissi and Wüllner performed, and Reinhardt staged *Die Fledermaus.* The concerts given by a steady stream of new soloists from within the country and abroad testified to the Riga public's untiring interest in music. There was hardly a world-class pianist or violinist who had not given a concert in Riga. Galleries invited the public to exhibitions of paintings, and well-stocked museums welcomed visitors. Native philosophers such as Celms or Weintraub gave lectures on problems of epistemology; Oswald Spengler spoke in Riga during the 1920s on the course of development of European history. During the 1930s Max Planck presented new insights into the structure of matter. It should also be mentioned here that Sholem Aleichem made two appearances in Riga before World War I, in 1908 and 1914, and read from his own works, receiving ovations from his ecstatic listeners.

The end of this cultural blossoming came almost abruptly. August 23, 1939, the day the German-Soviet pact was signed, became not only the day on which the fronts of a future war between the USSR and Germany became visible; it also became the day on which the destruction of our homeland's Jewish community began to loom on the horizon. This destruction occurred in two stages. The first stage was the Sovietization of the Baltic states, which resulted in the end of the free development of the national cultures of all the Baltic peoples. Here the Soviet regime's policy toward the Jews was double-edged. On the one hand, the Jews received for the first time the opportunity to enter the civil service; on the other hand, all Jewish schools were closed, as was the Jewish theater, and ownership of the Jewish Club's headquarters passed into the hands of the City Committee, that is, the state. The second stage began on the eve of the war, with the deportation of thousands of Jews together with their Latvian fellow citizens, and ended with our nearly total destruction by the Nazi regime.

There are still Jews in the Baltic states. Some saved themselves by going underground; others returned to their homelands after the war from German and Soviet concentration camps, as well as from places all over the USSR to which they had been deported or to which they had fled. After their return, they became witnesses of the already noted reversal of the USSR's policy toward its Jewish citizens, all of whom were gradually forced out of their positions in the cultural life of the entire country. Jewish names soon disappeared from places where they had once occupied a significant space: among the academics and musicians. Moreover, the Soviet regime denied its Jewish citizens, and of course also the Jews of Soviet Latvia, the right to maintain their own culture and even persecuted them for doing so. But it gradually became evident that the world, and especially the Jewish world, had changed after World War II, for from 1948 on there was a Jewish state—there was Israel. And for the Soviet Jews, who had before that time seemed to be hopelessly imprisoned in the USSR, there was now a refuge. The Jews began to emigrate. At first it was only scattered individuals, then hundreds, and finally tens of thousands. The stream of Jews emigrating from Latvia did not dry up after Latvia once again became a free democratic republic. The main reason is that the Latvian state has made no effort to the present day to include the small Jewish community of Riga (the Jews make up between 1.0 and 1.3 percent of the city's total population) into the cultural and political life of the state. Rather, it regards them as a foreign body. The state hardly cares about the social well-being of its Jewish minority. It seems to be content with the fact that the Jewish community lives on American and German funding. The fact that the Jews are Latvian citizens and have a right to be treated as such is a thought that seems not to have occurred in government circles.

In view of these circumstances, there will not be a rebirth of Jewish culture in Latvia in the foreseeable future. This chapter of Jewish history can be regarded as closed.

2

On the Political Situation of the Jews in Latvia

The tragedy of Latvia's Jews began not with the German invasion in June and July 1941 but much earlier. Certain preconditions for the genesis of this tragedy had already become evident during the first years after the foundation of the Republic of Latvia, though no one could have predicted the consequences at that time.

The Republic of Latvia, founded on November 18, 1918, was a state whose minorities composed about 25 percent of the population. The 94,000 Jews accounted for about 5 percent of the total population and thus constituted the second-largest minority ethnic group, after the more than 200,000 Russians. The Constitution guaranteed to all minorities completely equal rights, cultural autonomy, and freedom of religion. The Jewish citizens of this young, newly founded state, who had previously counted as second- and third-class citizens as long as the territory belonged to Russia, were certainly willing to support the Latvian state, which guaranteed them full civil rights.

But in actuality the state granted us freedom of religion and cultural autonomy without at the same time providing us in full measure with the civil rights guaranteed to us by the Constitution. That could be seen most clearly in the fact that we were de facto almost entirely excluded from all positions in the state civil service:

> In 1925 there were only 21 Jews among 5,291 civil servants, i.e. 0.4%, although Jews made up 5% of the total population. Only one of the 4,316 state-employed policemen in Latvia was a Jew, and when he walked the streets of Riga people ran after him to stare at him. There was not a single Jew in the judicial system, which employed 1,682 civil servants. In the

> postal system there was a total of 2 Jews; in the railway system, 33. All told, the democratic Republic of Latvia employed only about 200 of its ca. 100,000 Jewish citizens.[1]

Thus, the twenty-two-year history of the free Republic of Latvia—in whose foundation and subsequent international recognition the half-Jewish Zigfrids Meierovics played an outstanding role—included only a few people who were exceptions in this regard. Among these few were some figures who have already been mentioned: the jurist P. Mintz, who was a professor at the University of Latvia and served from 1919 to 1921 as state inspector and deputy minister of labor; Professor Centnerszwer, who occupied a tenured chair at the university; the physician Dr. R. Blumenfeld, who for many years headed the city medical service of Riga; and several state-employed musicians. But wherever there were Jewish civil servants, these were very isolated individuals. The rule that applied to Jews in general was that it was no use whatsoever for them to apply for jobs with state-paid salaries.

It is only natural that under these conditions our emotions toward the young republic were ambivalent, and this was to have serious consequences later on. On the one hand, we loved this country in which we had grown up, its forests and lakes, its fields and rivers, the Baltic Sea and the beach of Riga, and we believed there was nothing to compare to it in the whole world. The Latvians with whom we had grown up together, whose mentality and language many of us understood in all their fine points almost as well as our own, were closer to us than any other people. On the other hand, we faced the Latvians' state-supported refusal to regard us as people like themselves—a refusal that metamorphosed over the years into contempt and, later on, hatred. How were we supposed to behave in view of this complex situation, and how were we to make levelheaded decisions after being suddenly pulled into the whirlpool of world history?

It should not remain unmentioned that the social situation of the other minorities—the Germans, Poles, and Russians—was very similar. To be sure, the state did not reject them quite as strongly as it did the Jews, but they too were scarcely represented in the civil service or public life. Was this policy motivated by the fear that these minorities would crowd Latvians out of the professions? To some extent it was.

In any case, this fear certainly existed with regard to the minority candidates who wanted to study medicine. Because of the great number of candidates for the School of Medicine, which could not accept more than sixty to seventy students annually, there was an entrance examination for all candidates. For the Jewish candidates there was—unofficially, of course—a *numerus clausus,* or maximum number of possible acceptances. No matter how well-prepared they were—and they were excellently prepared—no more than one, at most two, of the Jewish candidates were ever accepted in any given year. To receive a license to practice in their Latvian homeland, Jewish doctors who had received their medical degrees abroad had to pass this entrance examination first, then register for the eleventh semester of medical school, and finally take their state certification examination once again. Certain professors at the School of Medicine, such as the gynecologist Dr. Putnins, were notorious for bullying their Jewish students during the examinations and giving them failing grades.

The fact that the civil service was closed to us led to a concentration of Jews in trade, industry, and the freelance professions. The Jewish masses lived in great poverty. The fact that there were prosperous Jewish merchants, doctors, and jurists hid this poverty only from those who did not want to be aware of it.

The result of the government's policy toward minorities was that, although they were represented in Parliament, they led a life that in a manner of speaking generally ran parallel to, but was isolated from, the life of the Latvians. There was no close contact. Instead, there was contact between the minorities themselves—for example, between the Jews and the Germans—which could probably be traced back to their shared language. The harmony between Jews and Germans is exemplified by the Stock Market Commercial School, built at the turn of the century (which is today the Academy of Arts of the Latvian Republic). The Germans built the school with partly Jewish funding, thereby accepting two conditions: that the school would accept Jewish children as well, and that the Jews' participation in its construction would also be expressed on the exterior. This explains why the facade of this building constructed in the Gothic style is ornamented to this day with two six-pointed Stars of David. In the Republic of Latvia there could be no talk of an integration of minorities.

Despite the aforementioned barriers, during the first ten years of the Republic's existence incidents of anti-Semitism were negligible. In their works portraying Latvian rural life, the old "classic" Latvian authors described the most frequently occurring Jewish figures, the village tailors and traveling peddlers, very benevolently and never made contemptuous remarks about them. The young Latvia of the 1920s followed this example. However, the *Latvis* newspaper was already publishing articles of an anti-Semitic tenor. On October 9, 1923, this newspaper even called for an anti-Jewish demonstration in Jelgava (Mitau) in which automobiles, wagons, and pedestrians were supposed to participate. Leaflets and pamphlets declared that to cross a Jewish threshold was to "betray" the Latvian people.

Increasing nationalism in Germany could not fail to affect a people that had developed for centuries under German influence. The bonds that had formed in the course of many years between us, the children of various minorities, were still there, but the issue of nationality, which had never existed previously, now surfaced. The word "Jew" was freighted with negative value. One day we boys were playing the old game that consists of intertwining your fingers with your partner's and trying, by squeezing his hand hard, to force your opponent to his knees. My opponent, a Latvian boy, did not want to fall on his knees despite the pain I was obviously causing him. When I demanded that he give up, he blurted out between clenched teeth, "I don't kneel to Jews."

A few years later, after the Nazis were in control, the world-famous singer Joseph Schmidt was giving a concert in Riga. To loud applause, Schmidt stepped onto the stage and bowed to the standing-room-only audience. As he was about to begin his first song, a voice from the balcony suddenly broke the silence, shouting in Latvian, "Jew!"

During the 1920s the Latvian intelligentsia was still at the beginning of its development. During the 1930s it became more self-confident, more nationalistic, and simultaneously more hostile toward minorities. At the university, the citadel of the Latvian intelligentsia, anti-Semitism soon became especially pronounced. Students of various fraternities joined together in Perkonkrusts (Swastika), a chauvinistic anti-Semitic organization founded in the early 1930s as a counterpart of the Nationalsozialistische Deutsche Arbeiterpartei, or

NSDAP (National Socialist German Workers' Party). The emblem of this organization, which propagated an undisguised anti-Semitism, was also the swastika. To be sure, President Ulmanis banned the organization, but the members paid no attention to the ban. They merely limited their activities slightly, but large swastikas continued to be displayed on the windows of their club headquarters in Bruninieku Street (Ritterstraße), and the government silently condoned them. Most of the organization's leaders came from the intelligentsia, from university circles, and were members of Latvian student fraternities, for example, Lettonija, Selonija, or Talavija.

Isolated instructors did not consider it beneath their dignity to indulge in anti-Semitic attacks. Thus, for example, the Latvian instructor Lindemanis refused during a meeting of the Academic Senate to take the empty seat next to Professor Centnerszwer, declaring that he didn't sit next to Jews. Professor Centnerszwer at once left the Academic Senate and resigned from the University of Latvia. He moved to Poland, where he became a professor at the University of Warsaw and a member of the Polish Academy of Sciences in 1929. He died in the Warsaw ghetto in 1943.

In 1933 Hitler came to power. In Latvia the leader of the Farmers' Party, Karlis Ulmanis, became head of state in 1934 by means of a coup carried out by the army and the Aizsargi, a paramilitary organization. He dissolved and banned all political parties. His policy toward the Jews cannot be called anti-Semitic in the conventional sense, but he was intent on enriching the Latvians, especially the merchants, at the cost of the minorities, primarily the Jews and the Germans. Numerous Jewish and German banks were taken over by the Latvian Credit Bank. Jewish companies—for example, the Linen Manufacturing Company in Jelgava (Mitau) and the Buffalo textile factory in Riga—were nationalized, and the import of gasoline and wheat was taken out of Jewish hands and transferred to the state. Import licenses were now necessary to import goods from abroad, and these were granted primarily to Latvian merchants, whereas Jewish merchants were able to get them only at high prices or at second or third hand. Jewish physicians lost their positions in the health-insurance companies. President Ulmanis did not like the Latvian intelligentsia because it considered him a mere peasant, and he did not encourage this group's anti-Semitism. On the other hand, he did little to hinder it and strongly stirred up the nationalism of young people in the rural areas.

The causes of World War II can be traced back to the Treaty of Versailles. It began de facto on August 23, 1939, when Molotov and Ribbentrop signed the German-Soviet pact in Moscow. Although the war did not begin until two years later for us, the inhabitants of Latvia, we were thus drawn without our knowledge into the preparations for the war as early as 1939. In early October 1939, representatives of the Baltic states were summoned to Moscow because the Soviet government wanted to negotiate with them for military bases for the Red Army in the Baltic region. According to the treaty signed on October 5, 1939, three such bases were to be built in Latvia: in Liepaja (Libau), Ventspils (Windau), and Pitrags. Almost at the same time, at the beginning of October, the German government informed its ambassadors to the Baltic states of the decision just made in Berlin to repatriate all Baltic Germans.

When I think back today to the two years that then separated us from June 22, 1941, I am amazed by the incredibly carefree way we lived our lives. Germany had been militarized and had annexed neighboring countries as Hitler's rabble-rousing speeches resounded over the airwaves. France had built the Maginot line, Germany the Siegfried line. Fruitless talks had been held in Moscow between the English and French and the Russians. All of this was reason enough to regard the future with deep concern. But we remained unmoved. "We" refers to the younger generation; but most of the older generation also seemed unaware of the impending danger.

When September 1, 1939, burst upon us, the feeling of excitement outweighed the feeling of fear. We felt pleasurable tickles of excitement in our bellies as we told one another of the calls for help that Radio Warsaw had broadcast to the whole world after the Germans' air attack on the defenseless city. I cannot remember hearing any warning voices during this time. We believed we were far from the scene of action. More farsighted people saw things differently. For example, the *Neue Zürcher Zeitung* (*New Zürich Newspaper*) wrote on October 10, 1939, that it was not hard to guess that the strikingly rapid deportation of the German minorities from the Baltic states was related to the danger of Bolshevik Russia absorbing the border states.

Yet even the *Neue Zürcher Zeitung* did not realize that behind this danger lurked an even greater one.

In the fall of 1939 I was drafted for regular service into the Latvian Army and dispatched to an infantry regiment in Krustpils (Kreuzburg). During the first few weeks after being called up, all the recruits, whatever their nationality, who had completed their secondary or university education were sent to the training school for instructors or officers—all of them, that is, except the Jews, who had to serve as common soldiers no matter what level of education they had reached and were ineligible for promotion. This treatment of the Jews was of recent date and characteristic of the Ulmanis era. In previous years there had been no such exceptions, and a considerable number of Jews had ended their tours of duty as officer candidates or reserve officers.

In the winter of 1939–40 the Russians began to reinforce their military bases in Latvia. Their freight trains, consisting mostly of gasoline and oil tanks, ran daily through Krustpils, which is on the main line between Moscow and Riga. They rolled from east to west, and we asked ourselves whether they would ever roll back.

Meanwhile, the anti-Soviet mood began to gain ground in Latvia. The Finno-Russian War, with the massive military failures of the Red Army, contributed greatly to our low opinion of the Russians. The USSR, like Russia before it, acquired the reputation of a "giant with clay feet." In the Latvian army, lecturers spread anti-Soviet propaganda in open or disguised form.

The fact that in the spring of 1940 we, the average citizens, did not suspect that our state's independence was soon to end should not be surprising. But it is remarkable that even government circles were not at all aware of it. For example, in the spring of 1940 Ulmanis extorted a tribute equivalent to one million U.S. dollars from the Jews of Latvia, not seeming to realize how endangered his own position already was. At any rate, the Soviet government did everything it could to lull to sleep the vigilance of the Baltic states' governments. For example, Soviet Foreign Minister Molotov said during the session of the Supreme Soviet in May 1940 that the Baltic states' political independence was not threatened by the USSR. According to the memoirs of the Latvian general Bangerskis, Stalin repeated this at about the same time in a conversation with the Latvian minister of defense, General Balodis. But according to other sources, in the spring of 1940 inflammatory articles against the governments of the Baltic states appeared in the leading Soviet newspapers. In mid-June armed clashes broke out on the borders between the USSR and the Baltic states; they had of course been provoked by Moscow. The Soviet government claimed that Latvia had blatantly violated the Latvian-Soviet pact, and it issued an ultimatum on June 16, 1940, to Latvia to immediately form a new government capable of guaranteeing that the Latvian-Soviet pact would be implemented.

That was followed by the Red Army's invasion and the annihilation of the independence of three democratic states. Ulmanis and most of the members of his government were arrested, and nearly all of them died in Russia. The world accepted the enslavement of six million people with apathy.

Each of the various social classes reacted in its own way to the loss of national independence and the change of regimes. The workers, especially the unemployed, were filled with hopeful expectations of a better future. By contrast, all those who owned any kind of property watched political developments with concern. The peasants—the Baltic states were agrarian countries—saw the *mene tekel* of collectivization on the wall. The merchants feared for their large and small businesses. The people in freelance professions feared for their independence.

I experienced the Red Army's invasion at Krustpils in the summer of 1940, and I can still remember today what an alienating impression it made. The officers wore squares instead of stars as collar patches. The soldiers' caps had points on top like spiked leather helmets. The soldiers themselves seemed very thin under their shirts; none of them had weapons, and they marched very close together, almost belly to back, in short, quick steps. Their singing sounded like the drawn-out howling of wolves. We felt as though we had been thrown back in time to the period when the Huns were storming Europe, and the number of Mongolians among them was in fact very large.

In the summer of that year my father managed to get me transferred to the military hospital in Riga; the object was to enable me to continue my medical studies while doing my army service. I was sent to the Department of Internal Medicine, where I worked as an orderly under the direction of Dr. Lusis and his assistant Dr. Blumbergs. Both of them treated me like a younger colleague, and the working atmosphere was extremely warm and pleasant. In the fall I was able, as I had hoped, to reregister at the university. Then the Latvian civilian doctors at the hospital were replaced by Russian military doctors. The head of the Department of Internal Medicine was now Dr. Kaganova, a stocky lady of middling height who used to appear every morning in full uniform. Her behavior toward me was correct until the day I made a few rash remarks that led her to conclude that I was a member of a revolutionary underground movement. As duty required, she denounced me to the Red Army counterintelligence, since denunciation was, according to Soviet law, the duty of every Soviet citizen who detected anything hostile or threatening to the state. The counterintelligence interrogated me from morning till evening and then, surprisingly, accepted my explanation that it was all a misunderstanding, yet it transferred me "for security reasons" to a unit in a rural district.

The interrogation had really shattered me. On that day I learned to fear and hate Soviet power. Without a doubt, I was only one of thousands who were mistreated in similar fashion by the counterintelligence or the KGB during those months in which Latvia was sovietized. At that time the methods of a totalitarian state, in which a harmless citizen can suddenly end up within the net of the secret service, were revealed to us clearly.

In the Latvian units that had in the meantime been integrated into the Red Army, Latvian officers were arrested with increasing frequency; some of them were shot, others deported to Siberia. Only a few of the latter saw their homeland again after the end of the war. Most of them died in the far north.

The much-feared nationalization process began immediately after annexation, and it accelerated quickly. Houses, banks, workshops, factories, stores—everything that people had built up through long years of arduous labor, literally by the sweat of their brows, all of this they now lost. The victims of the new regime included most of the Jews. On the other hand, there were also Jews who profited from the change of system. They now had access to all the places whose doors had previously been closed to them, especially in the civil service. Many Jews, in contrast to the Latvians, could speak Russian and were therefore preferred as coworkers.

Thus it was no wonder that Jews could now be found in many places where they had not been before, for example, in the police force. Later on the Latvians would say that "many" Jews had worked in the KGB. But of course nobody asked how many Latvians were part of the KGB apparatus even before the annexation of the Baltic states (many Latvians lived in the USSR) or how many joined the KGB after the occupation of Latvia. For many Latvians, the image of the hated Soviet regime doubtless began to merge during this period with the image of the Jew in a privileged position so as to form a single concept, namely that of the Jewish Communist. This concept was reinforced as arrests and deportations increased. The fact that the victims of the KGB also included numerous Jews did not concern the anti-Semites.

In the meantime, the repatriation of the Baltic Germans continued. In those days, we often saw on the streets of Riga the green uniforms of the Umsiedlungs-Treuhand-Aktiengesellschaft or UTAG (Repatriation Trust Ltd.), who helped the Germans about to be repatriated to pack and load their possessions. Through these men, some of whom were reputedly in the German counterintelligence, news filtered through in the winter and spring of 1941 about "certain occurrences" in the Reich. The word "war" cropped up with increasing frequency. Soon, the fact that Stalin did not want to acknowledge on June 22 but the boys in the streets of Riga had already known in April and May occurred: war with Germany was upon us. The men in the repatriation organization boasted that Germany was not even going to deploy the Wehrmacht against the Russians, merely the Berlin Fire Department—an assessment of the Red Army that probably went back to their analysis of the Finnish campaign of 1939.

On June 22 it came—the war had begun. German troops overran the Red Army, which stubbornly defended itself, and approached Latvia and Riga. These were decisive days and hours for the Jews of Latvia, and one would have expected all of them to flee to Russia with their entire families. But nothing of the kind happened. Most of them did not budge. Only about 10 percent sought refuge in flight. The rest stayed where they were and waited to see what would happen.

Had they really not heard anything about the persecution of the Jews in Germany? Was anything stopping us from fleeing to the east and there finding safety from the Germans?

The answer to the first question is that we were informed about everything—absolutely everything—that had occurred in Germany after the National Socialists seized power in 1933. The Baltic states' democratic press had reported extensively on the party's evolution and goals. We were adequately informed about the concentration camps and the fate of the Jews. We knew about Kristallnacht, the night of November 9, 1938, during which 25,000 Jews were taken to the Buchenwald, Dachau, and Sachsenhausen concentration camps. Moreover, countless emigrants from Germany and Austria had fled to and through Latvia. Among these refugees were some friends of our family, such as the music teacher Van Jung from Vienna and his companion Frau Mendel, and another friend of the family, Fräulein Lucie Rosenzweig. Van Jung died a few months after his arrival in Riga. Frau Mendel and Fräulein Rosenzweig, who married an Englishman, Mr. Page, both emigrated to Australia. The son of Dr. Otto Bauer, a specialist in forensic medicine in Vienna, also fled to Riga and went on from there to the United States. Another one of the refugees, the journalist Fritz Lachmann, became the founder and editor in chief of a new daily newspaper in German, *Europa-Ost,* which was financed by Jewish merchants. Its aim was to stand up to the two other German newspapers in Riga. At the beginning of the 1930s the *Rigasche Rundschau* had been joined by a second German daily newspaper which openly printed propaganda for National Socialism. The foundation of *Europa-Ost* took place in our home. Mr. Schapott, a friend of my parents, became the head bookkeeper, and Jacobson, a friend of my youth, was hired as a caricaturist.

All these refugees, and many others, told us in conversations that lasted for hours what they had experienced before leaving Germany and Austria. Today I can only admit, with horror and astonishment, how little we learned from their fates. We listened to them, full of sympathy, without realizing that all this should have been a warning to us. Only a few of us seemed at that time to be concerned about the future. I think of Otto Sachs, a relative, who was the director of the Riga Cement Factory. He had a subscription to *Das Neue Tagebuch* (*The New Journal*), which was now being published in Holland, and passed the issues along to us regularly. Although we often spoke at home about what was happening in Germany, on the basis of what we read in this journal and the reports in the newspapers and on the radio, this remained a discussion of sensational events from which we derived no consequences. Otto Sachs himself and his entire family were also finally overtaken by the fate of most of the Jews of Latvia.

Thus we had not the slightest reason to have any illusions about our future if we should fall into the hands of the Germans. Why, then, did we take that risk all the same? An answer to this question must take into account several historical aspects, at least as a starting point. A large proportion of the Baltic Jews, especially those in Estonia and Kurzeme (Kurland), were people who felt a bond with German culture. Their mother tongue was German, and they themselves had been raised in the spirit of the deepest admiration for German culture and civilization. Some of our families had been living in the Baltic states for centuries. It must have been this admiration that prevented most of us from recognizing the dangerous side of the Germans. For us they remained, in spite of all the news reports and personal accounts, "das Volk der Dichter und Denker"—the people of poets and philosophers.

There were other considerations as well. The year before the war, which we had lived through under Soviet rule, had done nothing at all to arouse our vigilance or caution regarding the Nazi regime. It had the contrary effect, for two reasons. In the first place, the sovietization of our entire lives, the transformation of all citizens into state employees, the nationalization of all private property, the complete restructuring of the entire financial system, and the nationalization of factories, shops, and banks completely occupied our attention and distracted it from many other problems, including the events in Germany.

Second, our formerly democratic press had become a standardized Soviet one, which since the Soviet-German pact of August 1939 cast a friendly eye on Germany and did not permit anything negative about Germany to be reported. It could have warned us. The Soviet authorities must have known about the persecution of the Jews in occupied Poland and about Eichmann's idea of a "Jewish buffer state" at Nisko, between the parts of Poland occupied by the Germans and the Soviets, for many Jews had fled from the German occupation zone to the Soviet one. But nothing about that was published. What we knew during the year before the war about the persecution of the Jews in Germany and in occupied Poland, we knew not from official sources but almost entirely from hearsay.

The one year of Soviet occupation had done little to kindle warm feelings in us for the USSR. The well-organized Latvian Republic had become a chaotic Soviet one. We now saw with our own eyes the fact that the huge country of Russia always lived on the edge of starvation as a result of this chaos. The comforting feeling of living in a state ruled by law had given way to fear of the KGB. Both the prosperous and the less-prosperous Jews, just like the other inhabitants of Latvia, had lost a large part of their property, and members of the freelance professions had become poorly paid state employees.

The number of Jews who had emigrated from Russia to Latvia after the Revolution of 1917, and who felt a bond with traditional Russian culture, was not large. But these Jews rejected the Soviet regime even more than we did. And they feared it more, because they had come to know it thoroughly during the Revolution and were now able to see that nothing about it had improved in the course of more than twenty years.

To everything negative that had previously been known about the USSR there was added one more significant event, which occurred a week before the war began: in mid-June the KGB began a large-scale deportation action throughout the entire Baltic region. In the course of three nights, 20,000 innocent citizens from Latvia and 20,000 from Lithuania—40,000 in all—were sent to Siberia, including about 5,000 Jews from Latvia and about 7,000 from Lithuania. During that time, numerous trucks rattled through the silence of the night in the cities of the Baltic states. In the open backs of these trucks cowered intimidated people who had just been pulled out of their homes and beds, with a few bundles and suitcases beside them, guarded by soldiers of the KGB holding fixed bayonets. In Riga they were brought to the Tornakalns (Thorensberg) railroad station and the Skirotava marshaling yard and there loaded into freight cars. This was the starting point of these unfortunate people's odyssey through the vast distances of Siberia and through Siberian concentration camps. Only a few of them returned after the end of the war. Six months later, the transports carrying the first Jews deported from Germany to Latvia arrived in the same Skirotava marshaling yard.

Obviously these events did nothing to foster love for the Soviet state among the citizens of Latvia. On the day the war began, the Jews of the Baltic states felt they were caught between Scylla and Charybdis. The overwhelming majority of us stayed put and thought the same as my father, who used to say, "Stay in the country and earn your bread by honest toil!" Sometimes he would add that he had survived one period of German occupation (he was referring to the occupation of the Baltic region by German troops during World War I) and would survive a second one as well. Others held similar opinions. The renowned surgeon Professor W. Mintz, who had returned from the USSR to his Latvian homeland in 1920, said very clearly, though without a great deal of reflection, "The Russians have already taken away my house and my car. What can I expect from them if I flee to the USSR?"

Similar thoughts might have motivated the Jewish bank director Jakobson in Jelgava (Mitau) during the Germans' advance as he stood in the marketplace with his arms raised and called out to the Jews—including the Salzmann family—who were fleeing in horse-drawn wagons, to see reason and return to their homes. He was one of the first Jews to be shot by the Latvians of Jelgava.[2]

Some Jews—may their naïveté be forgiven—counted on Germany to return to them their property which had been nationalized by the Soviet government. But some of them stayed where they were only because they could find no means of transport to escape. Others broke off their flight or preparations for flight because the rapid advance of the German troops blocked their path or because they were stopped by special KGB units when they crossed the border into Russia. Some overly disciplined party members remained behind because the Central Committee of the Communist Party of Latvia announced only days before the fall of Riga that everyone should stay at his post. This order was never rescinded, but the members of the Central Committee themselves fled.

The hatred and contempt for the Russians were greater than the fear of the Germans. A settled way of life and attachment to one's possessions stood in the way of cool reasoning. A certain justification of our blindness must also be seen in the fact that at that point the concept of the "final solution" was unknown to most people inside and outside Germany. After all, it was only on July 31, 1941, that

Göring wrote a letter on Hitler's orders to Reinhard Heydrich which contains the following passage: "[I] order you herewith to make all the necessary organizational, practical, and material preparations for a comprehensive solution of the Jewish question in the German area of influence in Europe."[3] But this was only the final step of the German leadership's already completed plans, for on Heydrich's orders the leaders of the Einsatzgruppen, or mobile killing units, had been informed as early as mid-June, and in some cases even earlier—in contrast to earlier campaigns—of the new tasks they would have to carry out, namely the immediate liquidation of the Jewish population and the active Communists. Everyone knew that Hitler himself was the author of these plans.

The fact that we were not the only blind ones during those years is impressively testified to by many pages in Stefan Zweig's *Die Welt von gestern* (*The World of Yesterday*).[4] Between 10,000 and 15,000 Jews fled from Latvia to Russia. Each one had his or her own reasons. Many understood the danger that most of us did not see. Some of them had worked in various Soviet governmental bureaus; others had been members of the government—all of them feared reprisals. Many of them died in Russia under various circumstances, some of them at the front with weapons in their hands. But many of them lived to return. However, of the 80,000 to 85,000 Jews who stayed in Latvia, only about 1,000 people survived.

3
Terror

A few days after the war began, the Red Army precipitately left Riga. On the streets there was unbelievable chaos. Tens of thousands of soldiers and civilians were trying, on foot or in cars or trucks, to leave the city as quickly as possible. Latvian snipers, who sporadically shot into the crowds from roofs and attics, increased the panic. Most of the people fleeing were citizens of the USSR who had resettled in Latvia after the annexation of the Baltic states, but there were also many Latvians who had worked together with the new regime in a variety of ways during the year of Soviet rule and who now feared being denounced as collaborators after the impending change of regimes.

The Germans' rapid progress increased the fear and the chaos. At that time men were the breadwinners in most families and therefore had the best opportunities to flee in the trucks of the firms where they worked. Flight was a head-over-heels affair. In most cases the men would show up at home totally unexpectedly, or they would suddenly telephone their unprepared family members to tell them to immediately pack everything that would be needed, since they had to flee at once. Many women, especially those with young children, could not bring themselves to take such a decisive step at a moment's notice. People hesitated, they thought it over, they asked other family members for advice while the precious minutes ticked by. Many a husband waited at the agreed-upon meeting place in vain. Others managed nonetheless to rush home and talk their families into leaving. The precipitate flight tore many families apart. Some relatives found each other again later in the wide expanses of Russia; others stayed behind, trapped. Thus it happened that many of the Jews who found refuge in Russia returned home after the war and only then found out that none of those who had stayed behind in their homeland was still alive.

Anyone who has never been in a similar situation, who has never experienced panic, who has never seen thousands of people full of fear streaming forward blindly, like a herd of sheep, should not condemn those who left behind their wives and children in this situation. They were overwhelmed by events more powerful than themselves. Moreover—and this is the essential thing—they could not have foreseen the fate to which they were leaving their families.

As for me, in the winter of 1940 to 1941 I had been transferred back to Riga, with the help of Latvian friends of my father's, from the Latvian countryside where the counterintelligence had sent me, and I had resumed my studies. Now the war had begun, and my unit was to leave Riga on June 27. That morning my father appeared unexpectedly in the house where we had been billeted and called me aside. He advised me urgently not to leave the country with the Red Army under any circumstances. "What will you do in faraway Russia?" he said, among other things. "Stay at home, that's much safer for you and we'll remain together!"

Before then I had done hardly any thinking about my future and had mostly followed my parents' advice, so now too I was entirely inclined to follow my father's instructions. The deportation of friends and acquaintances had aroused my hatred, and the arrest of many Latvian officers under whom I had served and with whom I had sympathized had also made me regard the Soviet regime with contempt and mistrust. Indeed, why should I now join the Red Army's retreat? I gave my father the consent he wanted.

That afternoon, when we were sent to a railroad station in a suburb of Riga to load ammunition, I used an opportune moment to take to my heels. A few steps from the railroad station I jumped over the fence of a large, quiet garden and found a hiding place there between dense bushes. I lay there until late evening and then made my way through the empty streets to our relatives, the Sachs family, who lived nearby.

My "great-aunt" Johanna Sachs, a cousin of my mother's, set before me a quickly prepared supper, which I attacked with a good appetite, feeling quite starved. Just after I had finished, her husband Otto Sachs came into the room and, after greeting me briefly, asked me what my arrival meant. After I had frankly told him the whole story, he looked worried and said, after some hesitation, "I doubt whether your father gave you good advice. But be that as it may, you can't stay here overnight. I'm responsible for all of the people in this house. If you're found here by Red Army soldiers we could all be shot!"

I was certainly afraid, but I left. It would have gone against my grain to beg for shelter. Outside, night had fallen, and in the dark the streets seemed even emptier than before. Not far from there lived Dr. Moritz Springenfeld, another relative of ours. Perhaps he would give me shelter. As I was passing through a small grove called the Agenskalna Priedes (Agenskalna Pines), heavy gunfire started up suddenly. Bullets whined around me in all directions and signal rockets rose into the dark, cloudless sky. But I reached my destination unscathed.

Dr. Springenfeld was not especially pleased by my arrival either, but he let me spend the night there. The next morning I borrowed a shirt and a pair of trousers from him, and in these civilian clothes I set out for home. On the Daugava shore, Red Army soldiers were checking the identification papers of everyone who wanted to cross the bridge to the other side of the river. I slipped past them unnoticed. My parents were happy to see me again.

On June 29 and 30 Riga was bombarded by German artillery. During this bombardment the famous wooden tower of St. Peter's church, the second highest in Europe and a symbol of the city, went up in flames. Afterward, some claimed that the Germans had shot at the tower, starting the blaze, because Russian observers were in it. According to other reports, German observers were in the tower to direct the German artillery fire, and the Russians set fire to the tower for this reason. The firefight between the Russians and the Germans was not very intense, but the city's inhabitants did not dare go out on the streets for two days. The Riga radio station was silent.

During the night of June 30 the rumble of artillery stopped, and in the early morning hours it became completely quiet. About six in the morning the familiar melody of the Latvian national anthem rang out from the radio; we had not heard it since the annexation of Latvia—that is, for more than a year. In the beams of the rising sun one window after another was opened, and "God bless Latvia" resounded louder and louder through the morning stillness. We didn't attach any importance to the fact that the Latvian anthem was followed by the Horst Wessel song.

The day was a hot one. The golden sun shone down from a cloudless sky on the happily excited city. Soon we saw the first German soldiers. They were strong, tanned fellows with rolled-up sleeves, who charged into the city along the house walls. Many of them had small bouquets of flowers in their rifle barrels and seemed a bit surprised by the warm welcome given them by the people of Riga, especially the women. They probably hardly realized that they were being greeted as our liberators from the Red terror.

In our home we were in good spirits. That morning there was an appeal on the radio for medical students to report for first-aid duty on the banks of the Daugava. It was an appeal for which, as I saw later, there was not the least need, for on the riverbanks only a few recently dug, and now abandoned, trenches testified to the battles that had taken place there. My father gave me a small medicine kit and a Red Cross armband, and I set on my way. The city had a Sunday air about it. Young and old strolled along the streets in light summer clothing. Friends and acquaintances greeted one another as though they had just survived a great danger together. A large semicircle of the pavement around the monument to Liberty, on which the words "For Fatherland and Freedom" still stand today, was covered with hundreds of bouquets. I stopped to look more closely at this splendid floral display, and as I did so I heard applause coming from nearby for a group of men who had just turned the corner of the Rainis Boulevard and were heading for the monument square. They were Jews. Young armed Latvians were guarding them. The thirty to forty Jews passed us in silence. The crowd applauded, and satisfied voices called out that it was time that the Jews too finally did something useful. Now they were being sent to the banks of the Daugava to fill up the trenches.

I stood there as though in a daze. What would these people do to me if they knew who I was?

What I saw there was the prelude to the mass murder of us Jews, which turned into a massacre and ended in a bloodbath on a scale that world history had never seen before. But "prelude" may be the wrong term, if one considers that large parts of Latvia had already been in

German hands for several days, and that there the Perkonkrusts (Swastika) and the Aizsargi (Defenders), organizations that have already been mentioned, had already begun to slaughter Jews and were merely continuing to do so in Riga. Had Perkonkrusts and the Aizsargi already planned the annihilation of the Jews before the beginning of the war and coordinated these plans with the Gestapo? We do not know. If there were no coordinated plans, this means that the Aizsargi, Perkonkrusts, and certain student fraternities began the slaughter spontaneously without having received any directives to this effect from the Gestapo.

An unchecked, unchained slaughter now began, and it lasted for years. Armed men forced their way, by day and by night, into Jewish homes. On the streets and in shops, factories, and workshops, they hunted us down. They startled Jews out of their sleep and shot them in their beds. Men and women, children and old people were herded into the little groves on the outskirts of large and small towns, forced to dig mass graves or stand at the edge of graves already dug, and shot by the hundreds and thousands. Those who were not shot on the spot were brought to jail and killed there. Newborn babies and infants had their skulls smashed against walls or were thrown into the air and shot at like clay pigeons or spiked on bayonets.

The center of the terror in Riga was the police headquarters. In the courtyard they herded together hundreds of Jews and tormented them for fun: they were beaten bloody or beaten to death, kicked, or forced to run up and down the stairs; old men were pulled around by their beards or compelled to clean the pavement or polish shoes with their beards or with toothbrushes. Women were forced to undress, humiliated, and raped. Some of the people who had been crowded together here were later brought to the central prison of Riga or the woods on the outskirts of the city and were shot there. Others were driven like animals to work in the city and herded together again in the evening in the courtyard of the police headquarters. Some were held here for weeks; only a few escaped from this hell alive. Synagogues were plundered and set afire, and Jews were thrown alive into the flames.

Lithuanian Jews who had fled from the Germans to Riga from Kaunas, Siauliai, Panevezys, and other cities had found shelter in the cellar of the Great Choral Synagogue on Gogol Street. On July 4,

1941, Latvian policemen drove Jews from the neighboring houses into this cellar as well and set the building on fire. Holy writings were torn up and thrown into the flames. Guards with machine guns surrounded the synagogue and shot anyone who tried to escape. It is difficult to estimate how many people died here. The figure of 2,000 victims that is given by the Soviet Latvian authorities is doubtless too high. The screams of the burning victims could be heard over a great distance and filled the souls of the people in the neighboring houses with horror. Some of them soon left their homes forever, because at night it seemed to them they could still hear the cries of the burning human victims. Film footage of the burning of the Great Choral Synagogue is included in German army newsreels (Wehrmachtsschau No. 567/30/1941). On the sound track, the narrator gloats triumphantly: "The synagogue in Riga, which had been spared by the GPU commissars in their work of destruction, went up in flames a few hours later."[1]

Nearly all the other synagogues of the city also went up in flames. They included the synagogue in Stabu Street (Säulenstraße), which was set on fire by the air force officer Herberts Cukurs (more on him later) and his thugs after they had pulled Jews out of the neighboring houses and locked them up inside. Eyewitnesses heard the people who were locked inside screaming for help and saw them breaking the synagogue's windows from inside and trying, like living torches, to get outside. Cukurs shot them with his revolver. The eyewitness I. Lancman testified that the victims of this bloodbath included the dentist Dr. Divlin and his wife, the sixteen-year-old Nisson Jakobson, and the two Loev sisters.

As early as July 17, 1941, Brigadier Dr. W. Stahlecker, the commander of Einsatzgruppe (Mobile Unit) A, reported that all of the synagogues in Riga had been destroyed.[2] The only synagogue in Riga that escaped burning was the Peitavas synagogue in the old part of the city; no one dared to set it on fire because it stood amid other buildings, including the Church of the Reformation, but it was desecrated by being put to use as a stall for horses.

In their unrestrained frenzy these gangs of murderers destroyed and burned down not only the synagogues; they also stormed the Jewish cemeteries, where they toppled the gravestones and smashed them to pieces in a wild rage. In the New Jewish Cemetery in Smerlis

(Schmerl), they locked Cantor Mintz and his family into the synagogue and then set fire to it (the Old Jewish Cemetery was in the Moscow suburb and after the ghetto was established it lay inside the ghetto).

In Riga itself the first executions took place during the night of July 1. The victims were the inhabitants of 19 Gogol Street, whose overly zealous custodian had reported to his local police station immediately after the Germans marched in that Jews lived in "his" house. That night several horse-drawn carriages full of students drove up to the front of the house. The students wore their fraternity colors and were armed. Guns in hand, they drove thirty-six inhabitants of the house into the street and shot them on the spot. Then they got into their carriages and drove away. As the victims were being carried away, two men who were still alive were found under them, Moshe Rosenberg, who was severely wounded, and a Mr. Dimkin. They were brought to the Jewish Hospital and treated there.

The murderers raged with particular fury in rural areas and in the small Latvian towns where everyone knew everyone else and everyone knew where the neighboring Jewish families lived. For this reason, in some places it took the gangs of murderers only days to exterminate the entire Jewish population. On the access roads they proudly displayed signs saying "judenrein," or "purified of Jews." In practical terms, the standard procedure was for the local authorities to imprison "their" Jews and herd them together in one place, but to leave the shooting to Perkonkrusts commandos who came from Riga and to the Latvian security police.

In some places the locals did not need the Perkonkrusts murderers' help at all. The historian M. Vestermanis's account of the events in the small town of Bauska (Bausk) gives an idea of the atrocities that took place in the provinces. On July 20, 1941, the first execution was carried out in Bauska. Twenty young Jews were the first victims of a German execution squad. That was followed by the expulsion of all Jews from the center of town and, after that, the implementation of one of the most appalling, maniacal ideas that National Socialist ideology ever had: the castration of fifty-six Jewish males, including ten boys aged from eight to fifteen years.[3] There is documentary evidence of the participation in this heinous crime by the Latvian doctor Steinharts, his medical orderly Plavinieks, the town's police chief

Druveskalns, and the local army commandant, First Lieutenant Nepil, a native of Vienna. It is also documented by the Soviet Special Commission to Investigate the Violent Crimes of National Socialism that this crime was treated in the town as a "festival of joy" and that the women of the town appeared on the streets "in their holiday finery."

Between July 25 and August 26, 2,000 Jews were executed in Bauska; 800 of them were natives of Bauska and the rest were from the countryside around the town. During the same period, 100 political (non-Jewish) prisoners from Islice near Bauska were murdered. Druveskalns and Nepil actively participated in these crimes as well. The victims were buried nearby in the forest of Vecsaule and exhumed and cremated in 1944 by the Germans as they retreated.

How did the average citizen react to these events in the country? Some indication is given by the minutes of a meeting of the foundation to rebuild the town of Viesite in southeastern Latvia, held on September 2, 1941. This document testifies to its writers' ingenious, yet crude, hypocrisy and serves as an example of many other similar documents from this period.

Four men were present at the meeting: the town's mayor N. Neimanis, the foundation's administrator J. Bitenieks, his assistant P. Rumbens, and the foundation's secretary E. Lejins. In the minutes of the meeting, which deal with the money and valuables of murdered Jews, it is stated that the Jews of Viesite had been "expelled" from the town to a nearby camp and that they had "departed from" this camp on July 19. The terms "expelled" and "departed from" stand for "forcibly deported" and "executed," respectively. At another point in the minutes the term "emigrated from" is substituted for "departed from." Farther on we read that the "departing" Jews—one cannot believe one's eyes—"donated" 5,609 rubles and 28 kopeks and that the town council used this sum for its own purposes.

The second part of the minutes deals with Jewish property, a portion of which is handed over to the town so that it can all the sooner "begin its creative work for the benefit of the Greater German Reich." Another portion of Jewish property is granted to those persons who have supported the army of the Greater German Reich. Five men are named, of whom three—Mayor N. Neimanis, the foundation's administrator J. Bitenieks, and his assistant P. Rumbens—personally took part in this meeting. The minutes shamelessly list the "services" performed by these men: Mayor Neimanis had helped organize the Jews' "emigration"; the fund's administrator Bitenieks had directed the Jews' "departure" from Viesite and its surroundings. His assistant Rumbens had organized the Jews' "expulsion" from Viesite to the camp and also implemented it. Of the other two members, who were not present at the meeting, Lieutenant P. Taurins and A. Silenieks, the former had participated both in the "expulsion" and the "departure" of the Jews from Viesite; the latter had organized and directed all of the actions and measures taken (no specific details are given) for the "purification" of the district of Viesite. In a word: murderers in official positions fabricated a document that was intended, infamously and insidiously, to camouflage theft and murder.

These minutes are dated September 2, 1941, and refer to events that had taken place one and a half months previously, between July 15 and 20. At that time, all the Jews of Viesite, together with those of Jekabpils (Jakobstadt) and Nereta, were murdered by an execution squad of the Perkonkrusts in the village of Kukas. Was there any retaliation for this bloody deed? There is a certain bitter irony in the fact that the "corpse-robbers of Viesite" were denounced by their own fellow citizens—obviously not on account of the murder of Jews, of course, but because they appropriated their victims' valuables for themselves instead of handing them over to the German authorities according to the rules.[4]

Children had been forced to watch as their parents were murdered. Women had had their children and husbands torn from them forever. Family members had disappeared without a trace, and those who remained behind made their way from one police station to another, from one prison to another, where the authorities refused to give them any information whatsoever about those who had disappeared. A reign of terror had invaded the whole country, but this was a reign of terror that affected only the Jewish population, while most of the other inhabitants of the country went on living their normal lives, which were still proceeding quite peacefully in spite of the war.

A very few Latvians who were accused of collaborating with the Soviet regime or suspected of being Communist sympathizers were overtaken by a similar fate to that of us Jews. Some were executed on the spot, while others were sent to concentration camps and stayed there for years. Among the latter was the Latvian writer Miervaldis Birze, who will be referred to again later.

In Riga, the woods of the suburbs of Bikernieki (Bickern), Rumbula, and Dreilini became the scenes of mass murder. Today a memorial stone in Bikernieki, erected by the Soviet government, testifies to the atrocities that were committed there. The inscription on the stone states that here 46,500 Soviet citizens died as victims of fascism. This was typical of the behavior of the Soviet regime toward us Jews, for nothing is said about the fact that, in the first place, those who died here were Jews and, in the second place, those who died included both native and foreign Jews, primarily from Germany. Here a deathly silence, in the literal sense of the word, has been spread over the tragedy of the Jews in the territory occupied by the Germans, as has generally been done in modern Soviet historiography in its entirety.

The memorial stone in Bikernieki is surrounded by parklike grounds within which lie the mass graves, which have been marked with concrete borders. All of this is in a totally neglected condition and is cleaned up a little only on state holidays if official wreath layings are to take place. In the winter, young people ski on top of the mass graves. On the grounds of the burned-down Great Synagogue on Gogol Street a green area was planted after the war. A memorial stone, which was not set up until 1989, informs posterity in blunt terms of the tragedy that took place here in the summer of 1941. In 1993, during a meeting of survivors of the Riga ghetto, a memorial was dedicated which looks like stylized walls and is meant to recall the foundation walls of the burned-down synagogue. The Soviet regime's lack of reverence toward the Jewish victims of Nazi terrorism is also revealed by the fact that, for example, in Sabile (Zabeln) the former synagogue was used in Soviet Latvia as a sports hall, as M. Levenstein, one of the surviving Latvian Jews, reports in his book *Du sollst sterben und nicht leben* (*You Shall Die and Not Live*).[5]

As the corpses of our Jewish fellow citizens, friends, and relatives piled up around us, as the blood of innocent people was spilled in streams, we looked for help to our Latvian fellow citizens, friends, and acquaintances, convinced that surely here or there a hand would be lifted to help us, surely a mouth would open to speak to us a word of comfort—but in vain. A bloody frenzy had overcome the country, and those who did not raise their hands to commit murder tried at least to harass us. We were thrown out of the electric streetcars and the buses (the official ban on our use of public transportation did not come until two months later); people watched for Jews standing in line in front of shops and tried not to sell them any food. "Suspicious-looking" people were made to say the word *kukuruza* (corn) to make sure they didn't have a rasping accent. M. Kaufmann tells of how outraged a woman streetcar conductor was over the fact that he and his son had dared, a few days after the city was occupied, to use the streetcar. She was completely beside herself with fury over the fact that Jews were taking the liberty of doing "this kind of thing," stopped the streetcar, and threw out the father and his son. Our Latvian friends, with whom we had only yesterday caroused and celebrated, acted as though they no longer knew us. Nobody sought us out, nobody comforted us, nobody did anything on our behalf. Suddenly we were alone; we had become strangers in our own homeland. People we had yesterday believed to be our friends denounced us to the police; cleaning ladies who had for years earned their bread by working for Jews threw their employers' possessions out into the street to express their "national" feelings; janitors informed the police of places where Jews were living who had not yet been noticed.

The Latvian press, especially the daily newspaper *Tevija* (*Fatherland*), which had been published in Riga since the beginning of July 1941, fanned the already blazing flames of anti-Semitism into an even brighter bonfire. Numerous authors, including in particular Raimunds Caks, Pauls Kovalevskis (who changed his name to Pavils Klans after the war), Arturs Kroders, and the Perkonkrusts member Adolfs Silde, poured out disgusting defamatory writings against prominent representatives of the Jewish community such as Albert Einstein, Sigmund Freud, Stefan Zweig, and others, and called absolutely openly for the annihilation of the Jews.

As we know, the results were not long in coming and enabled Silde to draw the following conclusion in 1942 in his annual review of events in Zemgale (Semgallen): "If we assess the most outstanding events of the past year, we cannot remain silent about the great joy we feel about the solution of the Jewish question in our country."[6] Silde died in Münster, Germany, in 1990.

A sea of hatred surrounded us. We asked ourselves what crime we had actually committed. Had we ever wronged our Latvian fellow citizens? Had we ever harmed them? What Latvian in the course of his life had never asked a Jew for help or, often enough, received it? Thousands and tens of thousands of Latvians had chosen Jewish physicians as their family doctors; thousands and tens of thousands of Latvians had been glad to work in Jewish workshops and factories in the certainty that they could count on the understanding and empathy of a Jewish employer precisely because he was Jewish. How often had Latvians poured out their hearts to Jewish fellow citizens, complaining about the hard-heartedness of the Latvians and admiring Jewish kindness and readiness to help?

It was not only a sea of hatred that surrounded us; it was also a sea of silence. Tens of thousands and hundreds of thousands were witnesses of the most horrible crime in human history and remained silent about it. Nowhere was the faintest voice raised to protest the universal bloodshed. None of the churches, neither the Lutheran nor the Catholic nor the Russian Orthodox church, tried to stop the killing. From not a single pulpit did condemning or critical words ring out urging people to levelheadedness or restraint. No judge let his warning voice be heard. The politicians also remained silent, the same ones who had granted us our civil rights twenty-three years before. If they believed they could make no headway against the Germans, why didn't they try to bring their own countrymen, the policemen, the Aizsargi, the bloodthirsty students back to their senses? This would have been the task of the country's intellectual leadership. But it was just this intellectual leadership that did nothing. Why not? Because most of the intelligentsia, together with the majority of the Latvian people, were entirely in favor of the "elimination" of the Jews and not only encouraged the mob to shed blood but also actively participated themselves. This does not mean that literally all the representatives of the intelligentsia approved of the killing. Not at all. But it still means that the majority welcomed the fact that now the Jews were at last going to be excluded from coexistence with the Latvian people. Thus it was no wonder that not a single official voice was raised to defend the Jews, that no Latvian Martin Niemöller was thrown into prison, and that no Latvian Alfred Delp was executed.

There were exceptions. J. E. Kroeger reports of the Latvian pastor Rozitis, who in the course of a so-called cemetery feast spoke a prayer on behalf of German soldiers and expressed the thanks of the Latvian people, but then also spoke of the trespasses of the Latvians against their Jewish fellow citizens. God would forgive them this sin only after harsh and sincere penance, he told them. Pastor Rozitis was denounced to the security police, where he was threatened with imprisonment and the concentration camp if he said "that kind of thing" again. The pastor answered calmly that for him there was no reason to repeat himself in a second sermon. It was thanks to an SS man who was well disposed toward the pastor that he was released with only a reprimand.

A list made by Einsatzgruppe A on October 15, 1941, states that at this point 30,025 Jews had been executed in Latvia. An additional 5,500 had been "eliminated" (to quote the report) in Latvia and Lithuania through pogroms. However, these are estimates rather than precise data. The actual number of Jewish victims was already much higher, since the number of Jews still alive at that time was about 41,000, of whom 30,000 were in the Riga ghetto, 7,000 in the Daugavpils ghetto, and 3,890 in the Liepaja ghetto. If we add to these numbers the figure of about 33,000 that is given by the Einsatzgruppe, we have a total of about 74,000 people. But at the time of the German invasion of Latvia there were between 80,000 and 85,000 Jews in Latvia, so it must be concluded that at the beginning of October 1941 not 33,000 but about 40,000 Jews had already been murdered.

How little the statements of Einsatzgruppe A correspond to reality is also indicated by the statement made by Lieutenant General Jeckeln, the senior SS and police chief of the Northern Army Group, who was sentenced to death by hanging, together with six generals, by a Soviet military court in Riga after a trial that lasted several weeks. The sentences were carried out on February 5, 1946.[7] When Jeckeln was asked in court about the number of Jews who had been murdered in Latvia, he answered, "The number of the Jews brought to Latvia from abroad is just as unknown to me as is the number of Jews who were killed in Latvia. So many Jews had been exterminated by the Latvians even before we Germans came to power that no exact figures could be established."[8] Jeckeln's explanations were based on the accounts of the Einsatzgruppe, which had reported, for example, from

Jelgava (Mitau) in the fall of 1941 that the 1,550 Jews still remaining there after the beginning of the war "had been completely eliminated by the local population."[9]

In his article "Die Mörder werden noch gebraucht" ("The Murderers Are Still Needed") in the German news magazine *Der Spiegel* (*The Mirror*), L. Olschwang presents a hideous picture of the massacre of the Jews in Lithuania after the German occupation in the summer and fall of 1941. His description of the events in Lithuania is totally consistent with what was happening in Latvia at the same time. In both countries it was primarily the local population—the Latvians and the Lithuanians—who murdered their Jewish fellow citizens.[10]

In this connection one should not leave unmentioned the writings of the Latvian author Miervaldis Birze about the atrocities committed by the Latvians during the period of German occupation. Birze, at that time twenty years old, was a fifth-semester medical student, and he was arrested in July 1941 in his hometown of Valmiera (Wolmar). He remained in prison until October 1943 and was then brought to the Riga airfield to do forced labor. From there he was sent in the summer of 1944 to Malachit, a satellite camp of Buchenwald, escaped from a marching column when the camp was evacuated shortly before the end of the war, and thus saved his own life. Birze's description of the Latvian terror—he primarily describes the terror of Latvians against Latvians—shows what cruelties Latvians inflicted on other Latvians only because they were Communists or were suspected of being left-wing. One can imagine what atrocities against the Jews such people must have been capable of if they were able to commit such crimes against their own fellow citizens.

The initial murders, he writes, were committed by Latvians against Latvians in Valmiera on July 26, 1941, with the Germans' blessing. The victims—about 250 Latvian prisoners—lie in three mass graves in the woods of Valmiera, where the murderers, as they themselves recounted, danced on the blood-soaked earth so that they could later say they had "danced on the graves of the Reds!" Birze quotes the chief of the Aizsargi, named Gulbis, who at one point during those days shouted out in his enthusiasm, "[Shoot] only the men? Bring out the women and children too! While we're at it, let's destroy them root and branch!"[11] One of the murderers was the lawyer Kakis, the son of a doctor who had settled in Valmiera. Birze remembers the date of the first executions so precisely because his own father was one of that day's victims. On the same day Kakis, who had been a leader of the local police since the first days of July, came into Birze's cell looking for Jews. There he spotted the Jewish engineer Joseph Lemberger from the Steizeler paper factory near Valmiera and had him taken away immediately.

In the spring of 1943 the Latvian police in Valmiera tied together 180 imprisoned women, men, and children—Gypsies, Russians, Jews, and Latvians—herded them out of the jail to the nearby woods, and executed them. Birze also describes how the former army lieutenant Arnolds Leopolds Runka, together with the German Rottenführer Sizius and Sizius's young son, who had a small-caliber gun in his hand, practiced target shooting at gypsy children, who died in the most horrible torment. Among the murderers of Valmiera, Birze also names Vilis Arvids Runka, the brother of Arnolds Leopolds Runka. The first of the two brothers is still living today in Oklahoma, the second in Adelaide, Australia. The Latvian writer Anna Pazare also writes of the cruelty of the Runka brothers in her book *The Grave Is Not Silent,* published in 1962.[12]

In 1941 and 1942 several Latvian police battalions were set up. The Latvian policemen in their "khaki-yellow uniforms with wine-red stripes on the collars" (they wore the uniforms of the former Latvian army) were notorious throughout the entire eastern sector occupied by the Germans. They turned up as execution squads in the Latvian countryside and in Slonim (today White Russia), and they rampaged in the Warsaw ghetto. They were also deployed against Soviet partisans in White Russia, Russia, and Poland. The battalions bore different numbers. No. 26, for example, operated in the Novgorod area, No. 18 around Minsk. The men of Battalions No. 18 and 21 were outstanding for their cruelty, especially in the torture of captured Soviet partisans. In 1972 some of them were tried in the Latvian Soviet Socialist Republic. Five of them received the death sentence, and four were sentenced to life imprisonment.[13]

On February 8, 1943, three Latvian police battalions were renamed legions, and this day was declared the founding day of the Latvian SS Volunteer Legion.[14] In memory of March 16, 1943, the only day of World War II on which two Latvian divisions fought shoulder to shoulder against units of the Red Army, the present Democratic Republic of Latvia has proclaimed March 16 Latvian Legion Day, a day of commemoration for the Latvian legionnaires. This decision was approved by the Latvian government—despite protests from within the country and abroad—in response to an initiative made by the Daugavas Vanagi (Daugava Falcons), a Latvian relief organization of former Latvian legionnaires.

After the war, especially during the 1980s and 1990s, an inept attempt was made to absolve the Latvian legionnaires of the justified accusation that they had murdered Jews. This was done in a very simpleminded way by arguing that Latvian legionnaires could not have murdered Jews because the Legions were not set up until 1943, that is, at a time when hardly any Jews were left in Latvia. It was a clumsy attempt to mislead naive people, since the Latvian Legions were built upon the foundation of the police battalions—as was stated by their chief of staff, A. Silgailis—and the latter had been practicing their bloody craft since 1941.[15]

One man who managed to make his way from eastern Europe to England during the war was asked in a BBC interview why nobody had bothered him on his long journey. He answered, "I was wearing the uniform of a Latvian policeman."

In his history of Latvia, the Latvian historian Arnolds Spekke attributes the massacre of the Jews in Latvia solely to the Germans. Whatever the motive may be that caused Spekke to present this version of reality, it does not correspond to the facts. Spekke states that there were protests when transports of Jews arrived from all over Europe and were then murdered in Riga. Although he speaks of protests, he mentions only one name, that of Archbishop Grinbergs. This protest could of course have been made only after the arrival of the shipments from abroad, that is, after January 1942. It has not been clearly proved what Grinbergs actually protested against. According to one report, he protested against the fact that foreign Jews were deported to Latvia and executed there. According to the second source, he protested against the assignment of baptized Jews to the ghetto, the opening of brothels, and the execution of gypsies. We can leave open the question of which source is more reliable. In any case, this was a verbal protest to the German security police or, as one of the sources puts it, "to the German masters," rather than an official measure. The fact remains that Grinbergs did not protest against the execution of his Jewish fellow citizens. In December 1941 and January 1942 it was in any case already too late to do so, for of the approximately 80,000 to 85,000 Latvian Jews who had lived on Latvian soil at the time of the German invasion, only about 5,000 were still alive.

The lecturer Nikolajs Valters writes in the Latvian Catholic emigrant newspaper *Dzimtenes Balss* (*Voice of the Homeland*), published in Chicago, about this subject as follows:

> There is a lovely legend that some Latvians—and their number is unfortunately quite large—were forced to commit these murders and that they inwardly resisted. Of course voluntary police units received orders of this sort. But in no case were there punishments, let alone the death penalty, for not obeying this kind of command. However, there were presents and honors for obeying them—and these were accepted[!] The possibility of not participating in these bloody crimes was in fact available. This opportunity was not used. But there were volunteers who themselves signed up for this executioner's work and who later boasted about it.[16]

A second Latvian historian, A. Bilmanis, devotes one single sentence to the horror of the period of German occupation in his history of Latvia, which ends with World War II. Of the fate of the Jews he writes: "The early arrival of the Gestapo in the Governorship of Ostland meant pogroms for the Jews. . . ." That is all. Bilmanis has nothing more to say about the murder of 85,000 of his fellow citizens and a similar, if not much larger, number of deported foreign Jews. This is incomprehensible and incredible. But almost equally incomprehensible and incredible is the portrayal of the fate of the Latvians during the same period in the second half of that sentence: "and for Latvian patriots the confiscation of their property, illegal imprisonment, the murder of hostages, extrajudicial executions, mass deportations, and mass executions of the inhabitants of certain provincial towns where German looters had been killed." It is generally known that the Latvians as a whole were among the Germans' most faithful allies and received favorable treatment in return; but this is apparently unknown to a historian who pretends to be writing the history of Latvia.[17]

The aforementioned Lieutenant General Friedrich Jeckeln, who became a Russian prisoner of war, was asked in court why Jews had been brought from all over Europe to Latvia in particular. He answered that Latvia had provided the "appropriate territory" for this measure.[18] And when asked why the execution squads mostly consisted of Latvians rather than Germans, he answered that the Latvians had had stronger nerves during the executions.

Some individuals already realized during the first days of the German occupation the hopelessness of our situation, and a few drew the logical conclusion by committing suicide. In our circle of acquaintances, the nose-ear-throat specialist Dr. S. Abramson and his sister, as well as the entire Friedmann family—husband, wife, and children—committed suicide. Hillel Friedmann was a dermatologist, his wife Rachel a surgeon. The older son was a painter and had worked in Florence for several years; the younger one was a fellow student of mine. During the first days after the German invasion, friends found the Friedmann family in their home unconscious. The parents had first injected their two sons with morphine and then themselves. They were taken to the Jewish Hospital, where they died. The philosopher Weintrob, who had just returned from a lecture tour in America, attempted suicide but was saved. Subsequently he made a second attempt and died.

Latvian emigrant circles have claimed that the literature published in the USSR and abroad concerning the bloodbath carried out by Latvians against their Jewish fellow citizens in Latvia is based on documents falsified by the Soviet regime, whose aim was to blacken the name of the Latvians who emigrated. This is nothing but an attempt to whitewash the facts. The contents of these documents match only too well what we saw with our own eyes and experienced with our own bodies. The fact that American courts have been unable to prove anything against such notorious persons as the Latvians Vilis Hazners and Edgars Laipenieks, who emigrated to the United States, only proves how difficult it is to convict someone of a crime after half a century has passed since the deed was done.

4
Imprisonment

During the first days of July 1941, a telephone call came from my mother's cousin Johanna Sachs, who has been mentioned before. She asked me to call on her younger daughter, Berta, who had been admitted to the Jewish Hospital. Berta, together with her older sister, Mary, and other young Jewish girls, had been pressed into forced labor by the Latvian police. They were forced to clean empty apartments whose inhabitants had fled from the advancing German troops. As the girls were burning old newspapers in a kitchen stove, an explosive device that had been hidden in the ashes exploded. Berta had suffered burns of the face, and her mother was afraid she could be permanently disfigured. Because the city was so unsafe, Mrs. Sachs did not dare to set out alone from Agenskalns to the Moscow suburb where the hospital was located.

I found Berta bedridden but otherwise in good spirits. The burns were superficial, and her mother's worries were groundless. Who could have imagined what trifles these worries were in comparison to the blows of fate that were to hit the family a few days later?

I knew my way around the hospital very well, because I had worked there as a student assistant a year before. In the Department of Internal Medicine, the Jewish doctors were just then handing over their patients to Latvian colleagues: the Jewish Hospital had ceased to exist. The new ward doctor was Dr. P. Lusis, my former superior from the military hospital. The warmth with which he pressed my hand did me good, and I realized he was making a very public effort to show me that he was distancing himself from the actions of some of the others.

In those days our family was living as though on top of a volcano because, what with the bad news arriving from all directions, we naturally had to ask ourselves when disaster would strike us as well. One day the notorious Latvian policemen forced their way into our apartment. They were holding weapons and wearing civilian clothes and red-white-red armbands (the Latvian national colors). Because of these armbands, they were popularly known among the Jews as the "Bändeldicken," or "armband wearers." In the hall the policemen ran into my friend Joe Abkin, who lived with us, and me. Joe came from China, could speak neither Russian nor Latvian, and told them in German that he lived there as a tenant. I explained to them that I lived there as a permanent resident. The policemen didn't quite understand who we were and left. Everyone breathed a sigh of relief.

One night—that summer was a hot one and I was sleeping on the ground floor with the window open—I heard a truck braking in front of our house. A voice said in Latvian, "38." This was our house number. I held my breath and thought, "Now they're coming!" But then the truck drove on.

At one point I had a peculiar encounter. I was a few steps from our house when I suddenly saw opposite me a former fellow pupil from primary school. His name was Mussel. We hadn't seen each other for about ten years, but we recognized each other immediately. He had grown tall and broad and was wearing a kind of boiler suit. His head was shaven. When I asked him what he was doing now, he answered with a Berlin accent, "Well, we're here to tidy the place up a bit for you!" With that we parted. Mussel was a Jew and apparently one of those whom the Germans at that time designated as WWJs (Wirtschaftlich Wichtiger Jude, or economically important Jew). As a rule, they were exploited and protected as long as they were needed. But no longer. I never saw Mussel again.

One day Mrs. Erna Krumins, the wife of a professor of architecture at the University of Latvia, showed up at our house altogether unexpectedly. Our families were very superficially acquainted. My father had treated Professor Krumins several times, and my mother had met his wife in an Italian course. Mrs. Krumins was appalled by everything that had taken place in Riga since the city's capture and cursed the Germans, with Hitler at their head, and her own compatriots for the atrocities they had committed. She offered to hide all of my parents' valuables in her home. My parents, who still did not realize the hopelessness of our situation, initially refused with thanks and assured her they didn't want the Krumins to get into any sort of trouble for their sake. But they finally gave in after Mrs. Krumins absolutely insisted on carrying out her intention. Doubtless Mrs. Krumins, who had extensive connections within the Latvian intelligentsia, understood much better than my parents did that a life-and-death struggle was taking place, that it was a question of survival or annihilation.

In the meantime, bad news came to us again from our relatives in Agenskalns. A Wehrmacht unit had ordered them to leave their house. The officers had been very polite but had requisitioned the space. Three generations had lived there since the turn of the century. Of the oldest generation, Mrs. Emma Sachs, Otto Sachs's mother, was the only one still living. She was a clever, active lady over seventy, the head of the family. Her pride was her children and grandchildren, her well-kept home, and her garden with its roses. My mother's cousin Johanna ("Hansi") was her daughter-in-law. She was an excellent pianist, a pupil of Godowsky. As a child, I had admired in her parents' house the laurel wreaths she had brought home from her concert tours. Godowsky, who died in 1938, had visited her in Riga shortly before his death.

Otto and Hansi had three children. Mary, the oldest, was twenty-one years old and a student at the university. Berta, the younger sister, whom I had just visited in the hospital, was eighteen. Both girls were extraordinarily beautiful. When they stood next to each other one was reminded of the angels at the bottom border of the painting of the Sistine Madonna, because their faces too radiated a strange, enchanting calm. When my father and I recalled our dead in later years, my father used to say he could not have imagined that people could exist who were able to shoot at such angelic creatures. Emanuel, the brother, was thirteen. Besides her son, Otto, Emma Sachs also had a daughter, Elizabeth, who had married the lawyer Alfons Heidemann. Their only child, a daughter, was also named Elizabeth, and was fourteen.

For years these nine people had lived in their beautiful villa surrounded by its large, well-tended garden. I too spent many hours of my childhood there. Now all of them had to leave their familiar home within twenty-four hours. To go where? Not far from them lived the already-mentioned Dr. Moritz Springenfeld, Johanna ("Hansi")

Sachs's uncle, in whose home I had found shelter the night after my flight from the Red Army. His wife had died in the spring of 1941, and since then the seventy-eight-year-old physician had lived alone in their four-room apartment. The displaced family moved in with him.

The rabble of murderers and thieves that constituted the so-called Latvian police force was precisely informed about where there was anything to be had. One night a few days after the Sachs and Heidemann families' involuntary move, the first marauders showed up in Dr. Springenfeld's apartment. Everybody was drummed out of bed, suitcases, wardrobes, and chests of drawers were torn open, and the most tempting items, from silverware and porcelain to carpets and suits, were stolen. The lawyer Heidemann's threats to press charges against the looters before Chief Stiglics of the City Police Force died away on the wind. The raids were repeated night after night until the families had been plundered nearly down to their bare skin. But this was still not the end.

On the morning of July 22 my aunt showed up at our apartment, sobbing. During the night the usual raid had been made on their apartment, but this time the perpetrators had not been satisfied with poking through the suitcases and wardrobes once again. They had ordered the men, Otto Sachs and Alfons Heidemann, to go with them. The bandits had said they would be taken to the police station to clear up a few questions. By the following morning they still had not returned. "Help us, Oscar, help us!" my aunt begged my father. It was a heartrending scene, whose tragic element we were unable to grasp in its entirety: at this hour we still did not know that the two kidnapped men were already dead. They had been executed that night in a grove, the Agenskalna Priedes (Agenskalna Pines), a few hundred meters from the house.

My parents tried as best they could to comfort Mrs. Sachs. My father was convinced that the two kidnapped men were in prison and said, naively, that it probably wouldn't be all that difficult to get two innocent people released. Although hundreds, even thousands, of us had already been killed, we still had not understood a thing. My father's intention was to find some well-known Baltic German among the Wehrmacht officers and to have our relatives released with his help. We walked around in the city for hours, taking our case to one officer after another. We did not meet anyone we knew. No matter whom we told about the incident, nobody knew how we could be helped. Finally an officer advised us to turn to the SS. And so we ended up in the former Ritterhaus, or Knights' Hall, of the Baltic German aristocracy, which had served the Latvian government as its parliament (Saeima), and into which the top echelons of the SS and the police had now been moved. Here we repeated our request and felt a certain relief when we were told to return at 3 P.M. and ask for First Lieutenant Junge. My father put on his black suit for the meeting with him. Later I described this ironically with the words: "He dressed in black for his own funeral."

I stayed at home, and my mother and I awaited the result of the interview, full of tension and restlessness. The hours crept by, and my father did not return. About six o'clock my mother, who was normally extremely self-controlled, wondered aloud where he could be. An hour later, when my father still had not returned, I mounted my bicycle and rode to the Ritterhaus. In the entrance hall I explained to two uniformed men that I was looking for my father. They listened to me in silence and then ordered me to get into the backseat of a jeep that was standing in front of the building. In R. Endrupa Street (Reimerstraße) a third SS man joined us. From my companions' conversation I realized that the third man was a Riga native, a Baltic German, who had previously kept silent about being from Riga. Doubtless he had done so because the Germans of the Reich treated their countrymen from abroad like second-class citizens. Now he was needed as a guide to the city. At first I had no idea where we were going. We drove along the quiet Brivibas Street (Freiheitsstraße), which seemed to be deserted, and turned the corner into Matijas Street (Matthaeistraße). As our car jolted over a railroad crossing, I suddenly realized we were on our way to the Central Prison. Was my father there? The iron gates of the prison opened. We drove into the courtyard and arrived at the admission hall of the prison, where a Latvian warder came toward us.

"Put this man into solitary!" barked one of my companions.

For a person who is deathly ill, in most cases it is a piece of luck if he is unaware of the inevitable fatal outcome of his illness. Just so, it was lucky for me that I had not the faintest idea of the total hopelessness of my situation. I did not suspect that death was in fact already at my heels. Who knows how I would have felt then in the cell if I had suspected what I only learned months later: that of the thousands of Jews who had been thrown into the Central Prison of Riga in July and August 1941, only ten or fifteen people left it alive. All the others were dead. Some Jews were executed in the prison courtyard and buried along the wall of the nearby Matijas Cemetery. Others were executed in the woods surrounding Riga. But because, as I said, I did not realize the hopelessness of my situation, I did not fall into despair. I neither screamed nor wept nor implored God to save me. I passed the time as best I could and tried to sleep as much as possible, sometimes up to eighteen hours a day, and waited for my release, which—yes, I had no doubts at all about it—was bound to happen. For a few days the cell next to mine was occupied by the well-known Latvian Socialist Bruno Kalnins, who is now aged and living in Sweden.

We were treated, I would almost say, humanely by the Latvian guards. The great suffering they saw here seemed to have made them sympathetic rather than harsh. One day as I was let into the washroom as usual after a "lunch" consisting of watery soup, I found a couple of slices of black bread on a small shelf above the sink. I brought them to Berkis, the guard, who was just then on duty, with the words, "Someone left them here." "Oh," he said, seemingly quite indifferent, "someone probably wanted to get rid of them. Just throw them away!" "I certainly won't do that," I answered, and took the bread with me, for the rations—200 grams a day—were quite meager. When a few days later I once again found a couple of slices on the shelf, and Berkis was once again on duty, I understood. I don't know how I had won his sympathy. Whenever Berkis was on duty I received my supplementary ration. If he hadn't been able to leave it behind for me in the washroom, I could be sure that the "food hatch" of my door would open at some point and Berkis would silently put the slices into my outstretched hands and slam the hatch shut again.

At night the building was totally still. Only once in a while a guard would shuffle by, open the peephole in the door, and look inside. Now and then a door was opened and loudly slammed shut, after which total silence set in again. By contrast, the mornings were pure hell. Hardly had we received our breakfast—a slice of bread and a mug of weak coffee—than the Latvian hangmen, who passed themselves off as examining magistrates, appeared about eight o'clock and the torturing began. The victims, who came from our building and other buildings of the prison, were lined up on the ground floor with their faces to the wall. I heard their names being called out and a "Yes!" or "Here!" called out in answer. Then the "interrogation" began. The muffled thud of rubber truncheons and the slap of whiplashes, followed by the screams, whimpers, and sobs of the victims, rose up to me on the second floor. This continued for hours, until finally about lunchtime the torturers' bloodthirstiness was quenched and the interrogations were broken off until the following day.

Eyewitnesses have seen people here with their faces beaten bloody, their teeth knocked out, and their jaws broken; some reportedly had internal hemorrhages after these "interrogations." In the afternoons everything was quiet, and I gazed for hours at the blue sky above the wooden box that stood before my window and blocked my view of the prison courtyard. It was an unusually sunny summer. Often sparrows sat on the edge of the box, preened themselves and twittered, while swifts, whistling as shrilly as street urchins, darted back and forth. Again and again I heard the drone of fighter planes, which led me to conclude, not incorrectly, that the front was still quite near.

Sometimes the afternoon calm was shattered by shots. Occasionally these were separate shots; then again there would be short rounds or the longer rattle of automatic weapons. I told myself the shots were coming from the police shooting range in the prison courtyard, and I think I actually believed this explanation. One day, horrible screams could be heard from afar. A human being was screaming like a stuck pig; he was screaming as though he were being skinned alive. The screaming was so appalling that it literally made me break out in a sweat. Horror overcame me, sheer animal fear. And not only me. As though upon command, all of the prisoners in our building began almost simultaneously to hammer on their doors. With the sweat running down my body I hammered too, in despair over the fate of that unknown man and my own fate, against the unfeeling iron door, until the screaming finally stopped and we gradually calmed down.

Lastochka was the name of a politruk (political instructor) of the Red Army who was marked for death. I knew his name because one day I was sitting beside him on the bench in the waiting room of the infirmary when an orderly called out his name. His body was covered with bruises from the blows of rubber truncheons. The previous day we had heard Germans, not Latvians, shouting "Out, out, you damned politruk!" force him out of his cell and chase him around the whole building. He had fled from them like a hunted wild animal, initially running back and forth on the ground floor, then up the iron steps to the second and third floors and then down again, where he had crashed to the ground and they had beaten him up. We couldn't see anything, but the slap of his bare feet and the trampling of the boots following him, as well as the muffled blows of the rubber truncheons, could be heard clearly.

A week had passed, and now about noon on July 30 the door of my cell opened and the guard who came in ordered me to follow him; he told me I had been released from prison. To my great astonishment and unspeakable joy, I saw my father in the entrance hall, standing there with his face to the wall. I was ordered to stand next to him, but I could not help peeking sideways now and then, full of curiosity. The hall was bustling with the comings and goings of policemen and civilians, Germans and Latvians, and between them moved prisoners accompanied by guards. A voice suddenly rang out from this din, calling out to me in Latvian, "What are you standing there for so proudly?" It came from a group of Latvian examining magistrates who were standing a few meters from me. At these words I immediately had a feeling something nasty would happen, for I suspected a trap. I answered modestly that I was just happy to be released. At that, the man turned to his comrades and called out mockingly that all of them had surely heard me saying I was proud to have been in prison. A unanimous "Yes!" resounded. "Come along!" he ordered, pushing me out into the prison courtyard.

There he took a stance facing me and said, while his right hand poked around in the back pocket of his trousers, "Now you won't be proud any more." I realized he was about to pull out his pistol, but my face remained motionless because I was too astounded by this rapid sequence of events. But the Latvian apparently didn't dare to shoot me, because of course I was a prisoner of the Germans. "Come along!" he ordered me again and pushed me back into the building with the single cells from which I had just come a few minutes ago. Here he and his comrades dragged me into one of their rooms on the ground floor. While some of them pulled a gas mask over my face, others threw me onto a plank bed and brought their rubber truncheons whistling down on my head, my neck, and my back. I doubled up with the pain but I couldn't scream, because one of the men was holding shut the air pipe of the gas mask. After a few minutes they paused and ordered me to stand up and follow a guard. I staggered behind him dizzily, got to the entrance hall again, and was led past my father, who didn't understand at all what was happening, into a big office. Here a German police officer was sitting at a desk. Two orderlies stood against the wall.

"Now, my young fellow," he yelled at me, "is it true that you said you were proud to have been here in prison?" I thought this over for a split second. If I denied it, I would be accusing the Latvian of lying, and he was more likely to be believed than I was. If I admitted it, I would simply be a stupid show-off. "Yes," I answered, "I said it." "Take off your glasses!" the officer ordered, and rose to his feet. He was at least 1.9 meters [6 feet, 2 inches] tall and weighed well over 100 kilograms [220 pounds]. He gave me a slap that sent me tottering to the wall, but a kick from one of the orderlies propelled me back to the desk. I received a second slap and flew to the other side of the room, from which another kick, this time from the second orderly, propelled me back to the officer. "So," he now said, "because you told the truth, you're released."

I rejoiced. I had made the right decision, then. Just after being led out of the room I found myself facing a second German police officer in the hall, who asked what was going on. "This is the case that we received the order about," was the answer, and immediately a Latvian civilian joined in the conversation. "If he say he proud," he said in broken German, "then he Communist!" "So," said the second officer, "then he'll just stay here!" I was led back past my father to the building with the solitary cells. In the guards' waiting room I collapsed onto a chair. "How on earth could you blabber such nonsense?" the older guard asked me reproachfully. "Do you really believe I said what they accused me of saying?" I answered. He was silent.

Led back to my cell, I palpated my head and neck. They were covered with thick welts. Months later my head would still hurt if I stroked my hair. I was overcome by a terrible, unquenchable thirst, accompanied by intensive urination, that lasted for hours. Fortunately the guards brought me water.

I did not find out until weeks later what had happened to my father. No sooner had he reported to the aforementioned First Lieutenant Junge than he was taken to the Central Prison more or less as I had been. There he was put into a cell in Building III, in which he found, to his great astonishment, a large number of Jewish colleagues who had been arrested before him. There were a total of forty-four Jewish doctors in Cells 11 and 12. They included Dr. I. Blechmann, Dr. A. Braude, Dr. M. Feitelberg, Dr. V. Goldberg, Dr. J. Goldring, the outside lecturer Dr. H. Idelson, Dr. V. Kretzer, Dr. L. Rabinovich, Dr. S. Rabinovich, and Dr. M. Wolpert. Some of the men were quite depressed, while others had not given up the hope of regaining their freedom.

Their chief pastime consisted of lecturing to each other on their areas of specialization. One day, July 30, all of them, including my father, were released from prison completely unexpectedly, without an interrogation. It remains unclear who had given this order. At the time, my father suspected that Baltic German doctors who had returned to Latvia with the Wehrmacht had intervened on behalf of their Jewish colleagues. I doubt that and believe it was a measure taken by the Gestapo, who feared that an epidemic could break out among the Jews of Riga, who at that point had no more doctors; that would have meant a serious threat to the army and the civilian population. One can judge how very justified this fear was from the fact that barely a half-year later there were already 157 cases of typhus among the German civilian and military population in Latvia and 4,825 cases in the population of Latvia, Lithuania, and White Russia.[1]

Thus my father had been released and could report to my mother only that for inexplicable reasons I had not been released. My father hoped to gain my release through the already mentioned fascist Perkonkrusts organization. To make contact with the right people, he turned to a Latvian colleague who had for years been his close friend and a good friend of the family. My astonished father now received from this "friend" a cool refusal, but that was not all. Worse yet, the colleague wrote a letter to the Perkonkrusts claiming that my father was collecting material about which Latvian doctors were Perkonkrusts members. Forty-eight hours after my father had been released from the Central Prison, Perkonkrusts men appeared at our home and took him away.

Some prominent members of Perkonkrusts had already been known by name before the war, for example, the philology professor J. Plakis and his son Dr. E. Plakis, as well as his son-in-law, the violinist E. Vinerts, and also Professor J. Vitols. The German invasion opened up for the Perkonkrusts leader Gustavs Celmins, his helper Adolfs Silde, and their followers Zilbergs, Buss, Stradins, Viktors Arajs, Kakis, the air force officer Herberts Cukurs, and hundreds of others a broad field for their rabble-rousing propaganda against the Jews. Some of them called for the murder of the Jews, while others themselves became murderers of Jews.

Years later, about 1955, in the concentration camp in Norilsk in northern Siberia I came upon the already-mentioned Kakis, who was there serving a twenty-five-year prison sentence for murder. Even a person who knew nothing about this man's previous history would have had a certain uneasy feeling about this gaunt, thin-nosed, silent man with his soft, shadowy movements. Even his compatriots, who otherwise, as was the custom in the camp, were not too particular in their choice of friends, avoided him. In the same camp another Latvian who was my patient confessed to me with a malicious grin that he had been sentenced to twenty-five years of imprisonment because he had participated in the execution of, as he put it, the "crooked beaks" (he meant the Jews). It cost me a real effort of will to treat a murderer effectively. But I did it nonetheless, and with the help of an exercycle specially built for him in a camp workshop I succeeded in strengthening his leg muscles, which had atrophied since he had had a stroke, to the point where he could walk on his own again.

Herberts Cukurs was an officer in the Latvian air force. He had become a famous figure in Latvia before the war when he dared to fly a primitive plane in 1933 to 1934 from Latvia to Gambia in West Africa, where there had once been a colony of Duke Jacob of Kurland. The flight was made in short stages because motor problems cropped up repeatedly. Cukurs's reports on his flight appeared almost every day in the newspapers. At that time we could not have imagined that the same man whose sense of adventure we admired would only a few years later earn himself the title "Butcher of Riga" for his murder of countless Jews.

The *Latvju Enciklopedija* (*Latvian Encyclopedia*) published in Stockholm in 1950 to 1955 does not mention Cukurs's war crimes: that is to say, it does not distance itself from him. It notes only that after the war he lived in Brazil.

Cukurs's mutilated corpse was found in the trunk of a private car in Montevideo in 1965. The identity of the person who settled the score with him remains unknown. Arajs was sentenced to life imprisonment by a court in Hamburg in 1979 and died in prison in Kassel at the beginning of 1988. During his interrogation he said, among other statements recorded in the court transcript, that he reported for duty in Riga with 500 men on July 1, 1941, and on the same day he was presented to Stahlecker at the police headquarters. He made a situation report to the latter, whereupon Stahlecker replied: "Carry on, in the same spirit!"[2] It is impossible to draw any other conclusion than that "carry on" referred to the executions of Jews and Communists, for what else could a man like Stahlecker have been interested in? The statement made repeatedly by the Jews of Latvia, that Latvians had begun to murder Jews even before the German invasion, is confirmed by this testimony. For days after the Red Army's retreat, large parts of the Latvian countryside were still no-man's-land and were in the hands of Latvian gangs that joined together in "self-protection units" and hunted down Red Army members, Latvian "Communists," and probably also Jews.[3] Without a doubt, Perkonkrusts and other nationalistic associations had a hand in this, because even before the war there were connections between them and the counterespionage posts of the NSDAP, as well as the Gestapo, which were maintained by the military attachés of the former Baltic republics in Berlin during the period of Soviet occupation in 1940 to 1941.[4]

When the Germans marched into Latvia, the hour of the Perkonkrusts criminals had come. Stahlecker let them do what they wished with the Jews, who had been declared outlaws. Perkonkrusts groups became real terrorist organizations. They proudly called themselves "Arajs's boys" and formed the core of the Latvian Schutzdienst, or SD (Defense Service), which took part in punitive expeditions in eastern

Latvia, White Russia, and, according to Birze, in western Europe as well. They set up their headquarters in the Jewish merchant A. Schmuljan's multistory villa on the corner of Krisjana Valdemara and Elizabetes Streets. In the cellar they set up a prison and on the top floor a storage depot for stolen goods. They used the remaining rooms as offices and meeting rooms and for their banquets. Here attacks on Jewish homes, synagogues, and small country towns were planned and subsequently implemented. They fell upon their unlucky victims like vultures, showed up unexpectedly in Jewish homes, arrested the inhabitants, and dragged out clothes and linens, bedding and dishes, children's toys and radios.

At the headquarters, their prisoners were forced to carry the stolen goods up to the top floor, where the robbers divided it up among themselves. For their attacks on synagogues they took along inmates from their prison, who were then forced to take out Torah scrolls, Bibles, candelabra, and other instruments from the holy places before the Perkonkrusts men set the buildings on fire and threw the Jews themselves into the flames. In the rooms where the stolen goods lay, my father saw a whole stockroom of ritual objects that had been brought together from the synagogues. It was Perkonkrusts members and Latvian policemen who attacked the Jews in the country towns, murdered them, looted their homes, and set synagogues on fire. It was also they who, as "examining magistrates," took delight in torturing prisoners to death in the Central Prison in Riga. The police sent some of their prisoners to work on the railroad, in the harbor, and in the turf moors near Riga, where many of them were forced to dig their own graves and then executed. At the headquarters themselves, imprisoned Jewish women had to clean the rooms, clean the toilets, and cook for the guards' canteen. At night all of the prisoners slept in the cellar on bare plywood boards. The daily ration consisted of 150 grams of bread and water.

During the day the gang of executioners took pleasure in "interrogating" old Jews, pulling their beards or forcing them to clean the streets or toilets with their bare hands. The robbers spent the nights in drunken orgies, raped Jewish girls, forced men "as a joke" to dig their own graves. Others were forced to dress in Red Army uniforms and kiss the earth, as they had allegedly kissed Soviet tanks when they invaded Latvia. One Perkonkrusts member who was asked by a student what the aims of the association were, answered laconically, "Three hundred Jews a night."

This was a gang of robbers who waded in blood in a frenzy of anti-Semitism and hatred of the Soviets. They were cruel, depraved men, and my father now found himself in their hands. Here he was interrogated, and here he saw in a Perkonkrusts member's hand the envelope with the return address of the man who had denounced him: Dr. K. Melnalksnis.

My mother was the daughter of a doctor who was formerly well known in Riga, Dr. A. Berkowitz. The Berkowitz family had resided in Riga as early as the eighteenth century, as is attested by old Riga documents. My mother had grown up within a sheltered family circle, and after she became my father's wife she had also led a life shielded from hardship. My father, always very actively concerned with his family's well-being, had as a rule taken off her shoulders all decisions concerning the family's practical life, and my mother had been able to pursue her very absorbing intellectual interests. Now she was suddenly alone for the first time in her life and left completely to her own devices. In the course of a few days she had lost her husband twice. She did not despair. Coolly and calmly she called on the German authorities and tried with their assistance to bring about my father's release.

In J. E. Kroeger's book *Eine baltische Illusion* (*A Baltic Illusion*), the entry for August 10, 1941, reads as follows:

> Just came in from headquarters of the Latvian chauvinists [he means the Perkonkrusts—B.P.] . . . The wife of a well-known Jewish doctor of Riga had turned to our department in her distress. Latvian right-wing extremists had arrested her husband. I accompanied a German first lieutenant as an interpreter. Most of the Latvians sitting there impressed me as being cruel and merciless. I could very well imagine what a fate awaited the unlucky man who fell into their hands. Although the first lieutenant made a very determined and energetic impression, nothing could be learned about the doctor's whereabouts.[5]

In the early 1980s I asked Kroeger whether he remembered the name of the doctor he had mentioned. The answer was negative. But for me there is no doubt that this passage refers to my parents, because the dates of my father's arrest and of Kroeger's notes match perfectly. After my mother's attempt to secure my father's release with the help of the German authorities had failed, she managed, thanks to the mediation of Professor Krumins, to make contact with Latvian intellectual circles who had a connection with Perkonkrusts. A Latvian lawyer agreed to accept her financial offers. Two Persian rugs and some other valuables from our house seemed to him an appropriate ransom for my father. The Persian rugs were more effective than the German first lieutenant's inquiry had been. Twenty-four hours after she had handed them over, my father was home again.

Another one of the countless victims of Perkonkrusts was the engineer E. Michelson, a friend of my parents. The bandits imprisoned him in the fall of 1941, when he was already living in the ghetto. They tortured him, but after a few days they released him. A week later they imprisoned him again, and this time he did not return to his family.

It is a known fact that Soviet documents deliberately avoid naming the murder of Jews as such. Reference is almost never made to murdered Jews, but only to butchered Soviet citizens. This results in the odd circumstance that in some publications of the relevant documents the German sources speak of executed Jews while the Soviet sources speak of executed Soviet citizens. In *Mes apsudzam* (*We Accuse*), a collection of documents about German atrocities in Latvia during the war, an attempt is even made to shift some of the blame for the Latvians' murder of Jews onto the Germans. For example, it is stated that in the Perkonkrusts prison in which my father had been, it was the Germans, not the Latvians, who had behaved like Huns and committed crimes against innocent people. As we have seen, that does not correspond to the facts. It is also stated that the "interrogations" (i.e., torture sessions) in the Central Prison in the summer of 1941 were conducted by Germans. That too is untrue. Until August 30, the day of my release, it was only Latvians who occupied themselves in this way. The Germans' chase of the politruk Lastochka, which was described earlier, was an exception.[6]

5

The Ghetto Is Established

In mid-July Dr. Rudolf Blumenfeld, a physician formerly with the Riga health service, came to see my father, Dr. Oskar Press, and discussed with him the question of how contact could be made with the German authorities in order to organize a ghetto so as to save the Jews of Riga from the annihilation that threatened them. They both agreed that they would have to consult with a few other men before joint action could be taken. A few days later my father was arrested. When he was finally released in mid-August the Jewish Committee, as it was called, had already been formed and had taken over the direction of Jewish affairs. Dr. Blumenfeld had persuaded the lawyers D. Elyashev and M. Mintz Jr., as well as Mr. Blumenau, Mr. Kaufert, G. Minsker, and Mr. Schlitter, an emigrant from Austria, to work with him. Some of these men had in the past received medals from the new Latvian state for their services at the front in the war of independence against the USSR. Perhaps they hoped this would give them a small but definite advantage in the Germans' eyes and protect them somewhat from the worst of the violence.

The Germans were also interested in establishing a ghetto, but for entirely different reasons. The extermination of the Jews would pose a threat to their economic well-being. Dr. Stahlecker, the head of Einsatzgruppe A, reported "that a total elimination of the Jews cannot be carried out, at least not at the present time, because in Lithuania and Latvia most of the skilled crafts are in Jewish hands . . . some professions are practiced exclusively by Jews, and it would be impossible to replace the Jewish workers with Lithuanians and Latvians."[1]

The inspector of armaments for Ukraine wrote to his superiors: "If we execute the Jews, let the prisoners of war die, leave much of the population of the large cities to die of starvation, and also lose part of the rural population in the coming year because of starvation, the question that remains unanswered is: who will then be left to produce economic goods?"[2]

The creation of the ghetto, which we believed would be a permanent institution lasting for the duration of the war, was for the Gestapo only a transitional measure. It was meant to enable them to exploit Jewish workers, but also—in the Gestapo's words—"to separate the wheat from the chaff," which meant that the "chaff" was to be liquidated. Moreover, if the Jews were crowded into the narrow confines of a ghetto, they would be forced to leave nearly all their property behind in their former dwellings, which promised a rich booty for the Gestapo.

The Jewish Committee was summoned to appear before the Gestapo and informed that the organization of a ghetto was imperative, since there was no other way to protect the Jewish population from Latvian pogroms. Of course this was only a perfidious game of lies on the part of the Germans, who wanted the Jews to believe they were being protected from the fury of the Latvians. At this very first meeting the Committee was presented with a four-point program, according to which:

1. the seven-member Jewish Committee bore the responsibility for the observance of all regulations affecting the Jews;
2. all Jews were to be resettled without delay in the ghetto as soon as it had been organized;
3. the able-bodied Jews were to be put under the command of an Arbeitsamt (Labor Authority), which was to be set up immediately, for purposes of registration;
4. all Jews were obliged to do the work assigned to them without opposition.

For the ghetto, the Gestapo had chosen some streets in the Riga neighborhood that lies upstream from the city center on the right bank of the Daugava and had been known as the "Moscow suburb" since the days of the czars. It was one of the poorest and least salubrious parts of Riga and consisted primarily of one- and two-story wooden houses, many of which had no sewage system or indoor toilets. The approximately 10,000 inhabitants, mostly Russian and Polish working-class families, were to be resettled so as to make room for about 30,000 Jews. In the best of cases, each ghetto inhabitant would have three to four square meters of living space.

According to a report sent by Generalkommissar Drechsler to Reichskommissar Lohse on November 20, 1941, the ghetto population consisted of the following categories (the figures were undoubtedly provided by the Jewish Committee):

a. Children up to the age of 14	
boys	2,794
girls	2,858
	5,652
b. Able-bodied persons between 14 and 65 years of age	
men	6,143
women	9,507
	15,650
c. Persons unable to work	
men	2,069
women	6,231
	8,300
Total:	29,602

A large school building at the end of Lacplesa Street in the Moscow suburb became the Jewish community's headquarters, or *kehilla* (the Hebrew word for "community"). This was now the meeting place of the Jewish Committee, whose task was to organize a second city government within the city limits of Riga for a second city—the ghetto—with all of its necessary areas of responsibility.

Mr. Blumenau became the head of the Wirtschaftsamt (Economic Authority), whose chief task was to provide the shops with foodstuffs that were apportioned to the Wirtschaftsamt by the city and transported to the ghetto by Jewish drivers. We received 175 grams of meat, 100 grams of butter, and 200 grams of sugar per person per week. The Finanzamt (Financial Authority) was headed by the lawyer J. Jewelson, who later worked in the Quartieramt (Housing Authority) after the Small Ghetto was created. A. Kehlmann headed the Sozialamt (Social Authority). Together with the Gesundheitsamt (Health Authority) he cared for the needy, the old-age homes, and the overnight shelter. The Malbishe Arumim, headed by Mrs. Elyashev, provided the ghetto's poor with clothes and shoes. Nobody knew the precise amount of living space or the borders of the future ghetto; nobody knew how rapidly the resettlement would proceed; nobody knew the exact number of Jews who were still alive in the city. (The figures on the ghetto population that are quoted in the foregoing list come from a period when the ghetto was already an isolated and fenced-in part of the city with registered inhabitants.)

That is why Mrs. Blumenfeld, the head of the Quartiersamt, was surrounded and besieged every day by hundreds of desperate, infuriated people who had just been evicted from their apartments, loudly clamoring for shelter for their families and themselves. While Russians and Poles took their time leaving their old apartments in the Moscow suburb, we were evacuated in a hurry, whole streets and neighborhoods at a time. In a few rare cases, we were even warned ahead of time. Latvian policemen threw some families out of their homes within minutes so that they, together with the custodians and neighbors, could plunder the possessions that were left behind. As a rule, in the ghetto a large family could expect to be assigned only a single room. Unattached people had to be content with a bed in the room of friends or strangers. Some were housed provisionally in dormitories, while others had to temporarily make do with a mattress in a corner of the community center until the authority finally managed to house everybody after a fashion. Strangers and families now lived cooped up together in one apartment, and their shared misery did not always guarantee peaceful coexistence. Discontent and strife broke out at the slightest provocation, such as the use and cleaning of the kitchen, bath, and toilet; because of small items that went missing, honest people accused one another of theft. This necessitated setting up a legal office, which was headed by the lawyer O. Finkelstein and had the task of peacefully resolving disputes among the ghetto's inhabitants.

The ghetto population did not obey all of the Jewish Committee's regulations without opposition. Some people understood that this was a life-and-death struggle and saw no reason why, under these circumstances, they should volunteer for unpaid servitude as well. But the Committee members had personally guaranteed that all able-bodied persons would in fact work for the Germans, and they were now forced to proceed against their own fellow Jews who refused. A small police unit of young men was organized; for a short time their chief was the jeweler M. Rosenthal. Later on, a Jewish refugee from Austria named Wand replaced Rosenthal as the ghetto's police chief.

Under the direction of the Gesundheitsamt, headed by Dr. R. Blumenfeld, the Linas Hazedek, or Jewish Women's Clinic, which was located within the ghetto, was converted to a general hospital. It thus took the place of the Bikkur Cholim, our previous hospital, because the latter could be seen from the ghetto's borders but lay outside them. The radiologist Dr. I. Haase was named hospital director. The Department of Internal Medicine was headed by Dr. V. Kretzer, the Department of Surgery by Professor W. Mintz. The Department of Gynecology was headed by Dr. Siegbert Joseph.

A children's hospital and an isolation ward were set up in the large apartments of a multistory house, for it was to be expected that infectious diseases could break out in the unhygienic conditions in which we lived. The children's hospital was headed by Dr. L. Blechmann and Dr. L. Rabinovich. The neurological clinic was directed by Assistant Professor H. Idelson and Dr. J. Krohn.

Since the Riga city authorities refused to provide services of any kind for the ghetto, the Committee also had to organize garbage collection and the emptying of the cesspits; it had large, deep pits dug, in which all the garbage was buried.

A difficult problem was posed by bedridden invalids who had previously lived alone and been cared for by friends and relatives or the Jewish social agency. The Committee established an old-age home for them in several large rooms of an old school building. Hundreds of beds were set up and the care and feeding of these poorest of the poor by nurses and relatives was organized.

The nose, ear, and throat specialist Dr. Jakobson became the director of one of the two ghetto outpatient clinics; my father was named director of the second one. Thus he had an official position, which enabled him to have contact with the director of the Arbeitsamt, which was located in a small two-story building only a few steps from the community's headquarters. The director of the Arbeitsamt was a young man who had a good reputation among the ghetto's inhabitants. It was common knowledge that he had personally intervened several times to ensure humane treatment of the Jews in their places of work, and that whenever possible he had arranged for them to receive meals there. Moreover, he tried not to send us to do work that could be life-threatening. People said that a group of Jewish workers who had been sent to cut turf on the turf moor near Sloka (Schlock) happened to meet him on the street as they were going there. They greeted him and came to a halt, surrounded him, and told him openly that they were going to their certain death, because thirty-two Jewish girls had been shot recently in the turf moor near Olaine (Olai). Thereupon he grew thoughtful and, after a moment of consideration, sent all of them back to the ghetto. When this man was transferred in the fall of 1941, Jewish workers presented him with a valuable cigarette case in recognition of his humanity. My father believed that this man must have been a Baltic German, for he seemed to know Russian and was familiar with local conditions. My father now turned to him and asked him to get me released from prison. He explained to him that I was a radiological technician and he needed me to maintain the radiological equipment in the outpatient clinic.

If we keep in mind what was going on at that time in the city and in the prison in particular, it borders on the miraculous that this man indeed managed to get me out of prison. On August 30, 1941, I was again brought before a German police officer, who told me I would be handed over to the Jewish Council—a term that meant nothing to me, because I had no idea what had been happening in the city during the previous thirty-eight days. But I told myself it would probably be better to sit behind lock and key at the Jewish Council than in the Central Prison. Once again I stood in the prison entry hall with my face to the wall, and once again they—this time it was the guards—amused themselves by trying to intimidate me. "A Jew isn't allowed on the street without a star," they told me, and asked, "How are you going to get into the ghetto?" I left the prison accompanied by an old guard and did not enter it again until eleven years later, after a Soviet military court had sentenced me to twenty-five years in a concentration camp and the loss of my civil rights for five years because of my intention to flee to the West.

The guard was not talkative. We marched side by side in silence and reached the Jewish community center. In the large courtyard of the former school building we were immediately surrounded by a curious crowd who had realized where I was coming from because of the guard's uniform. But there were others besides the merely curious. Again and again, anxious questions rang out from the crowd about whether I had seen this or that one in prison, and again and again I had to say no and explain that I had been in solitary confinement. We pushed our way through the curiosity seekers and walked down corridors and up stairways till we came to the conference room of the Jewish Committee. I knew most of the members, but because of my thirty-eight-day-old red beard they did not recognize me at first. But then they crowded around me, congratulating me on my release. Mrs. Blumenfeld pressed a sandwich into my hand. Someone pulled me into a side room where a barber—I don't know where he came from—pushed me gently into a chair and began to shave me. A few minutes later the door opened and my father rushed in and embraced me. In the meantime someone had sewn Stars of David on the front and the back of my jacket, and together with my father I started for home. At that time, my father had already found a room for us in the future ghetto, but the ghetto fence was still being built and many people, including us, still lived in their old apartments in the city. It took us barely a half-hour to get home, and then I was in my mother's arms. The hours until evening passed quickly. We had much to tell one another. I heard about my father's second imprisonment and my mother's efforts to get him released. I never told her that I was beaten in prison. On the following nights until we moved into the ghetto, I slept on a camp bed in the ghetto's outpatient clinic rather than at home. I had been advised to do so by the Committee, because I was officially in the community's custody and not a free man.

The ghetto's permanent borders had not been publicly announced initially, that is, in August and even now, in September, the Jewish Committee still did not know precisely which houses would finally lie within the ghetto limits and which ones outside. Some people who had managed to get hold of apartments had to leave them later on, after the ghetto was already crowded full, because it now turned out that these apartments lay outside the ghetto. The formation of the ghetto was not officially announced until October 23, 1941, in an order of Generalkommissar Drechsler that was published on October 24 in the Latvian newspaper *Tevija* (*Fatherland*).

Moving to the ghetto was difficult, because an order of Drechsler's forbade us to use the sidewalks, private means of transportation, trains, streetcars, buses, passenger steamships, or hired carriages. Jews were also forbidden to enter public swimming pools and nursing homes, parks and green areas, sports fields and playgrounds. We were not allowed to go to cinemas, theaters, libraries, or museums or to own cars or radios. Jewish doctors and dentists were allowed to treat only Jewish patients (this was published in *Tevija* on September 1, 1941). Moreover—and this was most probably an initiative of the Latvian police—our women were forbidden to wear hats or carry umbrellas; only headscarves were permitted. We wore the Star of David, which had to be at least 10 centimeters in diameter, on our chests and backs. But the police occasionally changed the order concerning which side of the chest. Woe to him who was not wearing the Star of David on the side dictated by the most recent order! The mildest punishment for this kind of crime was to be beaten up on the street. Some were arrested for it and disappeared forever.

All of these orders were meant to humiliate us, but we did not perceive them so—rather, they were a mark of shame for those who issued them. With heads proudly erect, we walked in the gutters, which were now our sidewalks, not reacting to the spiteful remarks that were sometimes directed at us by our fellow citizens walking on the sidewalks. If we met Latvian acquaintances, some of them only gave us a brief nod, while others preferred to cross to the other side of the street and pretend they hadn't seen us. Hardly anyone dared to speak to us on the street. We had to either carry the things we wanted to take with us into the ghetto or transport them on wheelbarrows. So we walked, loaded down with packs and bundles, in the gutters through the city to the ghetto and back again for many kilometers to our old apartment, in search of whatever things would be absolutely necessary. On the street we had to be constantly on the lookout and prepared to encounter the SS units that were out to beat us up. These SS people's main activity was to drive up to us Jews in an open car, jump out of the car, and attack us with rubber truncheons.

One day as I was on my way to the ghetto, loaded down with bundles of all kinds, the man walking in front of me suddenly turned around. I recognized Dr. Schomer, a colleague of my father's. "The car!" he shouted, and we and a couple of men and women dived into a courtyard. Peering carefully around the corner, I saw the German policemen swinging their truncheons as they attacked their victims.

The latter tried in vain to protect their heads with their hands from the blows raining down on them. A few minutes later, their work done, the policemen jumped back into their car and drove on. After that day, I never saw Dr. Schomer or heard anything about him again.

In mid-September came the day when we too had to leave our home. Our house at 38 Krisjania Barona Street had belonged to my grandfather. My mother had lived there her whole life, and I too had spent my childhood there. We walked out of our beautiful home in a euphoric state that made us regard the future hopefully, forget the horrors of everyday life, and repress any sighs or tears. I can still see before me today our apartment, our living room with its large, deep armchairs and its pictures on the walls. Among the paintings was one that depicted my mother sitting in a meadow with a large bouquet of wildflowers in her lap. On the opposite wall hung the portrait, darkened with age, of a woman with a crown on her head, who might have been a czarina. At that time we did not suspect that in the months and years to come our world would disappear, never to return, and that in the new world that was coming into being we would forever be strangers—that we would always look back at our past as at a lost paradise.

Our room in the ghetto was on the fourth floor of a six-story house in Maskavas Street (Moskauer Straße), only a few steps from Daugavpils Street (Dünaburger Straße). We divided it into two parts with some pieces of furniture we had brought with us. In the larger part, which had the window, slept my parents and our family friend Rosa Lurie, who, like so many others, had not found a room of her own. In the smaller part, I made my bed on a large old suitcase. In the neighboring room lived a Mrs. Kramer and her two adult sons, one of whom worked for the SS. The apartment had a third room, whose inhabitants I no longer remember.

When I left prison at the end of August the ghetto fence, a double barbed-wire fence 2.5 meters high, was already being put up. Holes were dug in the sidewalks and the pavement, wooden posts were hammered into the ground, and barbed wire was stretched between them. As late as the 1960s, one could still see the traces of the fence posts in places, even in streets that had been recovered with asphalt. The houses of the ghetto, which were resettled after the extermination actions, have remained largely unchanged until the present day;

thus they constitute the only completely preserved Jewish ghetto of the twentieth century. Only a few of the houses have been pulled down and replaced with multistory modern buildings.

The ghetto fence was built without haste, and as long at it was unfinished individual Latvians dared to enter the ghetto repeatedly. Some sold foodstuffs that had become scarce in the ghetto; a few others came to visit friends. Professor Krumins's wife came to visit us several times, accompanied by her older daughter, Velta, and brought my mother various things for the kitchen. Both of them expressed in vehement words their anger and bitterness over the injustice being done to us and called the persecution of the Jews an indelible disgrace for the Latvians and the Germans. During these ladies' last visit to us, just before the ghetto was closed on October 25, 1941, Mrs. Krumins handed me a large pair of wire clippers she had brought along in her shopping bag, advising me to use them if worse came to worst. She understood better than we, the threatened ones, what was still in store for us.

There were a few Jews who had not obeyed the order to move into the ghetto, in the hope that they could survive outside. During the second half of July, when all Jews were ordered to register at their local police stations, these Jews had not done so. They included the Abkin family, which consisted of the mother, a daughter Abigail, and a son Joseph ("Joe"), who has already been mentioned. The family had arrived barely a year before from China, where the father had died during a Japanese bombardment of Shanghai. The children, both in their mid-twenties, had grown up in China as "whites" or "colonizers." The fact that they were Jews had no meaning to them.

Joe had been living with us for many months. When we moved to the ghetto, he decided to stay in our old apartment, not believing that by doing so he was risking his life. He did not survive for long. Allegedly he was reported to the police by our custodian. He was arrested at the end of 1941 and never seen again. In Riga Abigail had married a Jew who was categorized as a Wirtschaftlich Wichtiger Jude (WWJ), or economically important Jew, after the German invasion. Together with his wife and mother-in-law, he stayed outside the ghetto. Yet they too met the fate that overtook most of us. But before these tragic events occurred, I saw Joe one last time.

It is hard to imagine that in those days, when death was our constant companion, we were at the same time still leading apparently normal lives. We laughed and joked, talked about books and films, and even made plans for the future. Human beings cannot dwell incessantly on even their darkest thoughts. Even on death row, condemned prisoners read books and forget, for minutes at a time, what is in store for them. This is the only explanation for the fact that we, prisoners in a concentration camp, visited one another and could sit together over coffee and tea and enjoy a good talk.

One day before the ghetto was closed a young woman I knew, Mira Israelit-Pasternak, invited me to afternoon tea at her house. One of the guests—there were perhaps eight or ten—was Joe Abkin. We were delighted to see each other again and shook hands heartily. It was to be our last meeting. We spent several pleasant hours together and enjoyed the cake Mira had gotten hold of somewhere. As usual, we indulged in reminiscences and spoke of the future as though we were unaware of the horrible present. We joked boisterously, and in this convivial atmosphere I made a date with a charming, slim, black-haired girl, Joe Ellis Levin, to meet at the Waldorf-Astoria Hotel in New York after the war. Of this merry company, the only survivors are my fellow student L. E. and myself.

In the city there were many sick and frail people who could not reach the ghetto on foot. Because we were not allowed to use public transportation of any kind, the Gesundheitsamt organized a transport service for these people, which consisted only of a pushcart and a wheelchair. Using these makeshift vehicles, three of us—my friends L. E., Jascha Kahn, and I—brought sick people and invalids to the ghetto from all corners of the city. Those who could travel in a sitting position were brought to the ghetto in the wheelchair, while the bedridden were transported in the pushcart. We carried the sick people from their apartments into the street on a litter and loaded them onto a mattress we had put into the pushcart. A few times we even transported two patients at a time on this mattress. Among the invalids who were transported to the ghetto in this fashion were the well-known Riga matzo manufacturer Gutkin and his wife. After we had settled them in their new dwelling in the ghetto, he thanked us most warmly and said that after the Germans were defeated we would always get from him as many matzos as we wanted. This was to remain a pious wish. He too was a victim of the murderers.

This work was not difficult for us, but it was a source of anxiety. As long as we were pushing the empty pushcart through the city we were barely noticed—people had quickly gotten used to seeing the Jews wearing the yellow star. But when we were on our way back to the ghetto we drew the curiosity of passersby. The stars on our jackets and our unusual burden informed them unequivocally about who was transporting whom and where. Outwardly calm but inwardly tense, looking neither right nor left, we strained to reach our destination. There was never any incident, but we always heaved a sigh of relief when the first houses of the ghetto came into view.

I had already known my fellow student L. E. for several years, but I only met Jascha Kahn in the ghetto. He was a friendly, clever young man, always in a good mood and ready to help, and we soon became friends. I can still see Jascha before me today: slim, wearing a blue pullover and a beige trench coat with a turned-up collar. A painful and tormenting memory, for one year later the Germans hanged him in the ghetto. Jascha's older brother had been a policeman and had been executed together with the other policemen for belonging to a resistance movement. Afterward the Germans suspected that Jascha knew about the movement and sentenced him to death by hanging. L. E. was present at the hanging, together with the other inhabitants of the ghetto. They were forced to watch the execution, which was supposed to "set an example." Jascha died speaking the words "Shma Yisrael, eloheno adonai ehod"—"Hear, O Israel, our God is the true God."

6

Daily Life in the Ghetto

The Riga ghetto, which came to be known as the Large Ghetto—for there was also a Small Ghetto later on—did not exist for long. Its gates closed on October 25, 1941, cutting us off completely from the rest of the city. On the same day came the first snowfall of the winter of 1941–42, and it started to freeze. At first there was only a thin blanket of snow, but it did not melt the way such an early snowfall usually does. Not until the end of March—that is, in the spring of 1942—did the thermometer rise above the freezing point again. It was an unusually long, hard, and snowy winter.

Although we had been forcibly resettled in the ghetto, a step that meant the destruction of our previous existence, nonetheless we tried to salvage something positive from it. We hoped that the barbed-wire fence would protect us from the worst attacks, and that it would be easier to survive as a community than as individuals scattered among our enemies. There were optimists who told us that life in the Warsaw ghetto was quite tolerable. Moreover, we hoped that now that winter had set in, the German dream of a Blitzkrieg in the East would soon peter out, and that the Germans would fare as badly in Russia as the French had fared before them. This optimism was partly justified, but partly we used it to keep up our courage and try to comfort one another. Of course we saw that we were caught in a trap, and in the worst of cases we would have no refuge anywhere. But what would the worst of cases be? We could imagine a slow decimation of the ghetto population, but not the total extermination of 30,000 human beings.

We could not suspect, let alone imagine, that what was happening here before our eyes was only a fragmentary picture of a comprehensive plan to exterminate us. But who, after all, could have imagined that what was happening here was the extermination of a whole people! And all the decisions had already been made. Whereas we still had the illusion that we would go on living and survive, the Gestapo had only the problem of how to technically implement the extermination plans.

The hope that in the ghetto we would be protected from attacks turned out to be an illusion. Very soon it became clear that we had to avoid the streets that ran along the ghetto fence, because there we were at the mercy of the Latvian guards on patrol who marched back and forth between the two barbed-wire fences. They shot some people down for no reason whatsoever and robbed others by using a primitive trick: they would beckon to their innocent victim to come to the fence and then ask him what time it was. If the person had a good watch, he would be forced to hand it over at gunpoint. In this way money, rings, and other jewelry ended up in the guards' hands. So people avoided these streets and got from one house to another by going through gaps they had made in the fences of rear courtyards and gardens. Thus a network of paths was formed between the houses, along which we could move safely. Because of the early winter, these slats broken out of the fences were followed by others. Because the state authorities provided us with neither wood nor coal for the large houses' central heating, more and more fence slats disappeared into kitchens and sheds until finally there were no more fences, but most of the ghetto's inhabitants had a small supply of firewood.

German, Latvian, and also Jewish policemen combed the ghetto repeatedly for men and women who were not working; of course blows would rain down if anyone was actually found. During these raids the Germans and the Latvians would pilfer things they fancied. Small objects we had saved and brought to the ghetto, such as carpets, pictures, and crystal, were sent to Germany as "the spoils of war." Almost daily the German authorities issued new orders whose obvious purpose was to rob us, who had already been robbed, even further. One decree would order us to hand over our bedding—sheets, pillows, and blankets—while the next one demanded musical instruments. Those who shirked working for the Germans and hid in sheds, cellars, and attics during the house searches did so in the conviction that they should save their strength rather than sacrificing it for slave drivers. Some devised very inventive hiding places, for example, behind woodpiles, where they would sit quietly while the policemen searched for them in vain. But most men and women went to work every day, mainly because of the additional meals that were provided at the places where they worked, bits of which they would smuggle into the ghetto.

Thus life in the ghetto acquired a certain rhythm. In the mornings, almost in the dark of night, thousands of ghetto inhabitants lined up at the gate in marching columns, were received by their German or Latvian overseers, and went off to work. Even the large columns numbering several hundred people were supervised by only two or three overseers. Sometimes even women or teenage boys accompanied the columns, since everyone knew there was no place to which we could flee. In the evening the columns returned. In the meantime those who had remained in the ghetto, mostly older men and women, did the housework. People cleaned their apartments, cooked dinner, and stood in line outside the shops.

A difficult problem was posed by the many children and teenagers who didn't know where or how to spend their time and were at risk of running wild. The community set up kindergartens for the youngest children and organized school classes for the older ones.

The well-known historian Professor S. Dubnow actively helped the community in these efforts. As has already been mentioned, he had emigrated to Latvia from Germany in 1933 and lived in Mezaparks (Kaiserwald), a suburb of Riga. He had an extensive private library. After the German invasion the Gestapo went to his house and interrogated him but left him untouched. Later he moved to the ghetto, while his large library was, to his distress, carted off to Germany. It was Professor Dubnow who advised my father—and probably not him alone—to write down for future generations everything he had seen and experienced in the ghetto. He was killed in the second extermination action on December 8, 1941. According to reports, the Gestapo officer who murdered him was a former student of his.[1]

After the resettlement of the Jews into the ghetto from the rest of the city was complete, the transport service for the sick was also finished. L. E. and Jascha Kahn found work in a Wehrmacht unit, and I started to work with my father at the Polyclinic, which was on Moscow Street in a multistory light gray house between Lacplesa Street and Katolu (Catholic) Street. I worked in the registration office recording house calls and outpatients and filling out filing cards. Every evening I put together an overview of the patients seen that day which, signed by my father, was sent to the ghetto's Health Authority. A nurse named Bobé and an elderly midwife worked with me. Every time an army motorcycle loudly rattled by on the street, the midwife would murmur, "May they ride and never reach their destination!"

Dr. Davidson headed the X-ray department; the consulting hours for internal medicine were handled by the brothers H. and I. Jawitz, Dr. Reimann, and my father. The usual analyses were done in the laboratory. The Polyclinic's pharmacy provided the patients with the necessary medicines, for the ghetto had no pharmacy. All the medicines came from Wehrmacht units, where they were slipped by army doctors to the Jews who worked there. Dr. Lämmchen and Dr. Rogalin made the house calls. From them we learned of the terrible conditions in which some ghetto inhabitants were living. For example, Dr. Lämmchen told us that during one house call the alarmed inhabitants had stopped her in the nick of time from hanging her coat on a nail. The seemingly brown wallpaper of the room got its brown color from tens of thousands of bugs that had infested the place for years and now defied all efforts to exterminate them. In the evenings, after consulting hours were over, Mrs. Drabkin tidied up the rooms. She was a cheerful young woman in her mid-twenties who had just graduated from the British Institute in Riga. She was glad to be allowed to work in the Polyclinic instead of doing slave labor for the Germans. Of my aforementioned coworkers at the clinic, the only ones who survived the German occupation besides my father and me were Dr. Davidson, Dr. H. Jawitz, and Dr. Rogalin. Mrs. Drabkin's husband, a dental technician, also survived.

The atmosphere in the Polyclinic was feverish and nervous, as it was everywhere in the ghetto. Quiet minutes and hours were followed by moments of extreme tension and fear. Sometimes we worked for hours in peace and quiet, until someone suddenly rushed in and panted that such and such a person had just been shot at the ghetto fence. "What for?" everybody would ask in alarm. The answer was always "For nothing at all!" Then again, someone would appear who had heard that machine guns had been set up at the ghetto gate, whereupon we looked at each other anxiously and our throats choked with fear. After a while the tension relaxed and everyone continued his or her work. Patients came and went. Some had been treated at their places of work and came to us with a written diagnosis from an army doctor.

In the evenings L. E., Jascha Kahn, and I would meet in a small room of the old-age home that had been fitted out as the outpatient department. The head of the outpatient department was Dr. Bruno Gottschalk. Here we were able to give first aid to emergency cases after the polyclinics had closed for the day. It soon became clear that our help was most often needed by men who had been beaten up by German or Latvian policemen at the ghetto gate as they returned from work. The ghetto gate was on the corner of Sadovnikova and Lacplesa Streets. A sign hanging above the gate proclaimed: "Jews provided for a fee. This includes Wehrmacht jobs."

Here the policemen waited for the Jews who were coming home. They would pick out a man or a woman at random from the work gangs, order him or her to strip, and frisk him or her. The policemen took special pleasure in frisking young women while loudly discussing their victim's physical advantages and disadvantages. A major pretext for beating people up was the constant attempts of the people coming home to smuggle food into the ghetto, which was strictly forbidden. Yet men and women dared to do so repeatedly, which was no wonder, because most of them had mothers, wives, and children in the ghetto who were starving while they themselves were fed at their places of work. Moreover, many of the Wehrmacht units did not mind if the Jews who worked for them stuck pieces of bread into their pockets.

Once the door of the outpatient department was flung open and someone shouted that we should get to the gate fast; a fellow had been nearly beaten to death there. We ran toward the gate immediately, but halfway there we were met by a children's sled pulled by a couple of men, on which the victim had been laid. His face was totally swollen from welts raised by blows made with rubber truncheons. We poured a bit of alcohol into his mouth and bandaged the wounds on his forehead. He came to slowly, opened his eyes, and sat up. Only then did I recognize him. It was Schneider, a pal of mine, with whom I had done army service in Krustpils (Kreuzburg) before the war. Twenty years later we met again. Schneider had become a butcher and worked in a butcher's shop only a few steps from my home. It was a great joy to see him again. Later he emigrated to Israel.

Another time we were summoned to the home of a man who had also been beaten up. When we arrived we were led into a small attic room, where an old man was sitting on a chair sobbing quietly to himself. It was the master tailor Milch. There was a huge cut on his head from a blow made with a rubber truncheon. In the dim light of a small electric bulb we cleaned the wound, which was sticky with hair, and bandaged it. During the whole time we were with him the maltreated man spoke not a single word to us. He seemed neither to notice us nor care about us, and when we left the room he was still quietly sobbing to himself.

Many of our friends and acquaintances visited us in the outpatient department in the evening, partly because they no longer had homes, whereas here it was possible to sit together in peace and have a talk. A frequent guest was the nose, ear, and throat specialist Dr. M. Wolpert. On the night of July 1 he, like so many other Jewish doctors, had been arrested by Latvian policemen and brought to the Central Prison, where he shared a cell with other Jewish doctors. When he was released from prison at the end of July and returned to his home, he found his apartment empty and deserted. He learned from the neighbors that his family had been resettled in the ghetto. He rushed there and found his little daughter Ina and his mother-in-law Mrs. L. Levin, but not his wife. A few days before she had been taken away by Latvian policemen, together with her friend Mrs. E. Goldring, from their shared ghetto apartment to police headquarters, from which the two women never returned.

After the loss of her mother, Ina, a blonde little girl of ten, became more attached than ever to her father, and in the evening she used to turn up at the outpatient clinic to wait for him there. Wearing a red knitted cap, she sat quietly and patiently on a chair, watching the adults around her. One evening, when her father was delayed longer than usual, she looked at us with big eyes and asked calmly, "Are there grounds for alarm?" These were distressingly mature words coming from the mouth of a little girl. Dr. Wolpert managed to save his little daughter. He himself also survived.

The daughter of Mr. Blumenau, the head of the Wirtschaftsamt, visited us almost every evening. She was a tall, cheerful girl and always brought along a girlfriend, whose surname, Vietinghof, was very unusual for a Jewish person.

Now and then Dr. Aron Bdiel would also visit the outpatient department. He was a slim young man with black hair, a dark complexion, and a small moustache. He had a very likable, quiet, and modest character. I had met him a few years before in the Jewish Hospital when I worked there as a student trainee. Before the war began he had lived in Latgale in eastern Latvia, and there he had witnessed the atrocities committed by Perkonkrusts and the Aizsargi after the German invasion. In the small town where he lived he was obliged to watch from close up while these murderers shot Jewish men, women, and children day after day. A great many Jews lived in the small towns of Latgale, and so there was a great deal of "work" for the mass murderers. We could get a sense of their callousness when Dr. Bdiel told us how they sometimes came to him in the evening after literally rubbing their fingers raw on their gun triggers in the course of the day, so that he could bandage their hands. For unfathomable reasons they let Dr. Bdiel live. And not only that: when there was nothing more for the murderers to do in that town and its surroundings, they put Dr. Bdiel on a train to Riga and advised him to save himself by going to the Riga ghetto, because there in Latgale he would not survive.

Years later I came upon Dr. Bdiel's name in the Latvian writer P. Vigants's notes in the anthology *The Salaspils Death Camp* (Salaspils was a village on the Daugava River about 15 kilometers upstream from Riga). In a short sketch entitled "The Strings Still Sounded," Vigants narrates how Dr. Bdiel was always able to convey comfort and hope to his patients even under the terrible conditions of the death camp, even when there was no longer any chance of their being saved. The inmates of Salaspils cherished Dr. Bdiel as a doctor and loved him because of his beautiful violin playing. The violin, writes Vigants, had belonged to a well-known Austrian violinist who had once given concerts throughout Europe and had left the instrument to Dr. Bdiel before he died in the camp. Vigants does not mention the name of the violinist. One evening, as Dr. Bdiel was once again gladdening his listeners with his violin playing, the camp commander's deputy Tekemeyer suddenly appeared in the barracks. When he was asked what the meaning of all this was, Dr. Bdiel explained, "We're making music. It's the only medicine that is left to us." "Wonderful!" shouted Tekemeyer, and smashed the violin against the wall, adding, "Don't forget that there's a gallows standing in the middle of the camp!"[2] M. Birze told me that Dr. Bdiel was shot in Salaspils in May 1943, together with the members of an underground movement.

Now and then Dr. David Berkowitz, a distant relative, visited me, sometimes in the outpatient department and sometimes at home. I now learned for the first time that he had fought in the Baltic Landeswehr against the Red Army. This was one of the reasons that had kept him from fleeing to Russia. He was convinced that in the USSR he would be arrested on some pretext and liquidated. He told me that as a Jew he had felt very comfortable among the Germans in the Landeswehr and that he had also sworn the oath of allegiance to the flag. When he pointed out that he was a Jew, the chaplain had answered that one swears the oath to the flag, not to a religion. Dr. Berkowitz had married barely a year before and his wife was now pregnant with twins. She would often complain of intense pains, and Berkowitz would joke that his sons were now playing soccer in their mother's womb, and that he would pay them back for it yet. When the children were born, my mother gave her a tin of cocoa as a present. The children died soon after their birth. I never saw Berkowitz again. After the liquidation of the Small Ghetto he was the camp doctor in the Dünawerke barracks in what used to be the Provodnik rubber factory. This was reported to me by E. Salzmann, whom he treated at the time for a phlegmon of the lower jaw and nursed back to health with touching devotion. Later he was sent to the camp in Dundaga, from which he, emaciated to the point where he was a walking skeleton, was sent to the Kaiserwald concentration camp. According to M. Kaufmann, he was secretly killed there.

Mrs. Eva Hoff and her children, five-year-old Marina and not-yet-three Leonard, also visited us at home a few times. Eva was the daughter of Dr. Berthold Pulvermacher, a respected doctor in Berlin. She had come to Riga in the mid-1930s and married Jacob Hoff, whose family she had been friends with for years. The Hoff brothers were well-known industrialists in Latvia. In 1938 her parents and her aunt, who lived in Berlin, visited her in Riga. And there they stayed, for Mrs. Hoff, who feared that something bad could happen to them at home in Germany, did not let them return to Berlin.

For five years the Hoffs led a carefree life in a patrician house on the Ganibu Dambis (Weidendamm). Then the USSR's annexation of Latvia forced them to move to a small villa in Mezaparks, a beautiful suburb of Riga. In early July 1941 the SS arrested Eva Hoff's husband, her father, and her aunt. The Gestapo had not touched Eva herself, who pretended to be a German, or her children; they lived in the ghetto in an apartment they shared with her niece, Ruth Budó. Mrs. Hoff, a tall, slim, attractive woman, impressed us as being very composed during her visits to us. She had not given up the hope of seeing her family again. Decades later, in the summer of 1984 in her apartment in Stockholm, she told me what a desperate struggle she had waged in subsequent years for the survival of her children and herself. Her path had led her to the Riga Central Prison and the Salaspils and Stutthof concentration camps and finally to Flensburg, where she had been saved and brought to Sweden by the Swedish Red Cross.

Once the dentist's wife Mrs. Feinmann visited us. Her son Dima, my friend and fellow student, lived outside the ghetto with papers identifying him as an "Aryan." Half a year later he was jailed in the Central Prison because someone had denounced him. Months later there were cases of dysentery in the prison. The sick inmates, including Dima, were shot. His wife Valentina, née Löwenstein, was saved by the well-known Baltic German publicist and former editor in chief of the *Rigasche Rundschau,* Paul Schiemann. The wife of Dr. R. Brennsohn-Meltzer, the daughter of the well-known historian of medicine Dr. I. Brennsohn, also visited us, and she and my mother exchanged memories of their youth.

The people returning from work brought news of the outside world into the ghetto. Mostly they told of minor events in the places where they worked, but occasionally there was also news of events at the front. The Blitzkrieg had stalled and reports of victories had grown increasingly scarce. "General Winter" had taken over the command. We saw, with malicious grins and full of satisfaction, how the German soldiers were freezing in their thin little coats, and we were quite amazed that the German leadership had allowed the situation to deteriorate so badly.

The mood in the ghetto was very depressed for some time after we learned that Jeckeln had caught several Jewish girls smoking in his headquarters in the Ritterhaus and ordered them to be punished by being shot on the spot.

One evening when I came home from the outpatient department I heard loud weeping coming from the room next door, where the Kramer family lived. My mother told me softly that Mrs. Kramer's older son, who worked for the SS, had been arrested. Sometimes it seemed to us that we were paying the price for the Germans' setbacks at the front.

Other news items—most of them concerned our personal fate and nobody knew if they were merely rumors—were called YWA (the acronym for "Yiden willen azoi"—Jews want it that way). According to one of these stubbornly recurring rumors, barracks were being built near Salaspils (Kurtenhof) and we were to be resettled in them. The only element of truth in this, as it later turned out, was that German Jews who had been deported to Latvia in the late fall of 1941 were in fact building a concentration camp there. Only a few of the Riga Jews were sent there after the extermination actions.

As I have mentioned already, the panicky flight at the start of the war tore many families apart. In most cases it was women with small children who had not dared to risk fleeing into the unknown and had stayed behind in Riga. Among these lonely women were Elena Bordó, the sister of Paul Sliosberg, a friend of my youth; Irene Fleisch, née Shapiro, a childhood friend of mine; and Samella Sverdlin, née Fishkin. Elena was the wife of Lev Bordó, who had fled to Russia—I don't know under what circumstances—at the beginning of the war, leaving his wife and their four- or five-year-old son behind in Riga. Elena, who had once been a young woman full of joie de vivre, was very depressed in the ghetto, and this condition slowly degenerated into despair. One day shortly before the extermination actions she slashed her child's wrists and her own. Someone surprised her doing so and it was possible to save her life. The child died, despite all efforts to save him.

Nikolai Bordó, Lev Bordó's brother, was also in the ghetto with his wife and little daughter. I saw him for the last time a few days after Pearl Harbor, that is, after December 7, 1941. I asked him his opinion on the significance of the United States's declaration of war against Japan. He was very depressed and only murmured that it probably no longer had any significance for us. His later path of suffering led him finally to Buchenwald, where he arrived in the fall of 1944.

Irene Shapiro had married my friend A. Fleisch. I often saw her on the street in the ghetto when she took her little son, barely a year old, for a walk in his carriage. She made no secret of the fact that she had refused to flee to Russia with her husband, preferring to stay in Riga with her parents. I didn't ask her what she thought of her decision now.

I had known Samella Fishkin for several years. When I met her by chance in the ghetto I found out that she had married my schoolfellow Sverdlin. She was in the final months of pregnancy. When I asked how her husband was she answered with a beaming smile that he was in prison and worked in an auto workshop. She said she had already seen him a few times as he passed her on the street in a prison truck, and they had waved to each other. Wasn't it lucky, she asked me, that he had such a good job? I agreed with her, though my throat had gone quite dry.

One day I ran into white-haired old Dr. Japhé walking slowly down the street. I was bound to his family by many years of friendship. I had known his daughter Ira since my earliest childhood, when we went to the same kindergarten. Since then we had grown up almost like brother and sister. In recent years, however, we had met less often, for she was studying agronomy in Belgium and returned to Riga only for the summer holidays. But our relationship had remained the familiar one of old. I knew that Ira and her mother had suddenly disappeared one day not long after the German invasion. Probably they had been picked up on the street and shot, like so many thousands of others. When I cautiously asked how he was living, the old doctor answered that he was doing well, he had a room of his own. "And," he added matter-of-factly, "when my wife and the sparrow are released from prison, there's enough room for both of them as well." When he said "the sparrow" he was referring to his daughter.

One floor above us lived the dentist Dr. S. Herzberg (known as "Lommi") with his wife Stella, his father, and his younger brother

Boris. We hadn't known one another previously but now we became friends. The two brothers worked for the Wehrmacht, while the dentist's wife worked as a cleaning lady in her former apartment in the city, in which two German officers were now living. Old Mr. Herzberg kept house. The dentist was still alive thanks to his courage. He told us that in early July Latvian policemen, the notorious "Bändeldicken," had forced their way into his apartment with the obvious intention of arresting him. In the hall the men were stopped by Herzberg's dog, a big snarling bulldog who made to attack the intruders. Without any ado Herzberg dragged the animal, barking with rage and possibly scenting their evil intentions, into a neighboring room and coolly scrutinized his would-be executioners. Perhaps they were impressed by the way this tall, black-haired, strongly built man had dealt with the vicious dog; nonetheless they ordered him, "Come with us!" "Gentlemen," answered Herzberg, "if your intention is to execute me, I ask you as an officer of the Latvian Army to shoot me on the spot." The men became suspicious and asked whether he was really an officer. "I will show you my commission," he answered. The men conferred briefly with each other and then left.

Stella, Dr. Herzberg's wife, was probably only a few years older than me, but she impressed me with her serene character, calmly weighing everything up. Once I asked her if she wasn't afraid of being frisked at the ghetto gate when she returned from work and she answered, "One should react to such things only when they happen instead of thinking about them beforehand."

Now and then I visited our relatives, the Sachs and Heidemann families, who lived in two rooms together with old Dr. M. Springenfeld. My father had said once, half joking and half in earnest, that he hadn't believed that the inhabitants of Agenskalns, the neighborhood in which Dr. Springenfeld had practiced his whole life—for fifty years, to be exact—would let him move to the ghetto, for this short, plump man had enjoyed a popularity among his patients that can hardly be described. He had the benevolent, almost childlike smile of a saint, and many believed him to be one. There were patients who kneeled before him on the street. He gave money for medicine to the poor people among his clientele and bought various household items for them.

The old gentleman, now seventy-eight years old, received me sit-

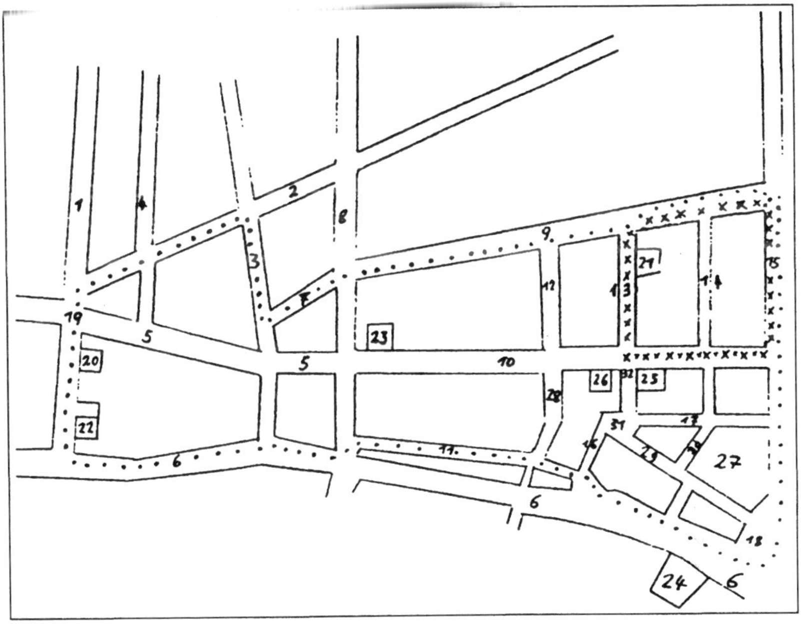

PLAN OF THE RIGA GHETTO

.... borders of the Large Ghetto
xxxxxx borders of the Small Ghetto

1. Lacplesa (Bearslayer) Street
2. Jekabpils Street
3. Katolu (Catholic) Street
4. Palisadu (Palisade) Street
5. Sadovnikova Street
6. Maskavas (Moscow) Street
7. Lazdonas Street
8. Daugavpils Street
9. Liela Kalnu (Great Mountain) Street
10. Ludzas Street
11. Jersikas Street
12. Maza Kalnu (Little Mountain) Street
13. Liksnas Street
14. Vilanu Street
15. Lauvas (Lion) Street
16. Sarkana (Red) Street
17. Kostromas (or Virsaisu) Street
18. Zidu (Jews') Street
19. Ghetto gate
20. Jewish community center in the Large Ghetto
21. Jewish community center in the Small Ghetto
22. Labor Authority and Maza Lacplesa Street
23. Linas Hazedek
24. Bikkur Cholim
25. Women's Ghetto
26. Ghetto command post
27. Old Jewish Cemetery
28. Berliner Straße
29. Kölner Straße
30. Bielefelder Straße
31. Blechplatz (Blech Square)
32. Prager Tor (Prague Gate)

ting on the edge of his bed, for there were hardly any chairs in the rooms, in which beds stood close together. My father always sent him a couple of cigarettes, which he appreciated greatly; cigarettes were scarce in the ghetto. His first words were always, "Well, old boy, what's new?"—whereupon I used to tell him all kinds of hopeful news items. I never met the young girls of the two families, because they worked in the city. Emanuel, the youngest, hung around on the street playing hooky. His watch, of which he had been very proud, had been taken away at the fence by a Latvian guard.

After losing their husbands, my great-aunt Hansi Sachs and Mrs. Heidemann were not very inclined to chat. Only once did I have a longer talk with old Mrs. Sachs, who at that time was seventy-four years old. I asked her how she thought the war would end, and she answered with absolute certainty that the Germans would lose. Her conviction was based on moral considerations. "A regime that sows only evil and tramples on other peoples will not triumph," she said. "But will we live to see it?" I persisted. She looked at me calmly and said, "But what does that matter?"

7
Extermination

The Large Ghetto had now been in existence for a month, and one might have thought that, despite all the rumors, it would continue to exist. Ghetto life, with all of its drawbacks, had become everyday life to which we had grown accustomed. But on Thursday, November 27, 1941, we were abruptly jolted out of this relatively calm mood by a printed announcement put up by the Gestapo. The announcement said that on Saturday, November 29, all the men had to appear at 9 A.M. in Sadovnikova Street for a roll call. Nobody could understand what this order was supposed to mean. We realized or suspected that nothing good could be behind it. But we could not deduce from the dry words what it could be or what threatened us. Would the men really be evacuated? For a long time now there had been rumors to that effect. And what was to become of the women and children?

One rumor followed another. On the next day, Friday, November 28, our anxiety grew when the inhabitants of the ghetto neighborhood bordered by Liela Kalnu Street, Ludzas Street, Liksnas Street, and Lauvas Street were driven helter-skelter from their apartments by the Jewish police and ordered to look for shelter elsewhere in the ghetto. At the same time a fence was hurriedly built around this neighborhood. Soon a new rumor was circulating. Now it was said that the neighborhood that had just been fenced in, the Small Ghetto, was the future work camp and that everyone who worked for the Germans would live there. What was to happen to the others was unclear.

At 9 A.M. on November 29, all the men stood lined up in rows in Sadovnikova Street. For a long time, nothing happened. People talked quietly. The mood was depressed. We were frightened without knowing exactly of what. Then the rumor went from mouth to mouth that machine guns were standing at the gates of the ghetto. About half past ten a few German police officers appeared and walked past our lined-up rows, seeming to be totally uninterested. After another long stretch of time the command to disperse suddenly sounded. Nothing had happened. We were still alive. We looked at one another laughing, as though we had been redeemed. On the way home my father and I visited Dr. Blumenfeld for a moment. He, his wife, and the psychiatrist and outside lecturer Dr. Idelson, who lived with them, had just sat down to lunch. My father asked Dr. Blumenfeld what he thought of that day's roll call and what he thought would happen next. Dr. Blumenfeld did not express an opinion, saying only that we could not expect anything good to happen. Dr. Blumenfeld's wife, the mother of my friend Arnold ("Bubi") Fleisch, said to me, "Look at me closely, my boy, for one day you will give my son my last farewell!" Her prophetic words came true in October 1944 when her son, who had fled to Russia in 1941, indeed came back with the Red Army and we celebrated a painful reunion. His wife, his little son, his mother, his stepfather, his parents-in-law, and many of his friends—all of them had been killed in Riga.

During our visit to Dr. Blumenfeld I noticed the very lavishly set lunch table with many open cans of every kind of food. I did not understand the meaning of this feast until years later, when Mrs. Ina Hait-Wolpert told me about a similar meal that took place at nearly the same moment in her parents' apartment in the ghetto.

We went home, where I laughingly told my mother that the Germans didn't know what to do with us. The euphoria did not last long. That same afternoon there was a new decree that the evacuation of the ghetto was to begin at 6 A.M. the next day, November 30. Suddenly everything became bitterly serious. That evening and far into the night, thousands of women sewed rucksacks and bags for themselves and their family members. In the families whose men were to move to the work camp, the Small Ghetto, but whose relatives were to be evacuated, there were desperate parting scenes. Some married couples considered committing suicide.

Later my father told me he too had suggested to my mother that they both end their lives with morphine. But my mother had refused, saying, "Who will avenge us if we all die?" Lone mothers first killed their young children and then themselves. Nobody slept that night.

To keep the Moscow suburb's civilian population from being eyewitnesses of the events now about to occur, the Gestapo began its extermination action in the late evening of November 29 and continued it throughout the night. What was exterminated was that half of the ghetto which lay closer to the center of Riga—that is, the half between Lacplesa Street and Daugavpils Street. Latvian execution commandos and Latvian policemen were deployed.

First the policemen, rolling drunk, forced their way into the old-age home and the neighboring houses. In the old-age home they machine-gunned old people, sick people, and invalids in their beds. They drove out of their apartments in the neighboring houses people who were still in the midst of their preparations for the supposed evacuation, with truncheon blows and shots, curses and threats. Anyone who did not obey fast enough was shot on the spot. Small children were hurled out of windows onto the street. In the dark of night Latvian policemen on foot and on horseback, including the already mentioned H. Cukurs, drove people down the street like a panicky herd of animals. According to an eyewitness report, Cukurs tore an infant out of its mother's arms and smashed the baby's head against the curbstone. As the mother threw herself with a wild scream on the lifeless, bleeding body of her child, he riddled her head with bullets from his revolver. Anyone unable to keep up was killed with a shot in the neck. Some of the old people were pushed into buses and driven off; these unfortunate ones had no idea where they were going. In fear and terror, those who were doomed to death were driven forward; they threw away their bundles so they could run faster, so they would not be beaten or caught by a bullet—not knowing that the bullet destined for them was already waiting for them in another gun barrel.

The people were driven down Sadovnikova Street and Ludzas Street and then out of the ghetto along Maskavas Street, kilometer after kilometer upstream, until they finally reached their destination, which was named Rumbula (not "Rumbuli," as reported by some authors). Rumbula, which until that day had been only a tiny railroad station, a point on the map, became during those days a meaningful name in the history of the extermination of the Jews, just as the forest of Bikernieki had been previously and the Kaiserwald concentration camp was to be subsequently. Here mass graves had been dug in the forest, which was surrounded by soldiers. Anyone who had reached this place alive suddenly realized in a flash what awaited him or her. In the bitter frost, everyone had to undress, lay their clothes in separate piles, and wait for the bullet that was destined for them, while in the meantime new columns were arriving constantly and the buses driving back and forth brought in new victims. According to the eyewitness A. Baranovskis, the Rumbula station chief, the action began at 8:15 A.M. on November 30 and ended at 7:45 P.M. the same day. On that day more than 15,000 people were slaughtered by the Gestapo and the Latvian police.

The Jewish police drove us out of our flat at 5 A.M., shouting, "Out, everybody out!" On the stairway we were caught up in the current of the other inhabitants of our building, who were streaming from all the floors toward the front door. Among them were the Herzberg brothers and their father. I didn't see Stella. It was completely dark outside. We followed the people in front of us through the dark courtyard, entered the next courtyard through a gap in the fence, and from there came out into Sadovniknova Street, which was empty of people. Latvian policemen drove us into the courtyard of the school at the corner of Sadovnikova Street and Daugavpils Street. Here we stood motionless in the darkness of the morning. As dawn began to break we saw several corpses lying lined up in the entrance to the school's cellar. The courtyard gate was guarded by two Latvian policemen in dark green uniforms. They were burly fellows armed with machine guns, with angular, bloated faces. None of us spoke a word. Only occasionally did a woman's "Oh God!" break the silence, followed by a brief "Scha!" (Quiet!).

When it was broad daylight, two German police officers appeared in the courtyard. They turned to us politely and said that the long trip to our new camp would perhaps be too arduous for some, and asked those who were old and frail to leave the group and go to the bus that stood ready to receive them. A few old men and women obeyed this request and were led away by a Latvian policeman. We stood there in silence until two other German police officers appeared and told us there was still room in the work camp, meaning the Small Ghetto, for those who were willing to work. Dr. Herzberg, his brother, and his father looked at one another and nodded. Then they looked questioningly at my father and me. I looked at my mother. She nodded to me and my father. "Go!" she said, "Maybe it's better this way." I embraced her and we kissed each other. I didn't know it was the last time.

A few more men decided to separate from their wives. There were about ten or fifteen of us, and we were now let out of the courtyard and marched to the Small Ghetto with a Latvian policeman. It was a lovely cold day. The sun shone down on us from a cloudless sky. The street, covered with ice and snow and empty of people, glittered in the sunlight. On both sides of it on the pavement and on the sidewalks lay hundreds of bags, sacks, and bundles that had been thrown aside by the people who had been driven along this street in the darkness. Here and there the snow was reddish-brown with blood. We were silent. Our eyes took in this image and never forgot it. The gate of the Small Ghetto was opened for our troop and closed again behind us.

The others, who had stayed behind in the school courtyard, had to wait there motionless in the cold for several more hours. Then they were let out and driven into the second half of the ghetto, whose "evacuation" the Gestapo had scheduled for December 8. That was how we escaped being shot that day. But for many it meant not salvation but only a delay, for death found them in Rumbula all the same. Because at that time we had no overview of the situation at all, it was no wonder that many connections became clear to us only years later. For example, we know today that there was a fateful connection between the arrival in Riga of the first railway transports of German Jews and the first extermination action in the Riga ghetto. The arrival of the transports at this time was not at all convenient for the Gestapo, because the reception camps at Salaspils (Kurtenhof) and Jumpravmuiza (Jungfernhof) were still not finished and there were still Latvian Jews in the Riga ghetto. The first of these transports arrived in Riga on November 29, 1941, and the Gestapo decided to liquidate it immediately in view of the aforementioned difficulties it would have had lodging it. That same night the German Jews, about 1,000 people, were brought to Rumbula, where preparations for exterminating the Jews of Riga had already begun, and shot on November 30 before the execution of the Riga Jews had started. This unforeseen operation led to a delay in the execution of the first Jews who arrived in Rumbula from the ghetto. The latter had to wait—and this is historically documented—for some time outside the grove in Rumbula until it was their turn to step before their murderers. Thus the execution process that had been painstakingly planned by Jeckeln personally was jolted out of its scheduled tempo. Not only the execution of the first columns coming from the ghetto was delayed; the whole plan of action was stalled. This explains why we were forced to wait for hours in the school courtyard instead of setting out for Rumbula immediately after leaving our houses. Because the Gestapo's schedule had been partly disrupted, we who straggled after the first half of the ghetto escaped execution that day.

In the chain of all the interconnected events that led to the fact that my father and I survived the war years, this delay plays a decisive role, for only thanks to it did we on that November morning get to the Small Ghetto, from which our path led us further to those who saved our lives, instead of plunging us into the mass grave in Rumbula. This delay also saved the lives of the Herzberg brothers and probably a few others. Only today, half a century later, do we know, thanks to information that has only recently come to light, about the curious interweaving of the fates of the Riga and the German Jews.

A second evacuation comprising the second half of the ghetto took place on Monday, December 8. It proceeded like the first one, except for the fact that there were fewer victims in the ghetto itself. This time the number of victims was about 11,000. All in all, about 27,000 people were killed on these two days.

Four young women initially escaped the bullets. Naked and trembling, they stood before their murderers' gun barrels and screamed in extreme mortal agony that they were Latvians, not Jews. They were believed and taken back to the city. The next morning Jeckeln himself decided their fate. One of the women was indeed Latvian and had been adopted as a child by Jews. The others were Jewish. One of them hoped for support from her first husband, Army Lieutenant Skuja. Asked on the telephone about her nationality, he answered that she was a Jew and he was not interested in her fate. She was murdered. The second woman received no mercy from Jeckeln, because she said she was the Latvian wife of a Jew engaged in Judaic studies. With this answer she signed her death warrant, for Jeckeln decided that she was "tainted by Judaism." Only the third girl, Ella

Medalje, was clever enough to give Jeckeln plausible answers and thus escaped with her life. A short time later her courageous and high-spirited friend Trine Hartmane confirmed that she was a "pure-blooded Aryan," whereupon the Gestapo ceased to bother her.[1]

Two or three women plunged merely wounded into the mass grave and lay alive under the dead. That night, when it had become quiet, they crept out from under the corpses, threw on a few of the pieces of clothing that were lying around by the thousands, and fled from this place of horror. They found shelter among heroic people. It seems that only one of these women, Frieda Michelson, survived the war. In her book *I Survived Rumbula* she tells the remarkable story of her rescue, which she owes to the Berzins, Pesla, and Viljumsons families.

The final action took place on the following day, December 9, and claimed 500 victims, who were shot at Bikernieki and in the Old Jewish Cemetery. These victims were people who had been flushed out of the cellars where they had hidden to escape being "evacuated." Among those shot was the merchant D. Michelson, although he and his son Max were already in the Small Ghetto. Two doctors, the internist Dr. Kretzer and the ophthalmologist Dr. Gutmann, attempted suicide. Dr. Kretzer's colleagues managed to save him.

The action was ended punctually at noon. The police officer who was supervising the action glanced at his watch and announced to the last Jews who had been herded together that they were to remain alive because he, in obedience to orders, had to end the action at twelve o'clock. The aforementioned Rumbula station chief reported that in April 1944 the Gestapo brought to Rumbula Russian prisoners of war, who dug up corpses and cremated them there. It is a known fact that Jews were also used for this work.

Now the Gestapo could send home to the fatherland the proud proclamation that "Latvia is free of Jews." Until the final moment, almost until the minute when they stood naked at the edge of the mass grave, the victims were told the fairy tale that they were being evacuated to another camp. Most of them believed it. When it came to the crude Latvian hangmen, we were prepared for anything; but the fact that these elegant German police officers, who offered buses to our old and frail people so they would not have to walk, were exactly the same rabble of murderers—that was hard to comprehend. Even if we had read Hitler's *Mein Kampf,* even if we had had an insight into the extermination plans that were approved a few weeks later at the Wannsee Conference, even then we would probably have scarcely understood what was happening to us in November and December 1941. To be sure, we knew from history that in the past entire tribes had been wiped out by their enemies. But we had grown up in the spirit of humanism and such concepts were alien to us. We would simply not have believed that a part of the German leadership began the Eastern campaign with the plan to totally exterminate the Jews. Nor would we have understood that for the Gestapo the Large Ghetto of Riga was merely a temporary solution meant to separate those who could work from those who could not.

The Gestapo's considerations are precisely recorded in the situation report written on January 25, 1942, by the Gebietskommissar (Area Commander) of Slonim (White Russia), Gert Erren, who had just "solved" the same problem there as his colleagues in Riga (20,000 Jews had lived in the Slonim area). He writes: "The action carried out by the SD on November 13, 1941, freed me of useless eaters, and the 7,000 Jews who are now available are being deployed in work processes without exception; they work willingly because of their continual fear of death, and in the spring they will be assessed and sorted out for a further reduction of their numbers." It should not remain unmentioned that 130 members of the Eighteenth Battalion of the Latvian police were also deployed in the liquidation of the Slonim ghetto.

At the place where the mass murders were carried out in the forest of Rumbula, one sees today a green area with several commemorative stones in the middle. The inscription on the oldest one says in Latvian and Russian that here are buried 50,000 victims of German fascism, political prisoners, and prisoners of war. Thus we see here, as on the commemorative stone in the Bikernieki forest, one of those half-truths that almost amount to lies, for only Jews lie buried in Rumbula as well as in Bikernieki.

We have always felt that this stone is an act of disrespect toward the Jews and a disparagement of our dead by the Soviet regime. Fifty meters deeper in the forest, where the long rectangles of the mass graves are located, the government permitted us in 1964, after long negotiations, to set up a second stone. "For the victims of Fascism" says the inscription in Latvian, Russian, and also in Yiddish, so that everyone who wants to understand the inscription will know who is lying here. A third, similar stone with the same inscription now stands near the road. Two small plaques at the edge of one of the mass graves bear the dates November 30 and December 8, 1941.

Once a year on the anniversary of the executions the survivors of those terrible years gather here to commemorate their loved ones. In the late 1960s and early 1970s, when the waves of Jewish national feelings began to rise, many young Jews of the postwar generation also came to the memorial services. Now and then words were said here that not only reminded us of the terrible days of the past but also condemned the Soviet regime for its veiled anti-Semitism. Because the KGB could not very well forbid a funeral ceremony in memory of the war victims, it did all it could to disrupt it. Participants arriving for the ceremony were photographed by KGB members, who also tried to drown out the speakers with loud music from loudspeakers hung in the trees. Some speakers pointed out, in barely disguised allusions, that some of the events occurring in the USSR reminded one of the eve of the Nazis' seizure of power in Germany. At times the memorial service was nearly transformed into a protest rally against the Soviet regime. A memorial service in November 1991 made one realize that even in the independent Republic of Latvia there is no deeper understanding of the Jewish tragedy (see chapter 11).

But it is not only on the days of commemoration that we visit this spot. Again and again, one or another of us makes the pilgrimage out here to the edge of the city and stands stunned before these graves. Stunned, because even today, after years and decades, it is incomprehensible that our dear ones and dearest ones lie here, and that murderers' hands robbed them of their lives only because they were Jews.

THE MARTYRS

8

The Small Ghetto

The Small Ghetto originally included only one neighborhood, which was bordered by four streets: Liela Kalna Street, Ludzas Street, Lauvas Street, and Liksnas Street. Later the adjacent neighborhood, which extended to Maza Kalna Street, and a few more buildings in other areas were added to the Small Ghetto, for example, the house in which the hospital's Department of Infectious Diseases was located.

Before the extermination actions the Germans had billeted several hundred women who worked for them—because of their work they were called "the seamstresses"—in the short-term prison. Now they were transferred back to the ghetto and billeted in the complex of buildings at 68–70 Ludzas Street, which was called the Women's Ghetto. Foreign Jews were lodged in one part of the Large Ghetto; almost all of them came from Germany.

The Small Ghetto was headed by an elder, Mr. A. Kehlmann, and his assistants, the engineer Mr. Hofshovitz and Mr. Berner. They were responsible for the various administrative areas, primarily the Wirtschaftsamt (Economic Authority), which supplied the ghetto's food stores. The rations were very meager, especially those of the old people and children who had survived to live in the Small Ghetto and could not work outside the ghetto. This was the reason for the workers' ceaseless efforts to smuggle food into the ghetto. The German Wirtschaftskommando decided on the following *weekly* food rations for the ghetto's inhabitants as of April 13, 1942:

Item	Nonworker's Ration	Worker's Ration
Meat	125 grams	125 grams
Fat	90 grams	90 grams
Bread	850 grams	1,700 grams
Sugar	75 grams	75 grams
Other foods	75 grams	75 grams
Coffee substitute	40 grams	40 grams

Not for nothing were these rations referred to as "starvation rations," for the nonworkers received just over 100 grams [3.5 ounces], the workers just over 200 grams [7 ounces] of bread a day.

The Wirtschaftsamt also included several hairdressers and a shoemaker's workshop, which was headed by a Mr. Josselovich and in which the lawyer O. Finkelstein worked as a shoemaker.

In the beginning, when they numbered about 4,500, the inhabitants of the Small Ghetto lived closely crowded together. Up to fifteen people would sleep packed together on the bare floors of small rooms. After a time the Wohnungsamt (Housing Authority), headed by Mr. Brandt and Mr. Margolin, remedied the matter somewhat. Moreover, the number of ghetto inhabitants diminished considerably over time thanks to the billeting of some of the large work gangs in barracks outside the ghetto.

The Technisches Amt (Technical Authority), headed by the engineers Mr. Antikol and Mr. Saslavsky, played a significant role in the daily life of the ghetto. Their capable coworkers included the architect Mr. Schneider, the teacher Mr. Lat, and the mechanic Mr. Botvinkin. The engineer Mr. Antikol had held a leading position in the Riga city administration and had remained in this position after the war started. But after a few days, when he realized the extent of the impending danger, he instructed his wife by telephone to leave the city together with their children. They never saw each other again, because when Antikol himself decided to flee it was already too late. He and his friend, the engineer Michelson, rode their bicycles toward the Russian border, but after a few hours German troops blocked their way. Although the later stages of his life in the ghetto are known, there is no detailed information about his death. During the final months before the liberation of Riga he and his friend Michelson, together with numerous other Jews, were billeted in the Armeebekleidungsamt, or ABA (Army Clothing Department). When there was no more doubt that Riga would be liberated within a few days, they both decided to flee. The engineer Michelson succeeded in escaping, but the engineer Antikol vanished. He did not appear in the apartment in which they had agreed to meet, and the Latvian apartment owner could report only that in the night she had heard excited voices and a shot in the street. Bloodstains were found on the pavement in front of the house. According to other sources, he was killed in Stutthof. His wife managed to escape. Russian soldiers in a railroad transport hid her and her three small daughters under the tarpaulin covering a railroad platform. Thus they reached Russia safe and sound, whence they returned to Riga after the war.

The men of the Technisches Amt managed to install shower rooms and a disinfection chamber, which served the Small and the Large Ghettos as well as the Women's Ghetto. The Technisches Amt renovated the ghetto apartments and put back into working order the water pipes and sewage pipes that had burst during the harsh winter of 1941–42 in the apartments of the Large Ghetto, some of which were standing empty and unheated. With the support of the Technisches Amt a kind of vocational school was set up which offered young people the opportunity to learn a craft. Also thanks to the Technisches Amt a small new hospital and a new polyclinic were organized, because the SS had requisitioned Linas Hazedek, the Jewish women's clinic, which had served as a general hospital in the Large Ghetto, for its own purposes and transformed it into an SS field hospital. Thus the doctors' collective headed by Professor W. Mintz was able to resume its activities, which were greatly needed. The number of surviving doctors was considerable. Whereas the older ones primarily worked in the ghetto, most of the younger ones worked for various Wehrmacht units.

Professor Mintz was ably assisted by his nephew, the surgeon M. Mintz, Dr. R. Blumenfeld, and Dr. I. Volpe. Dr. M. Mintz died in the ghetto of tuberculosis of the lungs after his powers of resistance had been broken by the tragic loss of his wife and child. Latvian policemen had arrested and taken away his wife Selma ("Fetty"), née Hoff, and his little daughter Leonore from the garden of the Jewish Hospital in the summer of 1941. It had all begun with Dr. Mintz's decision, in view of the terror that reigned in the city, to move his wife and child into his quarters at Bikkur Cholim, the Jewish Hospital, so as to have them constantly close to him and under his protection. Everything went well until the day his wife and his little daughter were surprised by Latvian policemen as they were taking a walk in the hospital garden. The policemen, always ready for cruelty, arrested the mother and child on the pretext that they were not wearing the Star of David—a severe violation of the regulations then in force. The hospital staff members who had rushed to the scene begged the murderers in vain to release the two on the grounds that they had not been on the street but in the hospital garden. It was of no use. They were never seen again.

Dr. R. Blumenfeld also died of tuberculosis of the lungs. In addition to those mentioned previously, the following doctors also worked in the ghetto: N. Berniker, H. Gittelson, B. Jakobson, N. Kahn, V. Kretzer, M. Magalif, G. Peisner, Dr. Rogalin, K. Thal, and the brothers H. and I. Jawitz. Outside the ghetto, the doctors P. Blatt, D. Blowetz, Dr. Davidson, J. Goldring, B. Ginsburg, V. Goldberg, L. Javorkowsky, B. May, L. Rudow, M. Solomir, and M. Wolpert worked for various commandos. Dr. L. Javorkowsky and Dr. May, who worked at the emergency reception center of the Wehrmacht, provided the ghetto's polyclinic and hospital with medicines from the German army's supplies.

Later on, some doctors from the countryside who had survived also found their way to the Riga ghetto; they were Dr. Sandler from Ludza, Dr. M. Sick and Dr. Weinreich from Libau, and Dr. Gurwitz. The latter had already been in a column of Jews in Daugavpils who had been designated to be shot, but a Latvian policeman had recognized him as the doctor who was treating his father. He pulled him out of the column and advised him to flee to the Riga ghetto, where he might perhaps survive.[1] The dentists working in the ghetto were Dr. Tumarkin, Dr. Cherfass, and the dental technician Ivnovitz.

In the city, the Riga Health Department had set up a special dental clinic for the civilian population where the dentists W. Frisch, Drs. Noim Sr. and Jr., Dr. Scheinenson, and W. Wigdortchik worked and the dental technicians Drabkin, Feldmann, Katz, Michalichek, Straschun, Tabak, and Cherniak did the technical work. Our neighbors from the Large Ghetto, the dentist Dr. Herzberg and his brother, who was a mechanic, worked together for a Wehrmacht unit.

The Berlin gynecologist Dr. Siegbert Joseph was appointed director of the Women's Polyclinic. When the Small Ghetto was finally disbanded in the fall of 1943, Dr. Joseph was moved to the ABA in Milgravis (Mühlgraben), where he headed a hospital. Dr. M. Wolpert, one of the Jawitz brothers, and Dr. Buchsbaum from Kassel worked with him there. In the autumn of 1944, shortly before the fall of Riga, the SS evacuated to Liepaja (Libau) the last Jewish prisoners, including Dr. Joseph and Mrs. H. Sherman, the author of *Between Day and Darkness.* Liepaja was constantly bombarded from the air by the Russians, and on December 22, 1944, Dr. Joseph was killed in one of these attacks. Dr. Wolpert experienced the end of the war in the Magdeburg concentration camp, where he had worked together with Dr. Jakobson and Dr. Javorkowsky. He returned to Riga in the winter of 1947 to 1948. Dr. Jakobson was killed shortly before the end of the war. Dr. Javorkowsky survived the war and became one of the most prominent hematologists in the USSR. Dr. Blowetz was saved by a Latvian woman he was friends with who sheltered him in her home. Dr. May was the victim of an aerial bombing attack on one of the last days of the war during the march from Magdeburg to Sachsenhausen. Dr. Gittelson died of starvation in the Zeitz-Remersdorf work camp, which was part of the Buchenwald concentration camp. Dr. Hirsch Javitz was deported to Germany and emigrated to Brazil after the war ended.

Of the others mentioned earlier, those who survived in Latvia were the doctors Davidson, Goldberg, Rudow, and Rogalin and the dentists Herzberg, Noim Jr., Frisch, and Wigdortchik, as well as the dental technician Drabkin. After the war, Dr. Goldberg became one of the leading urologists in the USSR. The doctors Noim Sr. and Ginsburg were shot dead on October 31, 1942, when the Gestapo avenged itself on the Jews for the shootout in the Kvadrats factory (which will be discussed subsequently).

One of the German Jews was a Dr. Aufrecht, who did not make a good name for himself in the Riga ghetto. The local Jews suspected him of collaborating with the Gestapo. H. Sherman calls him a lackey of the SS, and she is quite right, for he was a member of the Verband nationaldeutscher Juden (Association of National German Jews) and in the early 1920s signed a newspaper advertisement expressing support for General E. Ludendorff, who was at that time calling for the deportation of Polish Jews from Bavaria. In 1923 Ludendorff participated in Hitler's putsch.[2] After the war ended, Aufrecht was shot by the Russians after the liberation of the Lauenburg camp for "hard-hearted treatment of the Jews" (!). By contrast, Nurse Cartun, who worked in the polyclinic of the Large German Ghetto, was loved by all.

Although there were repeated actions, small and large, in the ghetto that were aimed at destroying old and sick people and children who could not work, a number of children had nonetheless survived. They were now taken to the Women's Ghetto, and a school was set up for them there. One of the teachers was a Mrs. Fiks.

The Small Ghetto was under the command of the Gebietskommissariat (Area Commissioner's Office). The deployment of workers was controlled by the Arbeitsamt (Labor Authority), which was headed by the German Stanke and the Latvian Dralle. Mr. Meisel, Mr. Kassel, and Mrs. Vishnievska represented the Jewish workers' interests. Affiliated with the Labor Authority were the Department of Statistics, an archive of addresses, and the Chevra Kaddisha, or Social Assistance, which was headed by the lawyer Mr. Wittenberg. In a word, in its structure the Small Ghetto was to a certain extent a miniature version of the Large Ghetto which had been destroyed, with the same institutions and tasks. It was a renewed courageous attempt to organize a normal life in a place where the Germans were trying to sow helplessness and despair.

The ghetto commandant, Obersturmführer Karl Wilhelm Krause, held absolute power over the camp and its inhabitants. According to J. Wolff, the author of *Mit Bibel und Bebel* (*With the Bible and Bebel*), he had been a former aide at the hospital in Herne, Westphalia, and later an estate owner in Upper Silesia; according to M. Kaufmann, he used to be a detective in Berlin. Krause was so cruel and bloodthirsty that only words like "incomprehensible" or "unimaginable" could approximately describe him. Murdering an innocent human being with a shot in the neck was for him a wholly everyday occurrence, a routine matter. His deputy in the Riga ghetto was named Gymnich. In the Salaspils (Kurtenhof) concentration camp, whose commandant

Krause later became, his deputy was a certain Viduss. According to H. Sherman, Gymnich was originally a taxi driver from Cologne. Krause and Gymnich shot and hanged their victims for the smallest offenses, for example, attempting to send a letter to Germany, which was forbidden. Of course, it was not at all necessary to invent a reason for a murder. In the best case they would send their victims to prison—where they were then, however, murdered by other SS people.

Later on, Krause was replaced by Unterscharführer Roschmann from Vienna. Of the German policemen who worked in the Small Ghetto, the ones known by name are: Danziger, Karasik, Kobello, Neumann, Tuchel, and Police First Lieutenant Heser. Whenever Krause, Gymnich, or Roschmann appeared in the ghetto with their trained attack dog, they would shoot at cats, pigeons, and human beings indiscriminately. Blood always flowed. If a ghetto inhabitant was busy preparing his meal when the three entered the ghetto, he would immediately throw it, dishes and all, into the privy just to be on the safe side, because simply cooking a meal could serve as a pretext for beatings and shooting. After the Kaiserwald concentration camp went into operation and the barracks camps were put under the Gestapo's command, these three made sure that killings occurred there again and again. But before they murdered the Jews, they still tried to extort from them their remaining money and valuables. One day the Small Ghetto's inhabitants were told they had to pay a monetary tribute. Krause and his henchmen set up wooden boxes for this purpose at the entrance to the ghetto, and the workers' columns had to throw in their mite as they passed by. When the gentlemen counted up their take and saw that it did not measure up to their expectations, they imposed a second tribute and threatened to execute people if they were "cheated" again. These were sums extorted not by the Gestapo but by Krause and Gymnich personally. None of this money ever went into the public purse. It all stuck to the fingers of these gentlemen. Greed took the upper hand over all other feelings and National Socialist ideals when they received confiscated jewelry from the head of the ghetto police force, Mr. Wand, not needing to share their stolen loot with anyone. Once the SS man Tuchel, feeling that he was being cheated by the Jew Aismann as the latter was handing over valuables that had been extorted from him, ordered Aismann without further ado to stand against the wall of the Jewish cemetery and shot him dead.

Now the defenseless Jews were frisked and beaten at the gate of the Small Ghetto, just as they had been previously at the gate of the Large Ghetto. The winter was cold, and the Germans took away the Jews' warm clothing so that they themselves would not have to freeze. The Jewish prisoners repeatedly tried to bring food into the ghetto. If they were caught doing so, blows rained down. If Krause or Gymnich was present, the "guilty one" would be taken to the ghetto's punishment bunker and was later, as a rule, shot at the wall of the Jewish cemetery. Others were led immediately to the cemetery, where they were forced to take off their outer clothing and kneel down with their backs to Krause, who then murdered them with a shot to the neck. Jews were hanged in the ghetto for the most minor offenses, such as bringing in a pack of cigarettes. One of the Gestapo's victims was Isidor Krohn, the younger son of the neurologist Dr. J. Krohn, because he tried to bring bread into the ghetto secretly. When the work gangs returned to the ghetto in the evening, they were led past the gallows—the hangings were carried out in the Large German Ghetto. If anyone did not look up at the victims hanging from the gallows, writes J. Wolff, he received "a blow under his chin, so that his head flew up by itself."[3]

Sometimes when the prisoners neared the ghetto gate and saw that the situation was risky, they secretly threw their hoarded food away before they got there; in such situations, whole mountains of food belonging to "nobody" were piled up. When the Large Ghetto was scaled down and the ghetto gate was moved, the SS patients in the former Linas Hazedek, which was now the SS field hospital, could see all this from their windows. Often they would use the opportunity to tell the SS people at the gate which of the Jews had "broken the law." The victims would then be received accordingly. Two German Jewish women were shot to death here because they had hidden butter under their clothes for their small children. Another one was shot for "theft of army property" after a tin dish was found on her that a compassionate railroad man had given her along with soup and a piece of bread. Mrs. Sherman reports that this woman's seven young children knelt down in front of Krause and Gymnich and begged for their mother's life. When the mother leaned down to embrace one of her children, Krause killed her with a shot in the neck.

The Gestapo had not forgotten the clothing of its 27,000 victims of November 30 and December 8, 1941. This clothing was now, in the winter of 1941–42, precisely sorted out and offered to the population of Riga for ridiculously low prices, together with furniture from the ghetto, at the ghetto fence itself. It is incredible but true that Latvians and Germans pushed and shoved each other here for weeks and actually bought these blood-spattered clothes full of bullet holes. The general of the Riga Command, Dr. Bamberg, also bought furniture here and sent it back to Germany. Some of the unsold clothing was altered to make underwear (as will be discussed subsequently).

In February 1942 the Small Ghetto's population was increased by 500 Lithuanian Jews, men and women, from Kaunas. In October 1942, 300 more Jews from Lithuania arrived. Their reports of the persecution of the Jews in Lithuania were completely consistent with everything we had experienced in Latvia. Just like the Latvians, the Lithuanians had taken the initiative in murdering the Jews even before the Germans arrived. In Lithuania as well, the year of Soviet rule, which ended with a large-scale deportation, had prepared fruitful ground for the ripening of anti-Semitic feelings. The Lithuanians and Germans had rampaged like monsters. The old forts around Kaunas, especially the ninth one, were notorious as places where Jews were slaughtered.

Among the Jews of the Riga ghetto, there was hardly anyone who still doubted that its fate was sealed. The only question was when death would overtake the individual. Everyone felt threatened, everyone wanted to flee as soon as possible, and hardly anyone had the opportunity to do so. In the winter of 1941–42 many believed the war would end soon. This belief was prompted by the stalled offensives outside Moscow and Leningrad. The entry of the United States into the war, which recalled memories of the year 1917, also contributed. Rapid flight seemed to be called for, but who had a place to flee to? For this reason, the Jewish work gangs continued to go to their places of work practically unguarded.

A few dared to flee. But some of them were immediately caught and shot, while others fell into the Gestapo's hands later on. A Span ish officer of the Blue Division may have thought of the shameful persecution of the Jews in Spain during the Middle Ages when he helped Jews from Riga, the lawyer B. Kaplan and two other men, escape to Spain. Unfortunately they were recognized by the Gestapo at the Spanish border and brought back to prison in Riga.

Other Jews were the victims of Gestapo provocateurs. A large group of Jews consisting of M. Srago, his mother and sister, Dr. Freidberg, the lawyer J. Jewelson, the singer Kristall, A. Levi, F. Sacharov, and several other people gave money and valuables to a "helpful" noncommissioned German air force officer and in exchange were supposed to be ferried across to Sweden in the summer of 1942. Hardly were these people on board the ship than they were received by Krause. Srago tried to resist and was shot dead on the spot. The others were sent to prison and never seen again.

In the Small Ghetto there was a resistance movement about which relatively little is known. The reason for this is that all of its leaders fell victim to the Gestapo, and the few surviving members did not know much about the organization itself. It seems that the intellectual initiator of the movement was the aforementioned lawyer J. Jewelson, who had been the head of the Finanzamt (Financial Authority) in the Large Ghetto. It was he who in early 1942 called on the younger people around him to stop letting themselves be slaughtered like defenseless animals and arm themselves instead. Jewelson was joined by the senior policeman I. Bag, O. Okun, who owned a textile factory in Daugavpils, the teacher I. Lat, the engineer Michelson, and the mechanic Botvinkin. I. Bag was the head of the organization. The men built up the resistance movement out of many small cells that knew hardly anything about one another. The procurement of weapons and provisions was relatively simple. Weapons that had been captured on the Eastern front constantly passed through the hands of the Jews who worked for the Wehrmacht (German armed forces) units cleaning, oiling, and sorting them. It was an easy task to pilfer these weapons and smuggle them into the ghetto. This was done with the help of the Jewish drivers who transported food into the ghetto every day. Provisions for the resistance organization in the form of canned food were brought into the ghetto the same way. B. Kramer, a medical student who worked at the health-services collection center, accumulated a supply of medicines. Well-camouflaged hiding places were set up; one of them could be reached only through an oven. In a cellar a shooting range was set up next to a smithy. The noise of the smithy drowned out the shots on the shooting range. Even an underground exit out of the ghetto, built by the engineer Antikol, is supposed to have existed or been planned.

Mrs. H. Sherman, the aforementioned author (*Between Day and Darkness*), also worked for the resistance movement. A German Jew from North Rhine–Westphalia, she had been deported to Riga together with her entire family. Here in the ghetto she met her future husband, the Riga pharmacist Willy Sherman, and his brothers Moses, Paul, and Salomon. Through Willy Sherman she became friends with many Riga Jews, including a number of ghetto policemen. The latter asked Mrs. Sherman, who at that time worked at the police headquarters, to get various things for them and smuggle them into the ghetto—for example, uniforms, collar ornaments, SS rank insignia, SS rune pins, woolen socks, and shoelaces. Together with a woman friend, Mrs. Sherman acquired these things for the ghetto policemen. One day Willy Sherman handed her the key to a ghetto hiding place and explained to her how she could get into it. It was a security measure in case the situation in the ghetto should become precarious. In this hiding place there were, he told her, food supplies to last for one to one and a half years, a radio transmitting station, pistols, and ammunition.

It is not known how information about the organization filtered through to the Gestapo. The creation of the resistance movement was hindered by several circumstances. For example, Jewelson, as has already been mentioned, was caught while trying to escape to Sweden. A decisive setback for the organization and the entire ghetto population occurred in the fall of 1942. On October 28, SD men stopped a truck at the Riga city limits near the Kvadrats rubber factory, in which several young Jewish men were riding. Allegedly they were trying to drive the truck to eastern Latvia and make contact with Soviet partisans. The truck driver was reportedly a Gestapo provocateur. When the young men saw they were surrounded, they did not surrender, but instead attacked the policemen with hand grenades and pistols. All of them were killed except for one named Elyashev, who died later on in prison. The Gestapo had lost three of their men, and they revenged themselves on the ghetto inhabitants. Apparently the Gestapo suspected that the Jewish ghetto police could not have been entirely uninvolved in the shoot-out. But it seems that this suspicion was groundless and that those who were killed constituted a small, separate group of foolhardy young men.

As has already been mentioned, a German Jew named Wand was the head of the ghetto police in the Small Ghetto. A. Nathan, who had been a schoolmate of mine, was the senior policeman. The task of the police force was to see to it that the regulations and decrees of the Jewish and German camp authorities were obeyed and fulfilled. Although the policemen could very easily have slipped into disfavor because of this work and been regarded as traitors by the ghetto Jews, nothing bad was ever attributed to them. On the contrary, they were regarded as nationalists and defenders of Jewish interests.

In the Women's Ghetto there were several Jewish policewomen, who were responsible to the Jewish policeman N. Goldberg. The police force of the Large German Ghetto consisted of German Jews under the command of the German Jew Frankenberg, who was assisted by Mr. Perl and Mr. Haar. Haar, a former boxer, had been promoted by Krause to senior policeman as a mark of gratitude for having saved Krause's life when a Latvian policeman pointed his weapon at him. Later on Haar became the police chief of the Large German Ghetto, but finally, like all the inhabitants of both ghettos, he ended up in the Kaiserwald concentration camp. M. Kaufmann has little sympathy for Haar and seems to have felt a certain satisfaction when Haar was drowned in the sewage of a latrine in the Kaiserwald concentration camp by Aryan capos who regarded him as a rival. Mrs. H. Sherman, however, sees him from another perspective. She writes that he entered the Kaiserwald concentration camp voluntarily because, as he said, conditions there were the worst and he could give the most help there.

According to J. Katz, this murder was the work of Mr. X (more on him later). A similar fate met Eisenstein, who, as the former camp elder of Salaspils, had more than a few Jewish lives on his conscience. He too was transferred from the Large German Ghetto to the Kaiserwald concentration camp, where many Jews had long been waiting for him. On the very day of his arrival he was twice beaten unconscious. Thereupon he was ordered by a capo to "fetch something" and while doing so he was "shot while escaping" by a guard.

Three days after the incident at the Kvadrats factory, on October

31, 1942, the Gestapo carried out its retaliatory measures, which were aimed at the inhabitants of the Small Ghetto in general and the Jewish ghetto police in particular. On that morning the entire population of the Small Ghetto had to appear for roll call while armed SD men searched all the houses from attic to cellar, broke into locked apartments, and dragged sick people out of the hospital. What happened next reminded the terror-stricken ghetto inhabitants all too vividly of what had happened there nearly a year before. They were ordered to go to work and the older and weaker men were forced to leave the columns at the ghetto gate. There were 106 men altogether. They were taken to the Central Prison and executed that same night in the woods of Bikernieki.[4]

The SD struck its second blow that same day against the ghetto police. First the policemen were taken off their posts along the ghetto fence and summoned to a roll call in the courtyard of the ghetto command headquarters. There it was explained to them that they no longer enjoyed the trust of the camp's leadership. They were frisked from head to foot and ordered to march to the Blechplatz/Blech Square under SD escort. At their head marched the senior policeman A. Nathan, for the Germans had ordered their actual chief, Wand, to step aside. Nathan apparently sensed that the SD men were up to no good, for when they reached the Blechplatz he shouted, "Run, boys, let's try to save ourselves!" His words didn't help, for SD men lying in ambush were already shooting at the fleeing policemen, literally riddling them with bullet holes. Thirty-nine of the forty-two Jewish policemen were killed on the spot.[5] One policeman, Genkin, who was only wounded in the foot, hid in a house but was soon found and executed. Two others could not be found at first. One of them, Damski, was found later, apparently because someone reported on him. In any case, a few months after this massacre Krause went to a certain house in the ghetto and there killed Damski with hand grenades. The three men who had sheltered him were also killed. They included the journalist H. Machtus and a man named Kohn. Escorted by Krause and Haar, they were led to the wall of the Jewish cemetery and executed there. Before his death Machtus is reported to have shouted at his murderers, "Don't think the Jewish people will die with my death. The Jewish people live and will live forever!" Both men died with the Hatikva on their lips.

The second policeman, Israelovich, managed to escape from the ghetto in a work gang. Friends hid him from the Gestapo in an attic until he found shelter with two Latvian women. But then someone betrayed him and he was brought to the ghetto by the Gestapo and forced to show them the location of the resistance movement's provisions depot.

The Gestapo left a few men, such as the engineer Hofshovitz, Berner, Dolgitzer, and the jeweler Rosenthal, untouched although they had been in the police force of the Large Ghetto. Rosenthal's wife was a German, but she was unable to help her husband. If he had fled from the ghetto he would have inevitably put her life in danger. Later he worked in the Heereskraftwagenpark or HKP (Army Vehicles Park), where Sturmbannführer Sauer arrested him in May 1944 and sent him to the Kaiserwald concentration camp. There he was tortured and subsequently killed.

The resistance movement was at extreme risk because of the arrest of so many people, some of whom certainly knew about it or were members of it. Nonetheless O. Okun, who had taken over the leadership after the departure of Jewelson and the death of I. Bag, did not give up.

We have already reported that the policeman Israelovich was arrested and that he revealed the location of the provisions depot. Furthermore, the police searched for a certain Mr. Freidberg and called on him to give himself up, which he did. The Gestapo arrested him, dug up the weapons depot, and at the same time arrested Okun. Roschmann personally drove Okun to the prison, and while he was doing so Okun attacked him in the car with a razor and wounded him. Apparently a list of the names of the resistance movement's members had fallen into the Germans' hands, which meant that all they had to do was to arrest these people. They executed Israelovich, Freidberg, and Okun and arrested the teacher Lat and the mechanic Botvinkin. Frankenberg, the Jewish police chief of both ghettos, arrested Elyashev, who worked for the Technical Authority and was caught attempting to cover up the traces of illegal activities in the room of his jailed comrade Botvinkin. Jewish prisoners made sure that Frankenberg paid with his life in Buchenwald.

The policeman from the Women's Ghetto, N. Goldberg, who had been arrested earlier, was brought from the prison into the ghetto and forced to give information about concealed weapons. Also arrested and shot in this connection were people who were billeted outside the city to cut turf. One man was even brought from Estonia to a prison in Riga. All in all, according to Kaufmann, 150 people were killed as a consequence of the shoot-out near the Kvadrats factory.[6]

For the Gestapo these events were a convenient excuse to make changes in the leadership of the ghetto police force. Wand was removed from his post. Months later, when the ghetto was dissolved, he was found murdered in a cellar of the Small Ghetto.

M. Kaufmann has recorded in his book individual events that led to the end of the movement. But the author expressly notes that even at that time the precise circumstances and connections were unclear. Today, fifty-five years later, new and very precise information has come to light about what was happening behind the scenes at that time, developments about which the Jews had no idea. The wire-pullers of the resistance movement and all the "covert" activities associated with it, from the smuggling of weapons into the ghetto to the ambush near the Kvadrats factory, were members of the Gestapo. Our present knowledge of the events of that time is very detailed, as can be seen from the fact that we even know that the Gestapo borrowed from the Wehrmacht a license place for the truck that was supposedly going to take the young Jewish men to the eastern part of Latvia. The Gestapo feared that a police license plate on the truck could have aroused the young men's suspicion.[7]

There are few other reports of Jewish acts of resistance against the occupying forces. We know from the interrogation protocol of Viktors Arajs that in mid-1943 an Obergruppenführer was buried in the Mezakapi cemetery in Riga after being killed in a "wild shoot-out" "after Jews who were about to be executed ran toward the execution commando and attacked the members of the commando."[8]

In the terrible desperation in which the ghetto inhabitants found themselves, many turned with fervent prayers to God. A few Torah scrolls from the Large Ghetto had been saved, and later these were even brought into the Kaiserwald concentration camp and several billets. Several rooms in the Small Ghetto had been fitted out as temples. Moreover, many people gathered regularly around certain personalities, for example, the lawyer Wittenberg, to pray and read the Talmud. Religious life in the Large German Ghetto was more richly structured. There was a synagogue with the requisite ritual implements where people met for religious services. There Jewish holy days were solemnly celebrated, with the congregation singing under the leadership of the cantor. The elder of the community from Hanover, Mr. Fleischel, was a Roman Catholic, and now and then he read the Mass for those who were Catholics like himself.

As long as the Small Ghetto existed it was possible, secretly of course, to bake matzos for Passover, with the Jewish ghetto police force making sure the bakery and the bakers were not discovered.

One of the most moving chapters in M. Kaufmann's book is the one about artistic performances in the two ghettos and the concentration camps of Riga. In a few pages Kaufmann manages to show how the artists, in pain and despair, did their best, and how their feelings made the souls of their audience, who were moved by the same feelings, vibrate in tune with theirs. The volume of artistic offerings is astonishing, and the number of great artists who perished in the ghetto is depressing. There were lectures on Jewish history, and Professor Weil, who had been a lecturer at the University of Vienna for many years, gave talks on Goethe's *Faust.* Plays were also performed in the ghetto, such as Lessing's *Nathan der Weise* (*Nathan the Wise*), the first act of *Faust,* and Hugo von Hoffmansthal's *Jedermann* (*Everyman*). Kaufmann calls the production of Stefan Zweig's *Jeremias* a pinnacle of artistic performance. Jeremiah was portrayed by the Viennese actor Diesendorf. The drama, which begins with the announcement of the imminent destruction of Jerusalem and ends with the message that a people can be conquered but not its spirit, must have made a deep impression on the audience. It also gave them the hope of survival. The words of Jeremiah sounded prophetic: "Woe to the destroyer, for he shall be destroyed, and woe to the robber, for he shall be robbed! He who has drunk blood in cauldrons, he shall drown in it; and he who has fed on the flesh of the people shall soon become the food of worms!"

9

The Large German Ghetto

The houses of the Large Ghetto stood empty and abandoned. German and Latvian policemen had plundered and vandalized the apartments. On the walls and floors were brown stains of dried blood. The remains of suddenly interrupted meals lay on the tables, and remnants of food supplies were still in the pantries. The doors stood open, and the severe cold of winter had seeped into the unheated rooms. Water and sewage pipes had burst.

Into this desolate ghost town the Gestapo now brought foreign Jews, primarily from Germany, who had been abducted to this place from their homelands on the pretense of resettling them. At home in Germany the police had told them that from now on they would live in the East, and most of these misguided people had believed this fairy tale. They had brought with them as many of their belongings as they could: clothes, underwear, bedding, mattresses, blankets, sewing machines, household goods, and food. J. Katz relates that his uncle quickly bought an iron stove before his deportation because he thought it would be cold in the East. Ruth Andreas-Friedrich's diary entries, which were published as *The Inner Front,* clearly show how naive a part of the German population, non-Jews as well as Jews, still was even as late as the fall of 1942, evidently knowing nothing about what had been happening in the East, especially in Riga, for the past year. In her diary entry for September 2, 1942, the author describes how she helped Jewish friends prepare for their deportation to the East: "Packed all evening in their room. Busy with scissors, needle and thread. Hundred-mark notes into coat lining, wedding ring into quilt, fountain pen under hatband, dollar bills between skirt seams."[1]

And all of this was happening at a time when thousands of German Jews already lay in mass graves in Riga and thousands more were dying of starvation.

In any case, not all German Jews had been struck blind. Many understood what lay before them and committed suicide. Thus a nurse, who has remained anonymous, writes in *Wir haben es gesehen* (*We Saw It*) that in October 1941 during the "transport period" the Jewish Hospital in Berlin was so filled with people who had tried to commit suicide that long rows of beds had to be set up in the corridors. "One night," she writes, "we had as many as 30 admissions."[2] Mrs. H. Henschel, the widow of the last chairman of the Jewish community in Berlin, reports that at the beginning of the deportations there were 1,200 suicides in Berlin.

The journey to the East took place in the most adverse circumstances imaginable. The winter was very cold, and some of the wagons, which were sealed shut, were not heated, whereas others were overheated. The deportees received no food or water, and they moistened their lips with the droplets of water that condensed on the windowpanes or scraped the ice off the windows. Many died during the journey, and many were shot dead in Riga as they were getting out of the freight cars after being driven out of them with whips and iron bars. Some of the freight cars containing the deportees' baggage never reached their destination, and others were plundered by the German and Latvian police in Riga. The Gestapo appropriated the best items and the valuables. The deportees could keep only what they were wearing on their bodies and carrying with them, if it had not been torn out of their hands. Thousands of kilometers from their homeland, the exhausted, starving, frozen, and frightened people—men, women, children, the old, and the sick—were now driven into the cold, empty apartments of our ghetto, which now became the Large German Ghetto.

One of the first transports from Berlin arrived on November 29, 1941. The new arrivals were killed in Rumbula in the early morning hours of the following day, November 30, the day of the first action, even before the Riga Jews (as described in chapter 7). Later the news filtered through that German Jews had already been deported to Latvia. On December 10, 1941, another transport of German Jews arrived. This group was brought to the ghetto that now stood empty after the second action had been carried out. Subsequent transports came from Berlin, Dortmund, Düsseldorf, Hamburg, Kassel, Cologne, Münster, Nuremberg, and Vienna. Jews from Prague who had originally been in Theresienstadt also arrived. The families from each of the various cities gathered around an elder: those from Cologne around Mr. Leiser, who later became the elder of the Large German Ghetto and the Small Ghetto, those from Hanover around Mr. Fleischel, who was a Roman Catholic, those from Prague around Mr. Steuer. Mr. Fleischel was not the only Catholic among the deportees. There was a whole group of them, and a few of them were already second-generation Catholics. Now they had all been made Jews again.

J. Katz describes Leiser as a not very likable man, with whom he once had a short conversation because he wanted to get clothing for Jews working in the Liepaja (Libau) harbor. Leiser received him in his office, where he sat behind a large diplomatic desk. He wore a gray-flecked suit with a matching tie and wore his hair closely combed back against his head. The tone in which Leiser conducted the conversation rather reminded Katz of Ghetto Commandant Krause. Fleischel was not very popular, either. His relationship with Krause was a shady one. According to rumors, they had known each other before the war. It was highly suspect that Fleischel was the only one of tens of thousands of dead Jews who not only was buried in a coffin but received a proper funeral ceremony in which soldiers on guard fired three salvos over his grave.

The foreign Jews who ended up in the Large German Ghetto were lucky in a certain sense in that they were billeted in houses and apartments in which people had recently lived under more-or-less normal conditions. But broken and smashed furniture, torn pieces of clothing, and spatters of dried blood on the walls and floors testified to the frenzy with which Latvian policemen had rioted here during the extermination actions. For fourteen days the unfortunate new arrivals received no food and nourished themselves on the bits of flour and groats they found in the pantries and the potato peelings and scraps of vegetables they scratched out of the rubbish piles. Their children stood at the ghetto fence and begged the Jews of the Small Ghetto for bread. The Riga Jews helped the German Jews as much as possible, shared with them their last pieces of bread, and even gave them milk for the children through the barbed-wire fence, which was quite a dangerous thing to do.

But thousands of other Jews from Germany and Western Europe never got a chance to see the Riga ghetto, for as soon as they arrived at the railway station in Riga the Gestapo loaded them into trucks and transported them to the woods of Bikernieki, where the first executions of Riga Jews had already been carried out in July 1941. Here mass graves had been dug beforehand, and here the unfortunate people who had just arrived were forced to undress completely. According to H. Baermann, here they were shot down with machine guns by Latvian execution units under the command of Viktors Arajs, who had been appointed a major in the Latvian SS.[3]

In the Riga ghetto the Gestapo rampaged among the German Jews just as it had done among the Latvian Jews. As early as December 1941 it sent 500 young German Jews, according to A. Winter,[4] or 200, according to H. Baermann,[5] from the Riga ghetto to Salaspils. About 500 other German Jews from southern Germany had already arrived there on a transport ending at Jumpravmuiza (Jungfernhof) near Riga. In the transport from the Riga ghetto was Mrs. H. Sherman's first husband, whom she had married only two weeks before, and two of his brothers. Of the three, only one survived the war—Alfred Winter. Some of the young people were deployed in the construction of the Salaspils concentration camp, while others were assigned to the so-called burial commando. Until that time, Winter reports, those who had been shot and other corpses in Salaspils had been buried in individual graves. To conceal the steadily growing number of corpses, the Gestapo now decided to bury all of them in mass graves and smooth down the layer of earth above them to match its surroundings. The burial commandos had to dig up the corpses and then rebury them in mass graves. While digging them up, the men also came upon the corpses of executed Russian soldiers and Russian women. The grave diggers had to work with their bare hands, and many of them contracted tetanus. On April 27, 1942, Winter, who was a member of this commando, buried his own brother, who had been infected with tetanus and had died of it.

In January 1942 the Salaspils concentration camp already had 1,500 inmates. Their daily rations consisted of 200 grams [about 7 ounces] of bread and some watery soup. At that time the commandant of Salaspils was the SS Sturmbannführer Rudolf Lange, commander of the Security Police and the Schutzdienst in Latvia and known as the "Bloodhound of Latvia." He was later succeeded by Krause. He was a close friend of Arajs and, according to rumors circulating in the officers' mess, once received from him as a Christmas gift a Christmas tree decorated with diamonds and rings.[6] The prisoners were shot or hanged for the smallest "offenses." Hundreds of emaciated victims perished of starvation, typhus, or dysentery. One day Lange, whose sadism during the final liquidation of the Small Ghetto is yet to be spoken of, played a despicable game with a German Jew who was about to be hanged. First he let him be hauled up on the gallows, then immediately let him down again and asked him how he had liked it up there. Only then did he finally have him hanged.

At the same time, sixteen other Jews were executed by a firing squad, including a fourteen-year-old boy named Sachs from Düsseldorf. A. Winter reports that he witnessed this scene from a nearby window.[7] Winter also relates that in January 1942 seventy Jews from Czechoslovakia arrived in Salaspils—what was left of a transport of 1,050 Czech Jews. Winter does not speculate as to what could have happened to the others but adds that three days later three freight cars of baggage and clothing were unloaded at Salaspils and that the Czech Jews recognized the clothing as belonging to their relatives who had disappeared. A fourth freight car was loaded with shoes and clothing, some of which was soiled with earth. Of the 200 to 500 young German Jews who had been sent in December 1941 from the Riga ghetto to Salaspils, between fifty and sixty returned as living skeletons to Riga in the spring of 1942. In Salaspils there were also many Russian civilians, adults and children, from the regions that had been occupied by the Germans. All of them died there of starvation, the cold, and infectious diseases.

H. Baermann, who has already been mentioned, was in the Salaspils camp from December 7, 1941, to August 2, 1942. According to his report, during this period 15,000 persons passed through the camp and nearly all of them were annihilated. Only 192 of them survived.[8]

The conditions in the aforementioned camp in Jumpravmuiza, where Unterscharführer Rudolf Seck and Oberscharführer Richard

Nickel rampaged, were even more terrible than in Salaspils. There, bunk beds stacked six or eight high stood in unheated barracks and stables. Transports from Nuremberg, Stuttgart, Hamburg, Vienna, and Würzburg arrived at this camp even before the first German Jews arrived at the Large Ghetto in Riga. Reportedly there were many pregnant women in the transport from Hamburg, and mostly children and elderly people in the one from Stuttgart. The unfortunate people who were brought to this camp by the Gestapo starved and froze to death there or were shot in the neighboring forests.

Originally all of the aforementioned Jews were in transports of 50,000 people, 25,000 of whom were destined for Minsk and 25,000 for Riga.[9] Consequently, by the end of November so many transports started to arrive almost simultaneously that there was no possibility of lodging the arrivals in Riga itself. Then and there, five transports comprising 5,000 people were rerouted to Kaunas, where all of them were slaughtered in the notorious Ninth Fort. The others were taken to Jumpravmuiza and, in early December, to the Riga ghetto, which was then standing empty after the extermination actions. The Jews who arrived in the transport on November 29 were shot at dawn the next morning in Rumbula (as described in chapter 7).

The Gestapo did not leave their newly arrived prisoners from Germany without work for long. Numerous workshops, for example shops for sewing and knitting, were set up for the women in the Large German Ghetto itself. If a person did not find work inside the ghetto, he was assigned to the work gangs of the Small Ghetto and went to work with the Riga Jews. The jobs at the Wehrmacht in particular were considered good work details, because the workers received meals and were not beaten. Cleaning the platforms and tamping the ties on the Latvian railway was also a popular job, writes J. Wolff, for there it was possible to trade items of clothing and underwear for food from the Latvian population.[10]

There were many children among the new arrivals, and the German Jews, like those of Riga, tried amid these desperate circumstances to provide them with a minimum of instruction. Schooling was organized for the older ones, and a kindergarten was set up for the younger ones.

Soon friendships arose between the young men of the Small Ghetto and the women of the Large Ghetto. To visit the Large German

Ghetto one needed a permit, but these were granted in most cases. Many women became pregnant, but because no births of Jewish children were permitted, the Gestapo forced the women to have abortions, which had to be done in advanced stages of pregnancy in some cases, and always without anesthetic. In many cases there was severe bleeding, in others infectious complications. Many women became sterile.

From then on, foreign and Latvian Jews walked together down the road of suffering that was to lead them a year later into the Kaiserwald concentration camp.

Many German Jews experienced the cruelty of the Latvian policemen soon after their arrival in Riga. For example, the Latvian policeman Danckops accused eighteen young Jewish girls of theft, for no reason at all, soon after their arrival and shot them on the spot. But the true murderers of the German Jews were Obersturmbannführer Gerhard Maywald, the head of Einsatzkommando 2C Dr. Rudolf Lange, and the ghetto commandant Krause. The first selection took place under Maywald's direction on February 5, 1942. He ordered those who had found no work so far—there were about 1,100 German and Austrian Jews—to take all their belongings with them and get into trucks that were allegedly going to take them to another camp. Of course the victims did not suspect that two days earlier the ghetto police had dug a mass grave in Bikernieki. Those who remained behind in the camp realized their relatives' fate only after trucks arrived filled with clothing, children's toys, and baby bottles full of milk. While sorting these things they came upon the belongings of their friends and relatives. Everyone understood clearly what this meant.

In February 1977 a court in Hamburg sentenced Gerhard Maywald to four (!) years in prison.

On February 10, 1941, Rudolf Lange received a transport from Vienna. It was bitterly cold, and Lange advised the new arrivals to use the buses that were waiting for them. More than half of them took his advice. They were killed in the buses with exhaust fumes.

But the cruelest murderer of the German Jews was the ghetto commander Krause. In an inhuman and bloodthirsty way he went about the business of exterminating his fellow Germans. To get rid of old men and women, he invented the following satanic game. He had his underlings tell the prisoners that a food cannery was being opened in Daugavgriva (Dünamünde), a few kilometers downstream from Riga, where the old people could live and work. They would be resettled there. His unfortunate victims of course did not know that no such cannery existed. The play-acting of the "resettlement" was staged on March 26, 1942. Old men and women had to approach in rows of ten and were taken away in trucks that supposedly drove back and forth between the ghetto and Daugavgriva. While some of the people were loaded onto the trucks, the others patiently waited their turn. The SS people even set up chairs for the very frail ones so that the waiting would not be overly strenuous for them. Initially Krause's unfortunate victims still believed in the fairy tale of the food cannery, but when the empty trucks returned after only twenty minutes to take away a new group of old people, these unfortunate people and their relatives understood what the "cannery" was all about. Loud weeping and lamenting broke out. The old and sick people tried to resist being taken away, and their relatives tried to pull them out of the Gestapo's clutches. The whole situation was a convenient excuse for the SS people to show their true faces. With blows of their truncheons and clubs, with kicks and punches, they brutally and mercilessly forced their victims into the trucks and, since now there was nothing more to hide, robbed them of their blankets, bags, bundles, and food as well. According to M. Kaufmann and G. Schneider, between 1,000 and 2,000 people were killed by the Gestapo in that incident; according to J. Wolff, it was 5,000.[11] All of them were shot by Latvian execution commandos in the forest of Bikernieki. Mrs. H. Sherman claims that the trucks were rebuilt refrigerated trucks whose exhaust pipes had been connected to the interior—that is, they were mobile gas chambers.

On the same day, another action involving a fictional resettlement to a food cannery was carried out in similar fashion in Jumpravmuiza. According to G. Schneider, 1,840 people were murdered in the course of this action.[12] The camp commander Seck was sentenced to life imprisonment on December 29, 1951, in Hamburg.

One day Krause and his deputy Gymnich burst into a room in which a Czech physician, Dr. Ranzel, lived with his wife and daughter. His elderly wife had a fever and was lying in bed. When Krause saw that she was smoking, he slapped her and dragged her out of bed.

Ranzel was outraged and hit Krause in the face, whereupon Krause set his dog on Ranzel. The dog wounded him severely. Krause pulled out his revolver and drove Ranzel before him to the ghetto command headquarters, where he "shot him before the eyes of the ghetto police," according to H. Sherman.[13] M. Kaufmann also describes this incident.

Krause's completely inconceivable cruelty is also documented in other recorded incidents. A woman was brought into the ghetto who had been in prison for a year and nine months, and during this time had not seen her two children, a girl of five and a half and a boy of three and a half. In the ghetto command headquarters Krause handed the children over to their mother, who wept as she hugged and kissed them. "Krause was all sentimentality, playing God the Father," writes H. Sherman.[14] On the following day the woman, together with her children and 300 Lithuanian Jewish women, was executed in the forest.

One day Krause saw a little girl sobbing on the street in the ghetto. When he asked her why she was crying she answered that she was freezing. "Just run along, I'll warm you up," Krause reassured the little girl, and then pulled out his pistol and shot the child, who was innocently pattering along in front of him.

Later on Krause became the commandant of the Salaspils camp, where his behavior toward Mrs. E. Hoff showed that a spark of humanity may at times slumber even in the breast of such a monster (see chapter 13). Because of this duality of his character, Krause was capable of personally killing twenty to thirty Jews on Saturdays in the Old Jewish Cemetery with a shot to the back of the neck, and hours later expecting to receive tender affection from his Jewish girlfriend Betty. This took place in his private apartment in Ausekla Street, where the ghetto policeman Haar had to bring her every Saturday evening and pick her up again every Sunday evening. Krause did not realize that Betty dreaded his attentions and his glassy blue eyes. He could not understand that to her he was nothing but a murderer, because he believed that murder was a duty which had been imposed on him. Yet he knew that Betty was at his disposal only because of her aged, frail mother, who had been exempted from physical work and from the extermination actions thanks to the relationship between him and her daughter. He also knew of Betty's passionate love for a Jewish ghetto policemen, Senja Safro, who was massacred by Krause and his men on October 31, 1942, together with all the other Jewish policemen (as described earlier). One week after this action, when Betty was again with Krause in his apartment, he asked her whether her lover had been among the murdered men, and she confessed that he had been. This did not stop Krause from then asking her if she had no feelings at all for him, Krause.

Months later, Krause was removed from his post as ghetto commander and sent to fight against the Soviet partisans. At their last meeting, he asked Betty again about her feelings for him. She did not dare tell him the truth, and with an effort managed to say that she liked him. This answer disappointed him very much, as he felt deep affection for her. Despite her coolness to him, Krause later saved her life and protected her mother from immediate death.

At a school where pilots were billeted and where Betty worked as a cleaning woman, a young officer had recognized her as a former neighbor of his in the Kantstraße in Berlin. When he heard that Betty had a woman friend in Berlin, he helped her start a correspondence with her. One of the letters was intercepted by the SS. Correspondence was punishable by death. Roschmann, Krause's successor, condemned Betty to death and had her imprisoned in the bunker, that is, death row. While this was happening in the ghetto, Krause, severely wounded, was brought to a camp hospital in Riga. Haar managed to get to him. A word from Krause was enough: the death sentence was commuted. However, Betty remained in the bunker, tormented by uncertainty. Krause survived and was sent to recover at home, whence he returned to Riga weeks later. On the day of his return, Betty was released from prison. Her new workplace was the Army Clothing Authority, or ABA, which was notorious as a "starvation work gang."

In the fall of 1943, Krause again took over for a few weeks the commandership of the ghetto, which was finally liquidated at the beginning of November. Two days before the end, Krause ordered Betty to be brought to him and advised her to take her mother, who had till then only done mending work in the camp, with her to her workplace at the ABA the next day. On that day, November 2, 1943, when those Jewish prisoners who, like Betty, worked outside the ghetto but still lived in the ghetto, returned from their workplaces in the evening, they found the ghetto deserted. All of their relatives—old men and women, children, sick people and invalids—had disappeared. This is how Betty's mother survived the mass murder that ended the history of the Riga ghetto.

Ten months later the rest of the German and Latvian Jews were evacuated under hair-raising conditions via ship, some to Liepaja (Libau) and some to Szezecin (Stettin). When they came out of the ship's hold into daylight again, they were so dirty they no longer looked like human beings. In Liepaja the prisoners, including Betty and her mother, were buried under rubble during a Soviet air attack and were dug out. On New Year's Eve Betty heard that Krause was dead. According to reports, he had been torn apart, quartered, and cut into pieces by partisans.

From Liepaja the prisoners were transported to Germany by rail in cattle cars. Betty's mother died in Betty's arms during the journey. Betty herself was near death when she was rescued near Kiel by the Swedish Red Cross. Previous to that, she had miraculously survived Auschwitz, Bergen-Belsen, and a death march of 100 kilometers [62 miles] and had experienced circles of Hell that even Dante could not have imagined.[15]

10

The Kaiserwald Concentration Camp

In the eyes of the Gestapo, the two ghettos commanded by the Gebietskommissariat (Area Commissioner's Department) did not completely fulfill their purpose. The inmates were not being exploited sufficiently or killed fast enough. Only a concentration camp organized according to tried and tested principles could attain both of these goals. Moreover, the shootout near the Kvadrats factory on the outskirts of Riga and the Gestapo's discovery of the weapons cache in the Small Ghetto had shown that a ghetto can sooner or later become an undesirable seedbed of resistance.

These and similar considerations must have caused the SS to build the notorious camp that received its name, Kaiserwald, from the exclusive Riga residential area in which it was located. Regarding the administration of the camp, there was a tug-of-war between the Gebietskommissariat and the SS whose origins were purely material in nature. According to law the inmates' wages and their entire possessions belonged to the camp's commanders. A camp was thus a lucrative source of income. The SS won.

When the first news about the building of the camp and the imminent resettlement filtered into the Riga ghetto, tremendous agitation seized hold of the ghetto inmates. Although their life was difficult enough, the four walls of the rooms they lived in still gave them a certain amount of protection and simulated the reassuring warmth of a home. When they came back from work and had the barbed-wire fence behind them, they felt secure on the streets of the ghetto and within the apartments among their acquaintances, relatives, and friends. It was only to be expected that things would be different in the barracks of a camp. In the summer of 1943 the ghetto inmates' agitation turned into a mood of veritable panic when they heard of the brutal reception of the first arrivals at Kaiserwald. The agitation was so great that the camp headman, Mr. Leiser, felt obliged to convene an assembly with the knowledge of the German camp commanders in order to calm down the inhabitants of both ghettos. He pointed out that in view of what had happened (he meant the shootout and the arms depot) "those in power" were acting very leniently, and that the Kaiserwald concentration camp was neither a paradise nor a hell. M. Kaufmann agrees with him to the extent that in comparison with the extermination camps to which many Jews were sent later, the Kaiserwald concentration camp was in fact not yet a hell. But only in comparison. In fact the regime was horrible.

The resettlement of the ghetto inmates in the Kaiserwald concentration camp was accomplished step by step during the summer of 1943. Many of the large work gangs of Jews traveled the long distance from the ghetto to Kaiserwald on foot. Most of the inmates carried small bundles. Larger sacks containing their last remaining belongings followed on trucks and wagons. At the entrance to the camp, the bundles and sacks had to be thrown into a shed. Their owners never saw them again. Moreover, these unfortunate people were even robbed of their very last pieces of clothing and belongings. Immediately after passing through the camp gate they were herded into shower rooms and ordered to undress within seconds. Then ice-cold or boiling hot water streamed down on them, after which the new arrivals, who were still wet—there was of course no soap or towels—were thrown rags which they were then supposed to put on.

The men received dirty and patched old jackets and trousers that were too large or too small, or torn, blood-smeared Soviet uniforms full of bullet holes. The women got skirts and blouses in similar condition, in some cases ball gowns with deep décolletés and high-heeled shoes. J. Wolff writes: "After we were dressed we looked as though we had been rigged out for a costume ball. . . . Tall women wore dresses that looked like dance costumes, with their underwear in full view; short ones wore dresses hanging down to the ground, with sleeves reaching past their fingertips."[1]

An X was painted on everyone's chest and back with white or yellow paint and a stripe was painted down their sides and trouser legs.

Some inmates got hold of a plank bed and a sack of straw for themselves, but others had to share a plank bed and a sack of straw with one or two comrades. The sacks were old, dirty, and torn, the straw black and rotten, the plank beds stacked three or four high. Many had to sleep on the bare floor; not everyone had a blanket. Within a short time, some people deteriorated to the point where they no longer had the strength to wash themselves. Everyone slept in his or her dirty rags. The barracks were full of vermin, and all the inmates had lice. The food was nothing but starvation rations, and the work was hard. If anyone was caught trying to bring food into the concentration camp, he was punished with truncheon blows. Smuggling in written notes from other camps was punished by death.

Something was continually being built somewhere in the camp, and the inmates had to carry bricks, beams of wood or concrete, and sacks of cement to the construction sites or load and unload the arriving and departing freight trains. This was soon beyond the strength of these emaciated figures, who resembled skeletons. Boxes and crates that a strong man could easily have carried alone were dragged along with great difficulty by three or four inmates. There were also the notorious, soul-destroying tasks such as loading sand or stones onto trucks which then had to be unloaded a few hundred meters away, loaded again, and moved back to the starting point. The aim of this "work" was, according to the psychoanalyst Bruno Bettelheim, to humiliate prisoners by making them perform senseless tasks.[2]

In the morning and evening—regardless of snow, rain, or severe frost—there were the notorious roll calls that lasted for hours. In the evening this was followed by a hastily swallowed bowl of soup. Going to bed began with a vain attempt to get rid of the lice. These unfortunates' entire bodies itched from louse bites, and they scratched and scratched themselves bloody before falling asleep, or sometimes sleeplessly throughout the night.

The camp commander was SS Sturmbannführer Sauer, who had reputedly owned a construction business as a civilian. He was assisted by the SS man Sorge, Oberscharführer Brüner, SS Sturmbannführer Dr. Krebsbach (who was sentenced to death at the Mauthausen trial and hanged), and the medical orderly Wisner. Other members of the camp administration were Blatterspiegel, Krötschel, Hirsch, Hoffner, Huck, Laris, Fischer, Meissl, Prate, Schiller (or Schuller), Schimmel,

Summer, and Schwartz. SS man Sorge, known as "Iron Gustav," who later became the commander of the camp at Dundaga (Dondangen), was also the barracks commander at Spilve, the Riga airport.

To exterminate the Jews, the Gestapo used not only hand-picked SS men but also the notorious capos, who had been recruited among sadistic professional criminals and criminals convicted of sex offenses. The capos of the women's camp were SS women, known as Blitzmädel (lightning girls), and convicted prostitutes. The first camp headman at Kaiserwald was Reinhold Rosemeier, the owner of a beer hall in Hanover, who had been sentenced to life imprisonment for a double murder. After a while he was succeeded by Hans Bruhn. The professional criminal Xaver Apel, a former member of the Saß gang in Berlin who had been sentenced to life imprisonment, was especially brutal; he was known as "Mr. X." H. Baermann, M. Kaufmann, and J. Wolff all tell of inmates whom Apel brutally injured with blows of his fists, young women forced to do his will, and feeble people whom he hurled into the Daugava, forbidding anyone to rescue them. Apel threw a man who had dysentery and had given someone else his food into a kettle of boiling water that was to be used for making coffee for the camp. The sick man was boiled to death; the coffee was nonetheless made with the same water.

The other capos who were known by name were Hannes Filsinger (or Vilsinger), Hans Marr, and a certain Mr. Schlüter. They beat the inmates with their fists, clubs, and rubber truncheons until the blood flowed, until the victims fell to the ground and were then kicked—in the stomach and the genitals. From morning till evening, blows rained down. Hardly a day passed on which the SS did not shoot or torture to death one of the horribly deteriorated, starving, and weakened Jews.

Despite all the selection procedures, there were initially also teenagers and children in Kaiserwald. Half-starving and dressed in rags, they hung around the camp, poked around in the inmates' possessions in the barracks looking for valuables, or tried to get hold of food in the kitchen so that they could prepare it for their fathers or mothers, who were at work. Later, all of them were sent to Auschwitz and Treblinka together with inmates who were weakened by old age.

Worn down by starvation and abuse, wasted away to shadows of their former selves, many inmates fell victim to typhoid fever, dysentery, typhus, tuberculosis, or festering skin infections. They were allowed to lie for three weeks in the camp infirmary, which had hardly any medicines or bandages. If they were still sick or unable to work at the end of that time, their fate was sealed. They were shot. The clinic was headed by a Polish medical student named Bolek, who showed great humanity and understanding for the sufferings of his fellow prisoners. Bolek was assisted by the doctors B. Jakobson, one of the Jawitz brothers, M. Weinreich, and M. Sick. The latter two were from Liepaja (Libau), where they had been eyewitnesses of the same horrible atrocities as those suffered by the Riga Jews. Dr. Weinreich had headed the hospital in the Liepaja ghetto. One of his most dreadful memories of that time was the visit paid to the hospital one day by the notorious murderer H. Cukurs. Cukurs, bent on finding able-bodied men and women who might be hiding in the hospital, had forced his way into the women's ward, where he discovered a newborn baby. Births were forbidden in the ghetto. Cukurs snatched the baby by its feet from its mother's bed, smashed its head against the wall so that the skull broke, and tossed the lifeless body to the ground. When the Liepaja ghetto was liquidated, Cukurs spared the lives of Weinreich and Sick, who had once been his own doctors, and sent them to Riga together with a few other Jews. Both of them survived the war. After the Daugavpils ghetto was liquidated, Jews from there also arrived at the Kaiserwald concentration camp.

The final liquidation of the Riga ghetto took place on November 2, 1943. Ukrainian and Russian soldiers who had been integrated into the Wehrmacht surrounded the houses of both ghettos, searched them, and drove the last inhabitants into the streets. There they were selected, in the Small Ghetto by Lange and Krause, in the Large German Ghetto by Krause and Gymnich. During the selection process Lange shouted mockingly at those who were about to be shot: "Faster, faster to Palestine! Throw a last glance at your arms depot!" Among the victims that day were the violinist Professor A. Metz and the lawyer A. Grey.

The selection process dealt a more severe blow to the German Jews than to the Latvian ones. The Latvian Jews were only a meager remnant of the Jewish inhabitants of Riga, for the majority had been exterminated in the two actions in November and December 1941. But among the German Jews there still existed, despite small and large actions during the preceding years, whole families consisting of parents, children, and relatives. According to the SS viewpoint, however, these were worthless lives. Now they filed in front of Krause and Gymnich, who decided who would go to Kaiserwald and who would be loaded into cattle cars at the marshaling yard (Skirotava) and transported to Auschwitz. The victims were primarily old and sick people, some of whom had been dragged out of their beds in the ghetto hospital. There were several thousand people in all, including many children. A. Winter estimates that the number of people evacuated at that time was 2,000,[3] J. Wolff 2,500,[4] and H. Sherman 4,000.[5] Latvian railroad workers claimed later that the transport never left for Auschwitz, but that the freight cars stood on the sidings until all of the people in them had frozen to death. On this subject, G. Reitlinger writes that a surviving witness reported that the train did leave for Auschwitz and that 600 of the 2,216 people on it died during the ten-day journey.[6] Reitlinger also quotes from the notes of Dr. Wolken, who made lists in the quarantine camp of Auschwitz-Birkenau and wrote that a transport of 596 people arrived from Riga on November 4. Of these, 476 were gassed. Obviously these were two separate transports.

Mrs. H. Sherman was with a small group of German Jews who were the very last ones to leave the Large German Ghetto, on December 20, 1943. The trucks had just started moving when women and children ran out of the surrounding houses; they had been hiding until then and nobody had known about them. They begged to be taken along. The SS people, unconcerned, drove their trucks out of the ghetto. Then shots were heard. Mrs. Sherman had counted thirteen women and sixteen children.

M. Kaufmann, who was among the last people to leave the Small Ghetto, spent his first night in Kaiserwald lying on the floor. He didn't even notice that an acquaintance, Professor Lemberg from Vienna, was lying next to him. The latter recognized him and said, "Kaufmann, I have no strength left, I want to die."[7]

But the ghetto now only seemed to be totally deserted. A few Jews, including two men named Adler and Miller, had fitted out a bunker in the cellar of the Entwesungsanstalt (delousing station) and stayed in it, well supplied, until the Red Army marched in.

Soon after the occupation of Riga in July 1941, many German

units had "billeted" the Jews who worked for them. The billeting consisted of providing them with accommodation in the places where they worked; here they lived from Monday through Saturday, and were allowed to spend Sunday with their families in the ghetto. Although the billeted Jews now and then fell victim to the SS, many of them, especially those who worked for the Wehrmacht, led a relatively tolerable life. That changed fundamentally when both ghettos were liquidated. From now on, all billets were under the command of the Kaiserwald concentration camp—that is, the SS—and their regime changed to match that of Kaiserwald.

There was a considerable number of large and small billets, only a few of which will be mentioned here. One of the largest was the Heereskraftwagenpark, or HKP (Army Vehicle Park), which included numerous factories and repair workshops for vehicles. Several thousand Jews, including some children and teenagers, were billeted here. In the HKP there was a large polyclinic headed by Professor Mintz. Other doctors working here included N. Berniker, H. Gittelson, V. Goldberg, L. Javorkowsky, B. May, and Dr. Gurwitz. Dr. Blowetz and Dr. L. Rudow worked at a branch of the HKP known as the Park. The German Jew Salomon, a retired army captain and bearer of the Iron Cross, was also at the HKP. M. Kaufmann mentions Madi Friedmann as one of the women who worked here. Once we had been good friends. A photo I found in 1985 in my friend P. Sliosberg's photo album shows four happy young people sitting in the sand on the beach at Riga. Among them are Madi Friedmann and myself. That was in the summer of 1938. We had no premonition of what was to come.

When the SS took over the command of the HKP, the regime increasingly worsened there too. There were extermination actions. Some of the HKP inmates were later sent to Strazdumuiza (Strasdenhof), where several thousand Jews were already billeted, including men and women from Lithuania. Most of them were German Jews who had been brought there after the liquidation of the Large German Ghetto, including the ghetto workshops. Actions of unprecedented cruelty took place there on July 28 and August 3, 1944. All the teenagers up to the age of eighteen and all the men and women older than thirty were murdered. Some of the victims were gassed in the shower rooms of the Small Ghetto; others were shot in the woods of Bikernieki. When the inmates were evacuated to Germany by ship on August 6, 1944, only a few hundred of the thousands originally billeted there were still alive.

Professor Javorkowsky, an eyewitness of the final action at the HKP, recounts that the SS suddenly appeared and immediately began to drag children as well as frail and old people out of the camp. With truncheons and fists, the SS men beat those who resisted, and drove them with kicks into the trucks. Screams and desperate pleas resounded in vain. Most of the victims were German Jews whose families fate had not yet torn apart. Weeping and lamenting people stayed behind in the camp. Among the victims of this action were the Pukin family, friends of M. Kaufmann, including the father Zhano (Siskind), the mother Rosa (Rachel), and their ten-year-old daughter Hilda. "The next day," writes Javorkowsky,

> we were loaded into trucks and brought to the Strazdumuiza billet, which we found empty. The Jews who had been here before us were either dead or already on the way to Germany by ship. Here Dr. Gurwitz from Daugavpils committed suicide. Two weeks later we were loaded into the hold of a steamship. Only when they handed down food or heaved up on deck the smelly tubs full of excrement did they open the hatches and let some air and light into the stinking room. We received no water, and when we landed a week later in Stettin we were close to dying of thirst. They brought us to Stutthof on lighters.[8]

Javorkowsky reached Magdeburg by a roundabout route and fled one night from the marching column on the way to Sachsenhausen.

Another very large billet was the Armeebekleidungsamt or ABA (Army Clothing Authority), located in Milgravis in the buildings of a former ultramarine factory. J. Wolff, H. Sherman, and Ph. Israelson (more on him later) worked there. The ABA's task was to mend worn and damaged articles of clothing and equipment. Wagonloads of torn and bloody uniforms, underwear, boots, field cooking pots, electrical apparatus, and so on arrived from the front and were washed, patched, and repaired here.

Those billeted Jews who, like J. Wolff and Ph. Israelson, worked in the infantry barracks of the prewar Latvian army in the Moscow suburb were brought to their workplaces every morning in cement barges that traveled for an hour up the Daugava River and back every evening the same way. Heavy physical labor such as loading and unloading ships was another task of the inmates. The ABA had a hospital headed by the gynecologist Dr. Siegbert Joseph, who has already been mentioned several times; one of the Jawitz brothers and Dr. M. Wolpert also worked there. The dentist Tumarkin and the engineer Antikol were billeted at the ABA. The regime here was just as horrible as it was in all the concentration camps. The Gestapo beat and murdered people day in and day out. Now Wehrmacht soldiers too often treated the Jews as badly as they could, mainly because they feared being sent to the front by the SS because of softheartedness. There were repeated extermination actions whose victims were the old and the weak. Once when they were selecting candidates for death, the SS brutes took pleasure in calling out "For a holiday!" as they made a new execution victim step to the side.

Mrs. Sherman just barely escaped death. She was lying in the hospital with an inflammation of the gall bladder, when one day Dr. Joseph ran into the room, pale with fear, and ordered her and another girl to get up immediately and follow him. Hardly had they left the room than the SS stormed the hospital and dragged all of the sick people out of their beds, pushed them down the stairs, loaded them into a truck, and drove off. Dr. Joseph had been able to save only two of his patients; thirty-five others were killed.

When the ABA was evacuated shortly before the fall of Riga—the thunder of artillery could already be heard in the distance—only 1,000 of the original 2,000 to 3,000 billeted Jews were still alive.

The lawyer O. Finkelstein, a friend of our family who had only a short time before been a successful and respected personality among the lawyers of Riga, worked at the ABA as a shoemaker. As a small boy I had often visited the Finkelsteins, admired the billiard room and the wall safe, which was camouflaged by a strip of wallpaper, and played "Happy Families" for hours with the daughter of the family, Tatiana. In later years I had seen Tatiana, who was studying law in London, less often. It must have been the summer of 1938 or 1939 when I visited her for the last time in the Finkelsteins' beachfront villa in Riga. When the war broke out, Tatiana and her mother, the singer Safonova-Finkelstein, were in England and the lawyer Finkelstein was alone in Riga. In the Large Ghetto he had still worked as a lawyer, but now he was a shoemaker. I saw him for the last time when we slept next to each other on the bare floor in the Small Ghetto. He was killed, together with the engineer Mr. Lubotzky, in the last extermination action at the ABA.

Thousands of Jews, including hundreds from Lithuania and some from Czechoslovakia, were billeted at Spilve, the Riga airport. The regime there had been tolerable as long as the billet was commanded by the Wehrmacht, but it became horrible after the SS began to rampage there, with Sorge, Kröschel, and Blatterspiegel running amok and Xaver Apel acting as the camp headman. Thousands of people perished in the Spilve billet. There was an outpatient clinic here in which Dr. M. Solomir from Riga and Dr. Klebanov from Kaunas worked. Solomir died in Dachau. M. Birze, who has been quoted earlier, was sent in October 1943 from the prison in Valmiera to do forced labor at the Spilve airport, where he saw the Jews who were working there. Birze writes: "The Jews who had not yet been exterminated, mostly young and still able to work, came wearing jackets with enormous sleeves and large ski caps that hung over their ears. . . . Around their calves they had wrapped cloths held together with wire. On their backs crosses had been painted with bright yellow paint; on their chests they bore the yellow star. Horror and endless exhaustion spoke out of their eyes."[9]

As has been mentioned, M. Birze was a medical student, and thus after some time he advanced to the position of medical orderly at the airport and treated those of his companions in misery who were ill. Most of them suffered from festering skin infections. The very ill among them were brought once a week to the hospital of the Salaspils concentration camp, with Birze accompanying them. Thus he met in Salaspils the dentist Shlotschower from Vienna, who was then fifty years old, and made friends with him. Birze writes: "Shlotschower felt continually threatened by death, because he was one of the few Jews who were still alive in Salaspils. Certainly he was being spared for only as long as it would take him to repair the teeth of all the commanding officers."[10]

Shortly before Birze was evacuated to Germany in July 1944 they met for the last time. "You will go to Germany, my homeland," said Shlotschower, "and I will stay here." And that is what happened. The retreating Germans shot him, about which Birze comments that he might have only just repaired the teeth of his murderer. Birze also reports that he and his comrades froze miserably while working at the airport and tried in various ways to protect themselves from the cold. They wrapped wires around the ends of their sleeves, sewed footcloths inside their shirts, and shielded themselves from the wind with paper from cement sacks. One day they received underwear brought from Salaspils. It was multicolored: blue, green, red. "One trouser leg was purple, the other white, as though we were supposed to go to a costume ball. The underwear had been patched together from items of clothing worn by Jews who had been shot."[11]

The Kaiserwald concentration camp continually "supplied" billets and camps with new people. For example, transports left here for the camps in Jelgava and the extermination camps of Dundaga and Klooga, where petroleum-rich shale was mined to produce petrol. There was also a labor camp in Sloka (Schlock) whose inmates were used for cutting turf. Here the eighteen-year-old Arthur Kaufmann, together with the Mordchelevitz bothers, was shot on May 20, 1943, by Roschmann and Gymnich because a bit of lard had been found on them. Jews were forbidden to hoard food on pain of death. When the inmates were ordered to line up, the Mordchelevitz brothers understood in a fraction of a second what was happening and tried to flee through the camp gate. Roschmann and Gymnich shot the fleeing men in the legs and then killed them as they lay on the ground. They ordered Arthur Kaufmann to turn his back to them, but the eighteen-year-old answered that he wanted to look his murderers in the eye. Roschmann shot him dead. Arthur Kaufmann was the son of M. Kaufmann, the author of the book *Die Vernichtung der Juden Lettlands* (*The Destruction of the Jews of Latvia*).

Now and then small groups of men, always new ones, were sent to the so-called base in Rumbula, where they were ordered to dig up and burn the corpses of those who had been murdered. They worked in chains. In the files they were designated as Kommando NR II89 and were under Roschmann's command. Not a single one of them was ever seen again. All of them were murdered after they had done their work.

In the spring of 1944 a transport of 4,500 Hungarian Jewish women, which Mrs. Sherman had seen in Riga and A. Shpungin saw in Dundaga, arrived in Dundaga via Kaiserwald. Both of them were shaken by the sight of these women, who had nothing on except their prisoners' uniforms, that is, they wore no underwear. Some were barefoot, while others wore wooden clogs. In Riga the Jewish women of the ABA threw two sacks of underwear for the Hungarian women over the wall of the Kaiserwald camp, which led to a fight among the unfortunate women. According to J. Katz, 2,000 of them were used to build runways at the Riga airport at Spilve.[12] Here these women, who hardly knew how to handle a shovel, were forced to do the hardest physical labor. The men of the Todt organization knew no mercy and beat the weeping women to force them to work better. After a few days all of them were shot.

Although the Germans knew they had lost the war, this was no reason for the Gestapo to show leniency toward its victims. The latter were evacuated to Germany in ships—the land routes were already under Soviet control—and during this journey the Gestapo's bestial treatment of the Jews remained the same. Most of the inmates of the Kaiserwald concentration camp were evacuated on August 6, 1944, in military transport ships, some of the others on September 22. The last Jews, prisoners of the Truppenwirtschaftslager or TWL (Troop Provision Camp), left Riga on October 11, two days before the Red Army marched in.

As has already been mentioned, the concentration camps and billets were a welcome source of income for the Gestapo apparatus, because the employers paid a fee for each inmate who worked for them. But these were funds that did not interest the individual SS people. What did interest them was the transformation of the war with all its alleged ideals and high-flown aims into a very ordinary looting expedition. The only aim they had in mind was to fill their own pockets, and at this they proved to be masters. The fact that Krause and his accomplices forced the Jews of the Small Ghetto to pay tribute to them was a small crime by comparison.

The SS leadership carried out their robbery on a much larger scale. In the Vorburg, formerly a posh Riga neighborhood inhabited almost exclusively by Germans, they set up a mammoth warehouse into which they dragged together everything they could lay their hands on, from carpets, lamps, chandeliers, furs, and fabrics to ladies' underwear and shoes. Here they piled up the possessions they had robbed from the living and dead Jews. Under the strict supervision of SS people, Jewish prisoners were forced to search painstakingly for hidden jewelry and gold coins and jewels that had been sewn into clothing. The Jews doing this work faced the death penalty if they did not hand over all the valuables they found. The lion's share of the jewelry, gold, and watches that were found went not to the state but into the pockets of the SS people, who, according to Mrs. Sherman, used to joke that this would be the foundation of their new fortunes after the war. It was a known fact that Jeckeln himself spent hours sorting jewels he had spread out on his desk.[13] In the SS "Alfred Rosenberg" commando, Jewish girls cataloged the paintings, sculptures, carpets, carvings, tapestries, and similar objects of art that had been accumulated there and were to be shipped to Germany.

Some of the warm clothing that the homeland (i.e., Germany) had donated for the freezing soldiers on the Eastern front also ended up in the warehouses of the SS. Soon the SS officers could be seen parading around in fur-lined coats and boots. The clothing, writes Mrs. Sherman, was sorted out and then sent back to Germany as "woolen clothing donated by our brothers, the Latvian people" for the people who had been bombed out of their homes in greater Germany.

In the Vorburg Mrs. Sherman saw workshops for uniforms, ball gowns, corsets, and underwear, a furrier's workshop, and sections for shoes, boots, and gloves. "All of the clothes that were produced there looked as though they were destined for the luxury-goods section of an exclusive shop, but they were exclusively for high-level SS officers, their wives, and their girlfriends."[14] The "reception clerk" here was the Riga tailor B. Rudow, the brother of the doctor L. Rudow.

The workshops in the Vorburg had been set up in the following way. Soon after the occupation of Riga the Gestapo sought out those Jews of the city who seemed to be useful for their private aims. In the process, the SS came upon the very capable tailor B. Rudow, who was made the head of a tailor's workshop. The SD man F. Sherwitz, the Gestapo's head of Jewish Affairs, soon realized that he could make capital out of men like Rudow. He made concessions to them, quartered the families of "his" Jews in a special building in the Large Ghetto, and later settled them in houses outside the ghetto on Washington Square (next to the Vorburg) and in Petersalas (Peterholm) Street. Workshops were set up, and Rudow himself was promoted to the position of private tailor of the SS leadership. In order to avoid the "offensive" contact between a Jew and non-Jews, Rudow had to take off the Jewish star. From now on he passed himself off as a non-Jewish foundling who had been raised by Jews, which might have appeared plausible because he was tall and blond. To Rudow's credit be it said that he never misused his altered status, but on the contrary helped his relatives and many others whenever he could.

In a similar fashion, F. Sherwitz[15] also made a non-Jew out of the Polish Jew Tamara Schermann. In the summer of 1944 the two Rudow brothers fled from their billets, the tailor from his workshop and the doctor from the HKP; that is how they saved their lives. Tamara Schermann also reportedly survived. The tailor Rudow was arrested immediately after the liberation of Riga by the Red Army, accused of "cooperation" with the Germans, sentenced, and deported—a fate he did not deserve. Years later he emigrated to Israel.

Thus the SS viewed itself as a state within a state and obeyed the teachings of National Socialism only to the extent that it found them convenient. This also applied to the doctrine of the purity of Aryan blood. In many SS commandos the SS people were not at all averse to having sexual relations with Jewish girls. The longer the war lasted, the more frequently many SS workplaces expressly requested pretty young Jewish women for themselves. The SS men left the hero's death on the field of battle to their comrades in the Wehrmacht. They themselves led a dissolute life and kept Jewish women, loose women, and capo prostitutes for their personal "needs." Although violation of racial purity was supposed to be the worst "crime of opinion," which in the case of an SS man could be atoned only by death, in Minsk SS officers publicly expressed their opinion that the restrictions of the Race Law were valid only for the German Reich, but by no means for the occupied Eastern territory. Some of the maltreated Jewish girls thus obtained more bearable living conditions for themselves, at least for a time, but sooner or later all of them were sent off to billets and most of them died there.

In Gebhard's *Handbuch der deutschen Geschichte* (*Handbook of German History*), K. D. Erdmann writes that the extermination of the Jews was entirely impersonal in nature and that the National Socialists aimed only to eradicate the Jews.[16] This view can only bewilder the reader and reveals total ignorance of what actually happened. Extermination accompanied by exploitation, robbery, torture, maltreatment, and death by starvation is hardly "impersonal" in nature. In fact, the extermination campaign of the Nazi regime and its accomplices had expressly sadistic features and was characterized by the hatred and contempt the Nazis had written on their banner since the beginning of the 1920s and in whose spirit they had educated the German people. For what other reason had they sung for years about Jewish blood splashing off the knife? The Nazis did not exterminate the Jews impersonally; rather, they delighted in tormenting them until the very last hour of the "Third Reich"'s existence.

11

Genocide in Latvia

For more than forty years, Soviet historiography ignored and labeled as taboo the subject of the murder of the Jews in the part of the USSR that was occupied by the Germans during World War II. Occasionally books about the murder of the Jews in the Ukraine appeared in the USSR, but thoroughgoing and extensive scientific studies were not published. In the Soviet Republic of Latvia, some brochures concerning the murder of the Jews did appear, but this was literature produced on order for the KGB for another purpose: namely, to denounce certain Latvian emigrants as fascists and accuse them of murdering Jews. The obviously partisan nature of these brochures requires one to treat their contents with caution. Serious works have begun to appear only in recent years (M. Vestermanis, H. H. Wilhelm). So it is no wonder that there is still great uncertainty about the victims' number and places of origin.

A declaration made by the Latvian Parliament on September 19, 1990, seemed to put an end to conjectures on this subject. In it, the murder of Jews within the territory of the Soviet Republic of Latvia during World War II was condemned and the participation of Latvians in these murders was deeply regretted. Moreover, in this declaration concrete information about the number of Jewish victims was provided for the first time by the authorities. According to the declaration, the number of murdered Latvian Jews was over 80,000 and that of foreign Jews was at least 200,000. One had to assume that these figures were based on detailed archival data. Moreover, it seemed inconceivable that a responsible government could thus incriminate the history of its country without having at its disposal weighty factual material to back up such a grave self-accusation.

Unfortunately, exactly that seems to be the case, for according to the authoritative conclusions of the historian M. Vestermanis, Latvian archives still contain no data to support the dismaying figure of an estimated 200,000 murdered non-Latvian Jews. It seems that these figures are based on the report written by experts of the medical service of the Sixty-seventh Soviet Army in December 1944, in which the number of foreign Jews who died in Latvia is in fact estimated as being more than 240,000. But these data are based on rumors, and besides, a few pages later in the same report the number of victims is given as "only" 100,000.

Implausible as it may seem at first glance, it must nonetheless be repeated and emphasized that the Latvian Parliament's declaration cited above is in this respect not a serious document. The situation is different with regard to the number of Latvian Jews who died. The number given in the Parliament's declaration is correct and matches our calculations and those of other authors.

As far as the number of deported German Jews is concerned, according to the information given by Sturmbannführer Lange of the Second Einsatzkommando, between 19,000 and 20,000 Jews from Germany had arrived in Riga by February 1942. According to the data of the International Tracing Service in Arolsen, 22,327 people had arrived by October 1942. R. M. W. Kempner estimates the number of German Jews who were forcibly sent to Riga at 30,000, but without citing his sources. All these data coincide with the numbers given by G. Schneider and R. Hilberg, according to whom there were 20,000 or 25,000, respectively. Hilberg's data refer to the late fall of 1941.

The figures given in the previous paragraph refer to those German Jews who were brought to the Riga ghetto or the Kaiserwald concentration camp, but not to those who were brought directly to other camps, for example, Jumpravmuiza or Salaspils, or were shot immediately in the woods around Riga or elsewhere in Latvia. The corpses recently found near Litene and Pitalovo, to name only a few places, probably are those of people in this group. In the mass grave of Litene only the corpses of women and children were found. It can be assumed that the number of German Jews who were deported to Latvia without being registered is about the same as that of the registered ones. This leads to the conclusion that about 40,000 to 60,000 German Jews in all were sent to Latvia. Latvian railroad workers also estimate the number of German Jews deported to Latvia to be 60,000. J. E. Kroeger, who had access to secret documents of the security police in Riga, estimates the number of Latvian and German Jews who died "before the gates of Riga" at 100,000.

In the summer of 1944, when the Germans were forced to withdraw from the Baltic countries, a few thousand German Jews may still have been alive. They ended up, like the Latvian Jews, in concentration camps in Germany, where most of them died of starvation or infectious diseases or were shot. Thus, at most probably only about a thousand of them survived the deportation to the East.

As for the number and origin of other foreign Jews who were murdered in Latvia, no official data of any sort exist, and rumors about them are still awaiting confirmation. As has already been indicated, in recent years numerous large and small mass graves have been discovered at various locations in Latvia, but these have yielded no new information because as a rule it was impossible to identify the victims. It must be pointed out here that a leitmotif in the relevant literature is the statement that Jews from France, Belgium, Holland, and even Norway died in Latvia besides those from Germany and the countries of Eastern Europe. Such statements can be found not only in the books by M. Kaufmann and M. Birze and the aforementioned KGB brochures, but even in the personal minutes of the interrogation of F. Jeckeln on December 14 and 15, 1945. These rumors are confirmed to a certain degree by the testimony of M. Morein which is stored in the archive of the Jewish Information Center in Riga. According to it, while looking for the corpses of his parents in 1946 near the village of Kukas near Krustpils, he discovered in a mass grave corpses whose clothes bore French labels. On page 156 of S. Zeitlin's collection of documents there is a photocopy of a French identity card issued to Adrien Prodhomme, which was found in a mass grave in Latvia.[1]

Mrs. H. Sherman tells of a transport from Westerbork, Holland, that she saw one day at the Riga train station. Bits of paper bearing pleas for water fluttered out of the air slits of the freight cars, which had been covered with barbed wire. The people inside were dying of thirst. Rings, watches, and money followed the pieces of paper, in the hope that someone would help them. The only things that arrived in the ghetto were the clothes of these people and some baby carriages with baby bottles full of milk. There was no longer any trace of the deportees themselves. Jews from Czechoslovakia were also brought to Riga and quartered in the Large German Ghetto. As has been noted earlier, A. Winter tells of the 70 Czech Jews who were the only survivors of a Czech transport that reportedly originally consisted of 1,500 people. In the list given by S. Weinberg, two Czech transports from Prague comprising a total of 4,000 persons are mentioned.[2] It is known from several sources that in January 1942 two transports from Theresienstadt arrived in Riga. The Jews from the first transport were quartered in Prague Street in the Large German Ghetto, and some of the men ended up in Salaspils. The deportees from the second transport were taken directly from the station to a small forest on the outskirts of the city and shot there. In E. Leiser's book *Leben nach dem Überleben* (*Living after Survival*) a railroad transport from Prague that reached Riga via Theresienstadt is mentioned.[3] A survivor of this transport tells of trucks in which the Jews were taken directly from the station to the outskirts of the city, where graves had already been dug for them. It is known that there were also Lithuanian and Polish Jews in the Riga ghetto and the billets. From the Kaunas ghetto alone about 1,000 Jews, men and women, were deported to Riga to do forced labor. Jews from Romania and Yugoslavia were also reportedly exterminated in Latvia.

We know about one transport of Hungarian Jewish women which was seen in Riga by Mrs. Sherman and J. Katz; according to A. Shpungin, some of them finally ended up in Dundaga. We can only surmise what the eventual fate of these women was. J. Katz reports that some of them, about 2,000, were killed after working at the Riga airport. We do not know whether these were the only Hungarians who reached Latvia. As has been mentioned, F. Jeckeln also claimed not to know how many foreign Jews had been brought to Riga. Thus the question of the number and origins of the Jews who were deported to Latvia and murdered there still remains largely unanswered. Nor do we have a precise answer to the question of how many of the Latvian Jews in the territory occupied by the Germans survived the war. In the days after Riga was liberated by the Red Army, a notebook lay in an empty school building in Akas Street in which the surviving Jews signed their names. There were 152 of them. Assuming that only half of those who had been saved signed the notebook, this number must be doubled to about 300. If a like number survived in the rest of Latvia, which is very unlikely, the number of survivors in Latvia as a whole would be 600. We estimate that about the same number could have escaped from the concentration camps on German territory. Thus the number of Latvian Jews who survived the Holocaust rises to about 1,000. M. Kaufmann likewise estimates the number of survivors to be about 1,000. But some are of the opinion that even this estimate is too high.

Wolfgang Scheffler writes in his book *Judenverfolgung im Dritten Reich* (*The Persecution of the Jews in the Third Reich*) that Polish Jewry probably suffered the most terrible fate under German rule: "Of the more than 3 million Jews living in 1939, only between 300,000 and 350,000 survived the war."[4] In other words, an estimated 10 percent to 11.5 percent of the Polish Jews survived. Only about 1.25 percent of the Latvian Jews survived.

I feel compelled to return to the declaration of the Latvian Parliament. It is obvious that this kind of declaration, even after a delay of forty-five years, is genuinely welcomed by the international public, by Jewry, and especially by the Jews of Latvia. We know that it was the result of the efforts of a number of prominent people, primarily Professor J. Stradins. But we cannot help pointing out that even today the Latvian press does not shrink from printing occasional anti-Semitic articles, that former Latvian SS legionnaires and members of the German-Latvian police hold meetings, and that fascist organizations such as Perkonkrusts (Swastika) and the Aizsargi (Guards) which had already been banned before World War II are becoming active again. At the same time, large sections of the Latvian population, especially the postwar generations, have received hardly any information to the present day about the tragic events that occurred during the war, and are growing up in total ignorance of this aspect of their own history. These facts are not outweighed by the Latvian government's gestures, such as returning to the Jewish community its former property which had previously been nationalized by the Soviet government, or opening a Jewish college-preparatory school, the only one in the entire Soviet Union. Nor can these gestures cover up the existence of a subliminal anti-Semitic current in the Latvian population. For many Latvians, the Latvian Parliament's declaration is only lip service, and the dark shadows of the blood-soaked events of the war years still mar the coexistence of Jews and Latvians.

But that is not all. In November 1991, on the fiftieth anniversary of the murder of the 30,000 Jews of the Riga ghetto, a memorial service was held in Rumbula, the location of the massacre near Riga. The parliamentary president of the Republic, A. Gorbunovs, also participated and made a speech. After the usual words concerning the death of the innocent victims, the president presumed to claim that the victims were themselves to blame for their death because they, the Jews, had shown goodwill toward the Soviet rulers in 1940 when the Baltic states were annexed by the USSR. In plain language, this is supposed to mean that the Latvians had every right to use the opportunity, when the Germans marched into Latvia about fifty years ago at the beginning of the war with the USSR, to settle accounts with their Jewish fellow citizens. The head of state himself was justifying the mass murder.

The president's words were silently ignored by the Latvian media, but hundreds of the bereaved, including the historian M. Vestermanis and the Member of Parliament M. Vulfsons, heard them with consternation, shock, and indignation. Was it an isolated faux pas or the opinion of a section of the official political structure? In 1995 the Latvian translation of Hitler's *Mein Kampf* appeared in Latvian bookstores.

THE SURVIVORS

12

Flight

After our small troop had been led to the Small Ghetto on November 30, 1941, we found an empty room on the ground floor of a small wooden house and set up our quarters there. We were ten or fifteen men, including the three Herzbergs, the lawyer O. Finkelstein, who had joined us in the Small Ghetto, my father, and myself. I don't remember the others. One of our neighbors in the other rooms was Dr. Bernicker's son Arian, a nice, tall boy of sixteen or seventeen. The room was completely empty. At night we spread blankets on the bare floor and slept wrapped in our coats. Our only possessions were the clothes we wore and some extra shirts, socks, and underwear.

The next morning we went to work. My father and I joined the Kabel work gang, which worked near the Kuznecovs porcelain factory a few kilometers upstream from the ghetto, where a narrow dam, the Krüdener Dam, stretches across the broad right riverbank toward the Daugava. For several days, a work gang had been digging a ditch for a cable along the top of the dam. Each of us was given a pickax. It was very cold, and we were forced to work hard in order to stay warm. As I swung my pick into the air high over my head and let it whistle down onto the frozen stones, I had to think of the slaves who built the pyramids. We too had been enslaved, our lives too were worthless, we too were doomed to die. Our overseer, a gaunt, elderly German in riding breeches and leather gaiters, walked up and down and forced us to work faster by occasionally whipping us with a riding crop.

There was a midday break, during which we received a thick slice of black bread and hot tea, which we ate and drank standing up outdoors at temperatures of about minus 20 degrees Centigrade [about minus 4 degrees Fahrenheit]. In the evening we went back to the ghetto. Great swarms of crows flew over us cawing. It made me shudder, because I imagined that they came from Rumbula, only a few kilometers distant, where our dead lay. One day, when the German at the head of our column took another route home to the ghetto, the thought flashed through me that we were now being led away to be shot. I didn't calm down until the ghetto fence came into view through the darkness in front of us. The work, to which we were unaccustomed, exhausted all of us, especially the older men like my father.

After a few days we were transferred to a work gang that was working on the railway. When the column of about 120 men left the ghetto in the early morning, it was pitch dark. The streets were not lighted, and all the windows were blacked out. We were guarded only by a couple of sleepy soldiers, some of whom marched at the head of the column while others marched at the end. At eight o'clock we reached the central administrative building of the railroad in Gogol Street and lined up there. After a while, German railroad workers who needed a few helpers appeared. Four of us, including my father and me, were put to work by three men who had to load a freight car with various products of Riga factories for the eastern front near Minsk. They brought us in a truck to the factories producing chocolate, cigarettes, shirts, shoes, and so forth in the city, and there we loaded crates of these goods onto the truck and brought them to the freight depot. There, over several days, we had to load a freight car full of hundreds of different kinds of products.

These men's attitude toward their work and toward us struck us as strange and incomprehensible. They worked with the same regularity and lack of interest as machines. At 8 A.M. it was time to enter the factories. At precisely 1 P.M. began the lunch break, which lasted till 3 or 3:30 P.M.; work ended punctually at 5 P.M. We saw no sign of the enthusiastic, self-sacrificing work for the front that was talked about so much in the newspapers and on the radio. Sticking to the prescribed working hours, especially the lunch break, was much more important to them than getting their task done. Their behavior toward us was correct, and they made sure we were fed well and in sufficient amounts in the kitchen of the railroad administrative building, where the cooking for a large canteen was done. Thus we were actually able to eat our fill. On the other hand, they showed not the slightest interest in our fate or in us as human beings. They seemed not to realize that only the day before we had been as proud and free as they themselves—it seemed not to have entered their minds at all. Once there was a brief exchange of opinions about the war, during which one of them declared melodramatically, "The Führer's already offered his hand in peace many times, but nobody's wanted to take it!" I smiled inwardly at such childish naïveté. Once, when my father briefly described our desperate situation to another one of them, the man replied unmoved that my father, being a doctor, could certainly get his hands on, as he put it, "a little powder" that would solve all our problems.

The mood in the camp was one of dejection. When we returned from work in the evening and met our friends and roommates, there was only one topic of conversation: the fate of the evacuees. The older men were convinced that they were in the Salaspils (Kurtenhof) camp and hoped to see them again; the younger ones had no illusions. One day my father showed me a crumpled piece of paper on which someone had written: Weintraub family all alive. He said the note had come from Salaspils and it proved that all of the evacuees had arrived there and were well. I answered that those few words proved nothing, but he stuck to his belief.

On December 8 the second "evacuation" took place. Only later did the word "action" in the sense of "execution" become part of the common vocabulary. As we, the inhabitants of the Small Ghetto, gathered at the gate at dawn to march to work, we saw through the barbed-wire fences the blurred outlines of the inhabitants of the Large Ghetto, whose "evacuation" had already begun. When we came back in the evening, the Large Ghetto was empty of people. Once again the word "executed" went from mouth to mouth.

On November 30, when my father and I had said goodbye to my mother, she had made me promise that, come what may, I would not turn to the Krumins family to ask for help. She felt that in such difficult times one had no right to become a burden to others. But now, after the second "evacuation," I was gripped by fear. I calculated that seven or eight days lay between the two "evacuations" and that on the following Sunday or Monday it would probably be our turn to be executed. On the spot, I wrote a letter to Mrs. Krumins telling her that I wanted to return a book I had borrowed from her and that I would expect to meet her on a morning convenient to her at the railroad administrative building on my way to work. I signed a Latvian name so that the letter would not contain anything incriminating if it should fall into the wrong hands. I was convinced that the Krumins family, who had certainly heard what had been happening in the ghetto, must know that it was now a matter of life or death, and would understand that my letter was a cry for help.

Two days later, when our work gang had lined up as usual on Gogol Street in the morning, opposite the central administrative building of the railroad, we saw Mrs. Krumins and her older daughter among the people who were going to work. They were discreetly eyeing our column from a distance. My father and I called out to the leader of our column that we wanted to warm ourselves up a bit, and we went into the administrative building. The two ladies followed us. We walked hastily up and down the long, wide corridors of the ground floor, my father and I in one direction, the two ladies in the other. Every time we passed one another we exchanged a few words. The Kruminses had only one thing to say: "The moment you believe your lives are in danger, come to us at once." After a few minutes we had to separate, to be on the safe side. The Kruminses left the building and we returned to the work gang.

After my letter arrived, there had been a very long discussion in the Krumins home. Professor and Mrs. Krumins and their two daughters, who were about thirty years old at the time, were serious and intelligent people. They were members of the Latvian intelligentsia, and thanks to extensive contacts at all levels of society they had realized long before we did that the Gestapo intended to liquidate us once and for all. Although all the family members agreed that they wanted to save us, there was nonetheless an unanswered question. For years the family's maid, Lina Pilsroze, had lived with them, and so far the Kruminses had not spoken to her at all about their intention to take us into their home. If she had refused to participate in the dangerous game of rescuing us, no one could have blamed her. The death sentence had been declared for those who sheltered Jews, and one could not assume that if the Gestapo discovered this conspiracy they would spare a Latvian professor's family and their maid. When the Kruminses finally divulged the matter to her, Lina's reaction was astounding. "Let them come," she cried, "the sooner, the better."

Sunday approached. Was a third "evacuation" in store? My father and I decided to act, for it was senseless to wait there any longer, when a bullet could catch up with us any minute. There were no preparations to make, for we had hardly any possessions, nor could we have taken anything with us anyway. On the evening of December 12 I snipped the Stars of David off our coats and stitched them on again very loosely, so that they could be easily torn off with a single pull.

The next morning we lined up in our column as usual. The soldiers appeared and received us. The ghetto gate opened and we left the camp. Daugavpils Street, along which we were marching, was dark and empty of people. After a few hundred meters we reached the dimly lit newspaper kiosk at the corner of Jekabpils Street where many of us left the rows of the column in order to buy the morning paper, which our German overseers never objected to. My father and I took advantage of the resulting slight disorder in the rows of the column to tear the stars off each other's backs. Then we pretended to run for a newspaper along with the others, tearing off the stars from our chests as we did so. I stood at the kiosk for only a fraction of a second, turned around, and pretended to be rushing back to my row. In fact, I only ran along the column and disappeared into the darkness of a park that lies there between two Russian churches. Nobody had noticed anything. My father did the same, but we lost sight of each other in the dark.

When I arrived at the Kruminses' building in Marijas Street, dawn was starting to break. I climbed the stairs to their apartment, not suspecting that I would not descend them again for two years and ten months. If we had known at that point how long we would be laying claim to the Kruminses' hospitality, who knows whether we would have sought refuge with them.

Nobody saw me on the stairs. As I reached the landing of the Krumins apartment, the door opened and Professor Krumins himself received me with a friendly smile. They had been waiting for me, for my father had already arrived before me. All the family members, and

Lina too, gathered in the hallway and clasped my hand with joyous excitement. Then we sat down at the breakfast table.

Professor Krumins, a tall, slim gentleman with a small graying moustache, was sixty years old at that time, but he was still very strong, agile, and lively. In the course of the years, we saw him less often than we did the other members of the family, because as a rule he left the house in the morning, came back at midday, but spent most afternoons at the university, where the Faculty of Architecture was his home away from home. He had been born into a peasant family, had studied at the beginning of the century in Riga and Karlsruhe, and later on had worked in Moscow for many years. He spoke perfect German, Russian, and a very cultured Latvian, and he loved to explain the derivations of Latvian turns of speech, many of which originated in peasant customs. His knowledge of the classical languages was excellent, and he also spoke English and French. Moreover, in recent years he had also learned Swedish. He had married in Moscow, and his two daughters, Velta and Ilga, had been born there. In 1920, after the founding of the Republic of Latvia, Professor Krumins had been offered a post at the Latvian University in Riga, where he was first an instructor and later a professor and dean of the faculty. In 1946 he became a regular member of the Latvian Academy of Sciences.

Professor Krumins was an architect and an artist. Many of his works, mainly landscapes, hung in the apartment. He was also very clever with pencil and pen. He often showed us his pictures and drawings, and I was astonished at the various techniques in which he worked. His comprehensive general knowledge and his outstanding special knowledge made him an ideal lecturer in his specialty, the history of architecture. He also offered courses in applied perspective, the theory of shadows, and elements of decorative art in architecture.

He had a fine sense of humor and loved to tell stories about all kinds of strange incidents involving students that he had experienced in the course of his long teaching career, or to tell the latest political joke—anti-Nazi, of course. His character combined goodness and kindness with decisiveness and stubbornness. This became evident within the first few minutes after our arrival, while we were still sitting at the breakfast table. Professor Krumins gave us a hearty welcome, saying that the entire family was glad to see us there safe and sound and that here we could calmly wait for the end of all the horrors—an end that would come much sooner than we believed. Today we know he was wrong, but who could imagine at the time that the end of Nazi rule was so far away?

"I place only one condition on your stay here," Krumins said then. "As long as you live here in hiding, you may never, under any circumstances, leave the apartment or show yourself at the window. That's all." He spoke these words in a friendly but firm tone, and in the years we lived under his roof we never broke this rule. Unfortunately, during the war years we heard of several cases where Jews in hiding were seen by neighbors and denounced to the police after they had broken just such basic precautionary rules, for example, by taking an evening stroll.

Whereas Professor Krumins was remarkable primarily for his intellectual gifts, Mrs. Krumins was spontaneity itself. Before World War I she had been an operating-room nurse in Moscow and had worked with Professor Mintz, among others. Although many years had passed since she had given up her medical activity, she had kept her interest in medicine, subscribed for years to *Lancet,* the leading English medical journal, and loved to talk shop with us. No less linguistically gifted than her husband, she had a perfect command of the three languages of the country, was widely read in English literature, had learned Swedish, and during the past two years had taken Italian courses, where she had met my mother.

Both of the Kruminses disliked the Germans, although they had grown up within German cultural circles, and they hated the Nazi regime not only for its inhumanity but also because they saw in it the rebirth of the colonial empire that had enslaved the Latvians for 700 years and now had taken away their independence once again. Both of them, but especially the professor, still remembered the punitive expeditions of 1905. In that year, during the first stirrings of the revolution in Russia, there were bloody clashes in many cities between the workers and the police. In the territory that was later to become Latvia there had been peasant uprisings which the Russian government put down using Cossacks, who were assisted by the Baltic barons. The Polytechnic College in Riga, where Professor Krumins was then studying, had been closed because of student unrest, which led him to leave for Germany and continue his education in Karlsruhe.

Both of the Kruminses were proud of being Latvians, but chauvinistic feelings were completely alien to them. Individuals from a great variety of nationalities, including many Jews, belonged to their circle of friends and acquaintances.

Today I believe that it was the clever Mrs. Krumins who realized during the first days of the German occupation what was in store for us Jews. She saw that it was necessary to act before it was too late. I think she was afraid of this "too late." She feared that one day there would no longer be anyone who needed her help, and that the whole family would then have to reproach itself for not having acted in time. From this thought, as well as an extreme sense of honor and the wish to thwart the Nazis' plans, sprang the plan to help Jews.

It was sheer coincidence that it was my father and I who, so to speak, fell into their hands. This was confirmed by Ilga, the younger daughter, in a letter she wrote to me in the early 1990s. Only thanks to her mother had the Presses lived in her house, she wrote—and not because her mother knew Mrs. Press well, but because when the terrible, fateful moment came her mother had cried out in a quavering voice, her eyes blazing, "We have to help, we have to rescue! We have to, we have to!"

Ilga was a few years older than me. From the first day of our stay, she regarded us as her personal protégés, so to speak, and did all she could to make our life in the "golden cage," as she jokingly called it, bearable. Her extraordinarily well-balanced character was a great source of support for us. As far as the comforts of daily life were concerned, our presence affected her the most, for she had given us her own room and now lived in her father's study. Ilga had a warm heart not only for people but also for animals, and had nursed many a wounded sparrow and many a lame pigeon back to health. From her I learned to tend flowers—a pleasant distraction in our otherwise quite monotonous existence.

Velta, the older daughter, was studying architecture and was the wife of the artist A. Meters, with whom she lived in a small apartment in the same building. She was an extremely lively and active woman, and used to show up at least once a day at her parents' apartment, where she usually sat with us for an hour or so, telling us about the latest events in the city and at the university.

Lina Pilsroze, the cook and maid, was a gray-haired woman of fifty with a pale, thin face and a somewhat weary, always friendly smile. Her quiet ways radiated patience and kindness. Although our presence in the house meant an additional burden for her, it seemed as though she never felt it. From the first until the last day of our stay, she remained invariably friendly toward us and never once let us know how very indebted we were to her. She washed our clothes, brought us our meals, and always gave us the same quiet, kind smile as on the first day of our arrival.

The Kruminses had decided after ample consideration to let only three people, whose discretion and reliability they were absolutely sure of, in on the secret of our presence in their house. They were the teacher Elza Mieleika and Mr. and Mrs. Stalbergs. We met Mrs. Mieleika on the day after our escape from the ghetto. She walked into our room, shook our hands with an enchanting smile, sat down in an armchair, pulled a cigarette case from her handbag, offered my father a smoke, and began to converse with us as though we were old friends. We admired the ease with which she could strike up relationships with new people. At that time she was in her late forties, slim and with a smile that made her pleasant face look beautiful.

Mrs. Mieleika played a significant role in our life: she helped provide the family with food, because given the scanty war rations it was not easy to feed two more mouths, my father's and mine. In those days, anyone who had even the most fleeting contact with Jews was putting himself or herself in the greatest danger. One day Mrs. Mieleika saw a column of young Jews. The emaciated young men aroused her sympathy, and in passing she pushed her lunch sandwich into one young man's hand. The next minute a Latvian policeman was standing beside her. Didn't she know that it was forbidden to make contact with Jews, let alone give them food, she was asked. Mrs. Mieleika confessed that she had felt sorry for the young man, adding that he was a former student of hers. Don't you dare to do it again, the policeman warned her.[1]

Professor Stalbergs, a colleague of Professor Krumins, and his wife, who was a pediatrician, came to visit occasionally and would then sit for a while with us too. Mrs. Stalbergs was a Jew but was not bothered very much by the Gestapo, if I remember correctly. This was probably due to the fact that Professor Stalbergs taught at the university; moreover, the couple was about fifty years old and childless.

This was the circle of people with whom we lived for three years. We got to know all the other visitors and friends of the family only through descriptions, or we recognized their voices penetrating through to us from the neighboring rooms. The Kruminses made constant efforts to bring diversion into our life. Now one, now another of them would appear in our room to have a brief chat or bring us another newspaper. We were in contact with the outside world not only in this way but also thanks to a radio that stood in our room. We listened to the BBC in German and English several times a day and drew fresh hope from the broadcasts again and again. I have often asked myself whether the employees of the BBC realized what tremendous moral support these broadcasts gave to all the oppressed people in Europe during the war. Only someone who himself has been on the edge of despair can fully appreciate the extent of this support. On the other hand, we know today that newspapers and radio stations in the West concealed a great deal from their readers and listeners at that time. Rarely did we hear anything about the death camps and their victims. Roosevelt and Churchill did express their outrage at the Nazis' atrocities, but nobody took any concrete steps to save the Jews. The cries of horror that resounded in 1945, when the world beheld millions of corpses and tens of thousands of living skeletons, came much too late. They did not bring a single one of our dead back to life.

The Kruminses and their friends supplied us generously with books, and we read a great deal. My reading consisted primarily of English books and medical literature. One book I read several times during this period was *Körperbau und Charakter* (*Physique and Character*) by E. Kretschmer, a gift the psychiatrist Dr. H. Idelson had given me through Mrs. Stalbergs, who was in touch with him.

The outside lecturer Dr. H. Idelson was one of the most striking personalities among the doctors of Riga. He was very popular with his colleagues of all nationalities, who valued him highly because of his intellect and education, and no less popular with his patients because of his kindness and readiness to help. He was married to a German woman and had two daughters and two sons. The sons were typical renegades, as is often the case with the children of "mixed marriages"; they called themselves Delson and were members of German fraternities. In the late 1930s they were presumably repatriated together with the Baltic Germans, for at the beginning of the war Dr. Idelson was alone in Riga. As I've mentioned before, Dr. Idelson headed the ward for the mentally ill in the ghetto hospital and lived with Dr. R. Blumenfeld, the former medical officer of Riga who was now a member of the [Jewish] Committee. My father and I saw him for the last time on November 29, 1941, after the men's roll call in Sadovnikova Street, when we went to Dr. Blumenfeld to hear from him how he thought things would probably develop.

Dr. Idelson survived the actions and lived first in the city, then in a small room at the Psychiatric Clinic on the outskirts of the city in Sarkandaugava until the fall of 1944, when all the Jewish prisoners were evacuated from the billets and the Kaiserwald concentration camp to Germany. Today we can no longer clearly determine thanks to whom he had received permission to live in the clinic. Some said it was his family's intervention; others said that German doctors had taken an interest in his research on patients with schizophrenia. Although faithful patients supplied him with food, he must still have had a very difficult time of it. In the summer of 1984 in Stockholm, the aged widow of Dr. Ogrins of Riga told me that Dr. Idelson had once called on her during the war and asked her for a small mug and a tin bowl. Mrs. Ogrins sighed deeply as she remembered this scene and added in consternation, "Such a modest request from such an extraordinary man."

His end was the same as that of most of Riga's Jews. When the last inmates of the Kaiserwald concentration camp were about to be evacuated by ship to Germany, the Gestapo got hold of him too. M. Kaufmann notes that Dr. Idelson was one of the last Jews from Riga to arrive in Stutthof, where he died of a heart attack three days after his arrival. The corpse was cremated immediately.

Thanks to the discretion of everyone involved and the Kruminses' caution, our life in the "golden cage" was never in danger, except for one single occasion. One evening in the winter of 1943 at about 10 P.M., as my father and I were about to go to bed, there was a frenzied ringing of the apartment doorbell. I heard Professor Krumins open the door, then I heard loud German voices and realized they were soldiers. All I could whisper to my father in horror was, "They're here!" As though turned to stone, the two of us stood in our room and waited for what was to come. After a few minutes the voices died out, the apartment door slammed shut, and both of the Kruminses appeared in our room. They were smiling with satisfaction because they had gotten rid of the Germans—it had been the military police. The soldiers had noticed a window that was not blacked out—because of the danger of an air raid a blackout had been decreed, under threat of severe punishment for noncompliance—and they had come to the wrong apartment in their search for the evildoer. "I told them they should check the apartment across the hall," beamed Mrs. Krumins. "Germans live there, but in *our* apartment every window is blacked out!" Thanks to Mrs. Krumins's confident manner and her fluent German, it didn't even occur to the soldiers to take a closer look at the rooms. I realized with amazement that the shock had literally paralyzed my father and me and prevented us from getting into our excellent hiding place, where only bloodhounds could have found us.[2]

In the winter of 1942–43, because of the shortage of coal, the house was not heated. We listened despondently as the water slowly gurgled out of the central heating system. We froze, until Professor Krumins set up in our room a little stove that we could stoke with wood, which spread a pleasant warmth when it was burning. He set up a similar little stove in the bedroom where he and his wife and Ilga used to spend the day. The maid's room where Lina lived was heated by the stove in the kitchen.

Our mood depended on the news from the front. If the Allies had won victories, we hoped for a speedy end of the war. If the Germans had been successful, it seemed the war would never end. We became truly hopeful after the Allied invasion of Normandy on June 6, 1944, and after the Red Army broke into Latvia from the east in the summer of 1944 and the reports from the front included Latvian place names for the first time. Nonetheless, the time until our final liberation stretched out endlessly. The focus of the Red Army's attack lay to the south of us, and the German troops did not surrender their northern positions for a long time. They did not pull out of Latvia until Marshal Maslennikov's troops broke through the German positions in Estonia in September and October 1944 and then, swerving southward, forced the German troops to retreat from Latvia. Valmiera, Cesis, and Sigulda fell in rapid succession.

On the evening of October 11 I stood at the window for a long time and watched the Germans' retreat with the greatest satisfaction.

Trucks loaded with boxes, wardrobes, tables, and crates filled the entire roadway. Now and then cavalrymen appeared, so exhausted they could barely stay in their saddles. Foot soldiers filled the sidewalks. Torches were flaming on top of the motor vehicles, illuminating this scene with their flickering yellow light. The Germans were actually fleeing.

In the late evening hours the stream of refugees dried up, and the street lay as still as though its inhabitants had died out. Toward midnight, just as I was looking out of the window once again, there was a flash of light outside. It was followed by a heavy detonation, and the walls of the room began to sway. The bridges over the Daugava—we lived only one kilometer from the river—had been blown up by the Germans. Then there was an air-raid alarm, and the Kruminses went down to the cellar as usual. On October 12 the city lay as though it were dead. Nothing moved. Only now and then did we hear at a distance the rolling of heavy artillery.

In the early morning of October 13 I stood at the window again and looked down at the street. It was deserted. Suddenly, at about 5 A.M., a soldier in a clay-brown uniform appeared. He was unarmed. He stepped slowly down the middle of the street, looking closely at the cobblestones. It was a Red Army soldier! We were free! I called my father to the window and said to him, "So we've lived to see it after all!" The tears were running down his cheeks as he answered, "We have, but the others haven't."

13
Freedom

We left the Kruminses' apartment and climbed somewhat clumsily down the four flights of stairs. We had to learn how to walk again. Months later I was still dragging my feet like a Belgian cart horse. As we took our first steps out into the street, we didn't know that the Kruminses and Lina were gazing down at us from the window. Ilga Krumins told me this in a letter she wrote to me in the 1980s: "To see both of you free on the street was for us the best reward for three not altogether easy years."

On the streets one saw hardly anybody but soldiers. Most of the Latvian civilian population had fled together with the Germans, and those who had stayed behind didn't dare to go out on the streets for days. They knew only too well what they had to answer for and feared a cruel revenge, a wave of arrests or a bloodbath similar to the one they had prepared for us three and a half years before. But nothing of the sort happened. It was as though people in the USSR had never heard of any massacres of the Jews. And yet eastern Latvia, where in some areas Jews had once comprised up to 57 percent of the population, had already been in Soviet hands for months, so the bloodbath in Latvia could no longer have been a secret. Nonetheless, nobody seemed bent on seeking out those responsible for the murders. My father gained access to the commander of the city, a Soviet general. The general had requisitioned for himself and his staff a villa in Henri Barbusse Street (previously Aristide Briand Street) that had formerly belonged to the Maikapar family. The Maikapars were Karaites and had owned a large cigarette factory in Riga, but they had been regarded as Jews by the Germans and had been forced to share the Jews' fate. It was said that the surviving Karaites, about 200 to 250 people, had collected a considerable sum and passed it into the hands of Reichsminister A. Rosenberg when he visited Riga at the end of 1941. At the same time Professor Steininger, the director of the Institute for Medical Zoology in Kleisti near Riga, wrote a report about the Karaites which might have been inspired by Rosenberg. According to the report, the Karaites were of the Mosaic faith but ethnically speaking they were not Jews, which corresponds to the facts. Accordingly, the Karaites were left undisturbed to the end of the war.[1]

The commandant had a cold and received my father and me lying in his bed, surrounded by his officers in the glow of a small electric bulb that lit the room only dimly. The electricity supply in Riga was very meager for months to come, for the Germans had severely damaged the Kegums hydroelectric power plant as they retreated.

My father reported to the commandant, using the notes he had made over the years, about what had happened here during the war. After a while the commandant motioned for him to stop. What my father had presented to him, he declared, did not correspond to the facts. The Latvian population was not responsible for what had happened here. With that we were dismissed. We left, very outraged and downcast. What the commandant had said was certainly not his personal opinion but very simply the Soviet government's attitude toward the murders in the areas that had been occupied by the Nazis. Whether it was in the Baltic states, the Ukraine, or in White Russia, wherever murders had been committed, the local population was not held responsible at that time for the atrocities, and it is not being held responsible for them today. Up to the end of the 1990s, not a single treatise by a competent historian that comprehensively covers the story of the murder of the Jews—of Latvia and other European countries—on the territory of Latvia has been published.

At that time we wanted not revenge but justice for those who had been murdered. Today we can demand only that the truth be told. But even for that we are probably waiting in vain. Not a single Jew has ever been able to accept this attitude of the Soviet regime and the very similar one of the Republic of Latvia. What is the reason, one wonders, for this strange stance? Why this totally open aversion to justice for the Jews, an attitude that stands in crass contradiction to what all the other European states have tried to attain, then and years later: an objective account of the atrocities committed by the Nazis and their accomplices against us Jews? Doubtless it was the anti-Semitism in the USSR, which was already gathering at that time, that was being expressed. In the years to come it became increasingly manifest and finally revealed itself so openly as to bring about an emigration that resembled a flight of tens of thousands of Jews from all over the USSR. Given this attitude of the Soviet regime, it is no wonder that the Black Book conceived by Ilya Ehrenburg and other renowned Soviet authors, which was to consist of eyewitness accounts of the atrocities committed against the Jews during the war, was printed only recently, that is, after a delay of fifty years.

We experienced the first days after the liberation in a condition of euphoria. We rejoiced over every person who had survived the hell of the past few years, and of course our joy was especially great when we met again old friends we had scarcely believed were still alive. Someone had placed a notebook on a desk in an empty school building at 10 Akas Street, and we, the survivors, signed our names in it. There were 152 people.

We who had saved ourselves and who stared at one another stunned by the miracle of our rescue and asked one another untiringly, "How did you manage to do it?"—we were treated with the greatest mistrust by the Soviet regime. Most of the survivors were summoned to be interrogated at night by the KGB. All were asked the very same stereotyped question: "Why did you survive when all the others were shot?" They also summoned to the KGB those of us, including my father, who had attended a memorial service at the Old Jewish Cemetery to honor the victims of Nazi terror. At the memorial service Lev, one of the survivors, had pointed out the place where Arajs and his accomplices had committed their murders and where a truck full of vodka had stood during the executions. Lev reported, "If anyone got tired from the shooting, he got himself a bottle from the truck, knocked off its neck with his bayonet, strengthened himself, and then continued his 'work.'"

As early as October 14 or 15, one or two days after the liberation of Riga, several high-ranking KGB officers came to the Krumins home, allegedly to congratulate them for saving us, but of course in reality to determine who was the rescuer and who the rescued.

In short, the surviving Jews were suspected of having collaborated with the Germans. Not the Latvians, but we Jews! The tailor B. Rudow and his brother, the physician Dr. L. Rudow, and Elga Burstein, all of whom had saved their own lives, were sent to Siberia. I never saw Dr. Rudow again, and I saw Mrs. Burstein only at the end of the 1950s when I myself returned from a concentration camp in Siberia. Also among the deported was a German woman, Mrs. Baumgart, who had lost her husband in the ghetto and had rescued the pharmacist Mr. Gurwitsch (or Gurewitsch) and his son. Yet another one was Mrs. Rosenthal, a German woman whose husband, a jeweler, had died in the ghetto. Who can say how many innocent people fell victim during those days to the KGB's, or the Soviet regime's, obsession with spies and its anti-Semitism?

During those days we heard for the first time of Zanis Lipke, his wife, Johanna, and their sons, those nearly legendary figures in the struggle to save the Jews of Riga. The Lipkes had kept Jews hidden in the cellars of several houses and brought food to them there. In some of the houses they had even walled up the doors to individual cellar rooms to provide security for "their" Jews. Over time, the Lipkes had then smuggled their protégés—there were about fifty or sixty of them—out of the city to reliable people in the countryside, where almost all of them survived. Yad Vashem minted a memorial coin in honor of Lipke, and on the occasion of a visit to Israel Lipke himself was permitted to plant a tree in the Avenue of the Righteous. He died in the spring of 1987, a man of the stature of the Italian Perlasca, the German Schindler, and the Swede Wallenberg.

In this connection one should mention Sch. Zeitlin's *A Documentary History of the Jews of Riga* (the original is in Russian), which names Russian and Latvian families who helped Lipke or who themselves saved Jews. Also mentioned are several mixed marriages where Latvian and Russian husbands protected their wives and thus saved their lives.

A few days after our liberation we moved into our old apartment in Krisjana Barona Street, now standing empty. We were told by our custodian that the two Germans who had lived there the whole time had taken our beautiful old furniture with them when they left. We made ourselves comfortable somehow. It must have been on the same day that I embraced my friend and fellow student L. E., with whom I had transported sick people into the ghetto, and whom on account of a newspaper story I had long believed to be dead.

On August 25, 1944, there was a brief article in the *Allgemeine Zeitung* (*General Newspaper*), published in Riga, that told of a Mrs. A. Pole, a Latvian, who had hidden several Jews, seven men and a woman, in her apartment at 15 Peldu Street. According to the article, the house was surrounded. Then there was an exchange of gunfire, after which Mrs. Pole and the Jews were arrested and sentenced in a summary trial. One can easily imagine what that meant.

Mrs. Stalbergs, who at that time was in touch with several Jews in hiding, found out that the Jews in Peldu Street had been informed on by neighbors and that L. E. had been one of those killed. Also among the dead were the three Lipmanowitsch siblings, twin brothers and their sister, their nephew Wange, S. Gurewitsch, the shoemaker Abel, J. Grundmann from Jekabpils, and J. Judelowich, the top-ranking Jew at the railroad commandership. But L. E. was not in fact among them.

I had seen L. E. for the last time on November 29, 1941, during the roll call of men in Sadovnikova Street in the Large Ghetto. He had dragged himself, weak and pale, to the roll call after having just recovered from diphtheria. He looked so frail that I was very concerned about his chances of survival. Fortunately I was wrong. When I invited him to live with us, L. E. accepted delightedly, and in the days and weeks to come he told me, bit by bit, about his fate.

Like most of the Jews of the Small Ghetto, L. E. had been deployed in various workplaces during all these years, and after the closing of the ghetto he had been taken to the Kaiserwald concentration camp. Until 1943 he had worked in the Quartiersamt (Housing Authority), where the workers were treated tolerably well, as they generally were in the Wehrmacht. The work there consisted of sweeping and scouring the floors, cleaning the toilets, chopping firewood, heating the rooms, and so on. In the spring of 1943 he worked for a while in a bank where Jewish prisoners sorted the valuables of murdered Jews: rings, watches, gold teeth, silver goblets, and ritual Sabbath candelabra from synagogues. The fact that stealing these objects was punishable by death did not stop L. E. from stealing a few watches he needed to pay for food. At that time, the threat of death was not a deterrent to any Jew, for all of them had become fatalists, living in the hope that fate would be merciful to them.

In the summer of 1943 the Small Ghetto and the Large German Ghetto were both dissolved and the inhabitants sent to the Kaiserwald concentration camp. The admission procedure to which they were subjected was beyond imagining. The capos beat and slapped the new arrivals and drove them in a rush through the showers, finally throwing them some rags to wear as clothing. L. E. was sent to work at a Luftwaffe arsenal. In November 1943 he found out he was to be sent to the notorious Klooga camp in Estonia, where oil-bearing shale was mined. For a long time already he had been toying with the idea of escaping, and he was well aware that in Estonia escape would be unthinkable, as he did not know the local language. But in Riga, as he knew where his friend Gurewitsch was hiding, he thought he could go underground. One afternoon while his work gang was busy unloading freight cars near the camp, he ran away as it was starting to get dark, without anyone initially noticing his escape. He hurried to A. Motmillers, a well-known and popular Latvian athlete, who also knew where Gurewitsch was hiding. Motmillers brought him to the janitor J. Ozols, who was already hiding five other Jews in the cellar of a building: the shoemaker Abel, Joseph Grundmann from Jekabpils, the Lipmanovitsch twins, and Gurewitsch. Here they stayed until the beginning of summer 1944, when they heard that the police might search the cellar rooms of the building. They had to look for a new refuge, and all of them except for L. E. found it in Mrs. A. Pole's apartment, where they died. L. E. wandered all summer from one hiding place to another. Finally he landed in a little empty wooden house in the Moscow suburb. Because the water pipes didn't work, he had to spend the final six days tormented by thirst until the Red Army marched in.

Soon afterward I met the Ozols family in person. J. Ozols was a plumber by trade, a tall, strong man with an extremely good-natured character. His wife, with whom he had four children, was small and delicate. Of course they knew what the penalty was for hiding Jews. I asked Mrs. Ozols why they had done so nonetheless. She answered only, "We felt so sorry for those boys." A. Motmillers not only helped

L. E. escape but also saved the lives of many other Jews, including the Ritovs, who were graphic artists, and their cousin.

In the days after our liberation I met Philipp Israelson through L. E. But he did not tell me the story of his rescue until forty years later in Berlin.

Israelson was sixteen years old in 1941 when the war between Germany and the USSR began. The very first days after the city was occupied by the Germans looked ominous for his family of four. First, the janitor, obviously authorized by the police, started to harass the Jews in "his" building. For instance, the Jews, including Mr. Israelson and his father, were forced to pull the garbage cart, which was normally pulled by horses, to the garbage dump on the outskirts of the city, accompanied by the approving looks and comments of passersby. Later on they were forced to do yardwork at the nearby First City Hospital, where Jews of all professions, craftspeople and academics, were digging ditches, glazing windows, laying pipes, and the like. Next, the janitor appeared in the Israelsons' apartment with three Bändeldicken (armband wearers) to arrest the father. Sharp words were exchanged. A German officer who was billeted with them drew his pistol and ordered the bandits to disappear or he would shoot them down. They left and never came back.

In mid-August 1941 the family had to move to the ghetto, and with heavy hearts they said goodbye to their maid Anna Apse, whom all of them called "Annina." She had lived with them for more than sixteen years, had raised both boys, and was a second mother to them. They wept as they parted. Annina took on a new job with the owner of the house, Mr. Stolterfoth. He had left Riga in the late 1930s together with the other Baltic Germans, but had now returned and moved into his old apartment in the building. When Annina saw during her visits to the ghetto that the Israelsons were beginning to starve, she started to pilfer Mr. Stolterfoth's food supplies and bring this and that to the Israelsons in the ghetto.

During the fateful hours before the liquidation of the Large Ghetto, Mr. Israelson and his father had decided to move to the Small Ghetto so that they could take better care of the mother and the younger brother. As the two of them were going to their workplace at the Heeressammelstelle (Army Collection Post) at dawn on December 8, 1941, they saw through the barbed-wire fence the inhabitants of the Large Ghetto who were about to be "evacuated." They saw their relatives among those who were walking past them, but they had no foreboding that this would be the last time.

At first the father and son worked at the Heeressammelstelle until they were taken to the Kaiserwald concentration camp in the summer of 1943. The treatment of the camp's inmates was truly a reign of terror. The capos beat and kicked the prisoners at will. To pass the time, they would take an inmate and shove into his anus a water hose that was attached to a hydrant, then fill his intestines with water until they burst. The notorious Mr. X sometimes beat people so severely that his victims fainted or even died. One of his victims was the husband of Jeanette Wolff, the author of *Mit Bibel und Bebel.* He fainted under the blows, but survived.

Mr. Israelson's father was later sent to the infamous camp at Dundaga. There all traces of him were lost. The few prisoners who returned to Kaiserwald from Dundaga looked more like skeletons than human beings.

In August 1943, young Israelson was billeted in the carbide factory in Milgravis, from which the prisoners were brought every morning on lighters to their workplace, which lay upstream in the Moscow suburb. In October, young Israelson managed to escape. As the lighters that were to bring the prisoners from their workplace back to the carbide factory made their usual run late in the evening, he swung himself silently over the railing and swam to land. It was the spontaneous action of a young man who had no escape plan and didn't quite know where he could flee. He reached the bank without being seen and walked, wet from head to toe, through the blacked-out city in which a curfew was in force. He couldn't turn to Annina, for everyone in the building knew him. Then he thought of Emilija Luse, Annina's friend, who had always liked him. He found her little house. Emilija and her husband took care of the wet and exhausted boy. The next day they told Annina, who rushed over and clasped him in her arms. It was she who after a while found a hiding place for him. She managed to convince an acquaintance, Mrs. Puce, to take the boy into her apartment. Mrs. Puce lived in an apartment that included a cellar room which could be reached only through a trapdoor in her living room. No stranger could ever have suspected that there was a cellar door under the living-room carpet. Israelson spent a year in this room by the glow of a small oil lamp. It was a long year for the elderly lady and the boy. Nor had the years passed over Annina without leaving their traces. One autumn day as she was once again visiting the two, she fainted away and died a few minutes later.

A month later Riga was liberated. Not until the 1970s, when Mr. Israelson had emigrated from the USSR to Germany, did he manage to find Mr. Stolterfoth, his former landlord. In the course of the correspondence that now began, Israelson discovered to his amazement that Stolterfoth had noticed the disappearance of cigarettes, coffee, and food at that time, but had silently overlooked it because he understood who was being provided for.

I saw our neighbors from the ghetto, the Herzberg brothers, again in the aforementioned school in Akas Street, where we signed our names in the list of survivors. Both of them were pale and could barely stand up. They had spent the last few weeks before the liberation of the city almost continually in a lying position. Their father had fallen victim to one of the selections. At his workplace in the Heereskraftfahrpark or HKP (Army Vehicle Park), Boris, the younger brother, had made friends with a young Latvian woman whose name was Mikki. Mikki wanted to save her Boris's life at any price. In August 1944 the two brothers escaped from the HKP and were hidden by Mikki in a cellar that was part of a large store and served as a stockroom for paint and wallpaper. Here the brothers had to lie rolled up in wallpaper during the daytime without a break. Only at night could they move around a bit. Thus they managed to survive. Mikki and Boris stayed faithful to each other after the war as well.

When I asked Dr. Herzberg whether he knew of the whereabouts of Stella, his wife, he told me the following story.

In the summer of 1941, when the Herzbergs were still living in their apartment in Valdemar Street, two German officers were billeted with them. Usually in such cases the Jewish men and women had to be their servants. But the two German officers refused to accept such services from the Herzbergs. When the Herzbergs finally had to move to the ghetto like all the other Jews, the officers offered to hire Mrs. Herzberg officially as their cleaning lady. This was meant to give her the opportunity to return to her apartment every day from the ghetto. The officers expected nothing in return. Their wish was to give her the opportunity to go on with her normal life in her former home. Thus Stella Herzberg was able to pursue her private activities in her apartment during the daytime, read books, listen to the radio, or do sewing. She spent only the nights in the ghetto. This went on until November 1941, when the officers revealed to Mrs. Herzberg that her life was in danger in the ghetto. They told her she could go back there only once more, to say goodbye to her husband. After that they would bring her to her uncle in Switzerland. And that is what happened. Stella Herzberg experienced the end of the war in Switzerland. Later she resettled in Germany.

Two colleagues of Dr. Herzberg, the dentists Dr. Frisch and Dr. Noim, had also survived. The former had been saved by a Latvian woman who was a friend of his, the latter by a Russian woman. Dr. Rogalin, who had worked in the ghetto polyclinic, survived by similar means.

The university had resumed its activities a few weeks after the liberation of Riga. One of my first teachers was Dr. Goldberg. He too had been billeted in the HKP and had escaped from it in the summer of 1944. He had found shelter in the house of a friend, the renowned Latvian actor Janis Osis, and had hidden there until the Red Army marched in. Together with his wife M. Klaus-Goldberg, a German, he emigrated at the beginning of the 1970s to Germany, where he died in 1978.

I did not learn of Professor W. Mintz's sad end until the late 1950s in a letter from Paul Sliosberg, a friend of my youth, who himself had been deported from Belgium to Buchenwald in June 1944. There he heard of the arrival of a transport from Latvia. He sought out the new arrivals and met Nikolai Bordó, the brother of his brother-in-law. Nikolai told him of the sad fate of his sister and her son and said that Professor Mintz was also among the new arrivals. A short time later, when Sliosberg was brought to the camp infirmary because of an illness, Professor Mintz, also ill, was placed on the plank bed next to his. They hadn't heard anything about each other for years, but now they met again on the "manure heap of the Reich." As early as the beginning of the century Mintz, then a young man in his thirties, was one of the leading surgeons of Russia. The *Soviet Medical Encyclopedia* mentions his contributions to the field of stomach and pericardial surgery as well as his introduction of the operative therapy of acute appendicitis. In 1918, when Lenin was wounded during an attempt on his life, Professor Mintz was one of the doctors who treated him, and in the bulletin concerning the state of Lenin's health Professor Mintz's name was the first one to be mentioned. In the ghetto as well, he operated with brilliant success under the most difficult circumstances.

Mintz's condition deteriorated rapidly. About November 1944 he was carried out of the clinic. Nobody asked what had happened to him, but many knew that he was killed with an injection they called "the death shot." Phenol or Evipan was used for this purpose.

Nikolai Bordó's traces were lost in Buchenwald. Paul Sliosberg survived, apparently thanks to an Allied air attack in which several bombs fell on the camp, destroying, among other things, the camp's card file. From then on he claimed to be a Belgian and thus survived.

One of the old acquaintances I met shortly after our liberation was G. Zivian, the son of the internist Ch. Zivian, who had acquired false identification papers at the beginning of the German occupation and gone as a male nurse to the town of Indra on the Latvian-Russian border. There he had worked together with A. Schönfeld, the son of the psychiatrist M. Schönfeld, founder of the Atgasen Psychiatric Hospital. Schönfeld had received from the SS center in Berlin a certificate testifying that his mother—who had committed suicide shortly after the Germans marched in—had been Russian. Dr. H. Marnitz, head of the Department of Health and Public Welfare at the commissar general's office, advised him to go to Indra as the district doctor. According to Zivian, Latvian militiamen shot him down in Indra during a drunken brawl. But Marnitz writes that he was taken by SD men to the prison of Daugavpils and shot to death there.

I was told by my father in the late autumn of 1944 that the children of Eva Hoff were alive, whereas her own fate was as yet unknown. Years later I heard that Mrs. Hoff was then living in Sweden. The story of her rescue, which she told me in the summer of 1984 at her home in Stockholm, resembles a miracle.

After the German invasion, Eva Hoff had always insisted to the authorities that she was a German. After the first action she repeated this to the ghetto commandant, bribed him with a valuable ring, and as a result was allowed to leave the ghetto together with her children. For her that was the beginning of years of wandering from one hiding place to another. Whoever sheltered her would sooner or later become frightened and ask her to look for a new shelter. First she and the children stayed with nuns in a cloister, then with a farmer in a small house on the outskirts of the city. For a while she lived in a Latvian's one-room apartment together with a young Jew who was also on the run. Janis Bataitis, her former janitor, gave her refuge for a few months, and after that Mr. and Mrs. Celmaraugs sheltered her for a long time. When her presence there seemed to be arousing suspicion, she moved in with a Mrs. Wagner. Here she was arrested by the Gestapo after she had evidently been recognized by somebody. She landed in the Gestapo prison and after that in the Riga Central Prison. Despite all attempts to intimidate her, she continued to insist that she was a German. Together with her children she was taken to the Salaspils concentration camp, where she was forced to leave her children behind when she herself was brought to Stutthof by ship. In April 1945 she was evacuated from Stutthof to Flensburg. During the days of liberation she, once a fine figure of a woman, weighed only 44 kilos [about 97 pounds].

Months later she heard that her children were alive and well. The commandant of Salaspils, Krause, had given her his word to bring the children to acquaintances in Riga and had kept it. The children lived for many years with their foster mother until Mrs. Hoff managed to arrange for them to emigrate from the USSR. Not until 1978 were the three of them united in Stockholm.

Ina Wolpert, the little girl with the blonde braids and the red hood, who used to wait patiently in the ghetto clinic for her father, also survived, as did Dr. Wolpert himself. Ina was saved by Mrs. Rudzitis, whose acquaintance I happened to make in Berlin in the 1980s.

Several times during the weeks after the liberation I saw the electrical engineer Michelson, who owed his life to his quick wits. He had gone underground and had no identification papers. One day he got caught in a police passport checkpoint near the Russian cathedral in the center of Riga. On the spur of the moment, Michelson fled into the church, threw himself on his knees in front of an icon, and stayed motionless in this position as the policemen entered the church. They left him alone, for he wore a long beard at the time, and they took him for a Russian Orthodox believer at prayer. His wife Frieda, whom he married after the war, was one of the very few Jewish women who had miraculously survived the actions in Rumbula in the year 1941. In her book *I Survived Rumbula* she describes her rescue.

One of the few survivors of the Dundaga concentration camp, about which hardly any detailed descriptions exist—simply because there were hardly any survivors—was Abraham Shpungin, who was brought from the Kaiserwald concentration camp to Dundaga. Together with 200 other prisoners he was transported there in a freight train. They had to hold out for three days in a freight car, standing pressed together, without food or drink. Several people died during the journey.

Conditions in the camp were ghastly. The rations consisted of a slice of bread in the morning and watery soup in the evening. For shelter there were tents of pressed cardboard that were sunk into the ground to a depth of 50 centimeters [about 20 inches]. In the summer it was damp in the tents, and in the winter it was cold as ice. The Germans built a giant training area for tanks in Dundaga, using about 1,000 Latvian and 1,000 Lithuanian Jewish men and women, as well as several thousand Hungarian Jewish women whom they had brought there from Auschwitz, and whom Mrs. Sherman and J. Katz had seen in Riga. The Jewish prisoners' work consisted of clearing the forest, and it was far beyond the strength of these weakened and undernourished people. The SS men and the capos beat them and murdered them for the slightest "offense." Shpungin remembers a man who had brought some food to his son and been caught by a patrol. The camp commandant Kröschel tied the man to a post. SS men poured water over him. It was January. They repeated this until the man had frozen to death under a crust of ice.

The mortality rate in Dundaga was appalling, and new transports came almost daily with people meant to replace those who had died. Instead of burying them, Kröschel had the idea of having them sunk into the sea through a hole in the ice. When the ice started to melt in the spring, the corpses floated to the surface. Now Kröschel became frightened that the corpses might be carried across the Baltic Sea and end up in the hands of the Swedish Red Cross. This could have led to inquiries directed at the German government or even to reports in the international press. Therefore he ordered his prisoners to fish the corpses out of the sea. Wading in ice cold water up to their necks, they had to salvage the corpses of their dead comrades and burn them on the beach. Many caught severe colds doing this and died of pneumonia.

Because of this affair, Kröschel was fired from his post and replaced by Hauptscharführer Gustav Sorge ("Iron Gustav"), who had formerly been a cat burglar. Sorge's "career" had begun in 1938 when he ordered a German minister to be buried alive in a concentration camp. After the war he was brought before a Soviet military court which was then sitting in Berlin. He was sentenced to a twenty-five-year prison term—the death penalty had been abolished from the Soviet penal code at that time.

Together with his friend Matiss Frost, Shpungin managed to escape from the camp in the summer of 1944. They had to hide in the hayloft of a barn for nine more months until the end of the war, that is, the day of the German army's capitulation. In later years both of them emigrated to Israel.

Afterword

The end of the war was a happy awakening in a world which greeted us, if not exactly coolly, then at least with a certain reserve. Unconsciously we had prepared ourselves, full of hope, for a new life, although of course we understood that the pain of our terrible losses would overshadow everything. It soon became apparent that those around us had scarcely any interest in our fate. One reason for this was certainly the amount of misfortune that the people in Latvia and the USSR as a whole had themselves had to bear as a result of the war's devastation. In any case, the Jews who had survived the ghetto experienced only the empathy of the Jews around them. There was no material or emotional assistance either for us or for the other Soviet citizens.

We had survived and now we had to go on living. Freedom, which just a short while ago had been a distant dream, had now become a reality. But for a long time to come it remained the stuff of dreams, which intoxicated us—something the people around us couldn't understand at all because they accepted their own freedom as something that was self-evident. They hardly realized that we, the survivors, needed additional weeks and months before we could regain a foothold on real life. Some of us never managed to do so.

In the meantime, life went on around us like a giant conveyor belt. In spite of the war, little had changed, which was a great disappointment for many. They had hoped that a catastrophe of such dimensions, which had ended with the explosion of atom bombs, would bring about a new world with better relationships between human beings. This was a vain hope. We were forced to adjust to the conveyor belt of life, and nobody noticed that we were like invalids who, sitting in wheelchairs, were trying to compete with healthy people.

But could we be fit competitors, wounded as we were in body and soul?

Many were emaciated and had famine edema; countless others had contracted tuberculosis and died of it just after the war or years later; some struggled with its aftereffects until their old age.

The fact that we had lost our relatives years before did not make our losses any easier to bear; our reason understood that they had been slaughtered, but our souls could not come to terms with it. Our souls developed a split that kept us from entering into natural relationships with non-Jews who had come into contact with the Nazi regime. Secretly we always directed at them the question of what attitude they had taken during that period. If they were too young to be suspected of any misdeeds, there was nonetheless the gnawing suspicion that they might be dishonest. Thus the life that we had saved remained tortured by doubts.

We were lonely, we had lost our families and our homes, and we longed for the warmth of a family hearth. Bizarre and generally temporary relationships were struck up between people who had scarcely anything in common except their loneliness. The worst off were the young people and the old ones who were unable to enter into such relationships and shuddered from the cold world around them, while this world showed not the slightest understanding of their problems, because it had no idea of what they were.

Lucky were the young people who were cared for by relatives who had survived. But for those who were entirely alone and without financial means, the bright future they had once hoped for, with all its high-flying dreams, was over once and for all. All that remained was everyday life with its meager earnings and the usual material cares. The old people were entirely alone with their memories and their pain, isolated from the present day and from the people around them, who were striving forward and had their own problems. They didn't care about the old people, not because they were without feelings but because they didn't understand them at all.

In the euphoria of victory during the postwar period, many had hoped there would also be a drastic change in the political life of the USSR, that the USSR could become a free, democratic state. The signs of this which some believed they had detected soon turned out to be an illusion. The Iron Curtain that had opened up a bit during the war fell shut again and hermetically sealed off the country. The KGB continued to rampage, with its old cruelty, until Stalin's death. It arrested and sentenced some of us, so that after the end of the war many Jews, instead of enjoying the freedom they had longed for, only exchanged the German concentration camp for a Soviet one. The Soviet regime looked with mistrust upon the relationships that the Jews of the USSR were forming with Jews in foreign countries, and it showed only a certain conditional trust in its Jewish citizens, which decreased to the same degree that the significance and prestige of the state of Israel increased for the Jews.

Thus in the last analysis freedom and peace had by no means brought the survivors all the things they had hoped for while they were suffering and struggling for their lives. Now they saw they had been clinging to illusions when they believed that after gaining their freedom they would build up a postwar life that would be more or less a continuation of their lives before the war. Hardly anyone managed to do that. Only the ruins of the past remained; life did quickly sprout again from the ruins, but our new existence had little in common with life before the war.

The psychic wounds we had endured were severe. To be sure, there is some truth in the saying that time heals all wounds. The piercing pain felt by the body is replaced by the dull pain of the scar. At the beginning of the 1980s in Israel I made the acquaintance of an elderly lady who had emigrated from Poland to the United States after the war. She told me how she, together with her relatives, had been forced to wander around without respite for years during the German occupation, and how her parents had kept her and her brothers and sisters now in one cellar and now in another. She was the only one who had survived. Although forty-five years had passed since then, tears rolled down her cheeks as she told her story.

It is this grief that has made it so difficult for us to find a way of connecting with life after the war.

Notes

Preface to the English Edition

1. G. Reitlinger, *Die Endlösung: Hitlers Versuch der Ausrottung der Juden Europas 1939–1945* [*The Final Solution: Hitler's Attempt to Exterminate the Jews of Europe, 1939–1945*] (Berlin, 1983), p. 225.

Chapter 1: On the History of the Jews in Latvia

With the exception of well-known cities such as Riga, Berlin, and Moscow, names of places throughout this book use Latvian spellings with German equivalents in parentheses.

1. "Mordechai Dubin," in *Encyclopaedia Judaica* (Jerusalem, 1971), vol. 6, p. 246.
2. As quoted in Max Kaufmann, *Churbn Lettland: Die Vernichtung der Juden Lettlands* [*The Destruction of the Jews of Latvia*] (Munich, 1947), pp. 160–66.
3. Through her personal choice of new releases Mrs. Esther Ettinger, the owner of a large bookstore, influenced the taste of her large circle of customers, who were primarily Jewish. Evidently she enjoyed a good reputation among her Latvian colleagues as well, because when the City Hall caught fire during the battle for Riga at the end of June 1941 and the valuable book collection there was severely damaged, she was summoned from the ghetto to help with the restoration work. However, this recognition of her professional expertise did not save her from the fate that finally overtook nearly all the Jews of Riga.

CHAPTER 2: ON THE POLITICAL SITUATION OF THE JEWS IN LATVIA

1. M. Bobe, S. Levenberg, I. Maor, and Z. Michaeli, eds., *The Jews in Latvia* (Tel Aviv, 1971), p. 274.
2. This incident was told to me personally by E. Salzmann in 1993.
3. Raul Hilberg, *Die Vernichtung der europäischen Juden* [*The Destruction of the European Jews*], 2d ed. (Frankfurt am Main, 1990), p. 420.
4. Stefan Zweig, *Die Welt von gestern* [*The World of Yesterday*] (Stockholm, 1944), pp. 354–94.

CHAPTER 3: TERROR

1. Bundesarchiv microfilm 140490KW-Wpr Aufn. 493784–87.
2. Cf. A. Ezergailis, "Araja komanda" ["The Arajs Commando"], *LPSR Zin. Ak. Vestis* [*Bulletin of the Latvian Academy of Sciences*], no. 10 (495), 1988, pp. 113–30.
3. M. Zvonov, "Po evreiam—ogonj!" ["Aim at the Jews—Fire!"], n.p., 1973.
4. J. E. Kroeger, *So war es* [*So It Was*] (Michelstadt, 1989).
5. M. Levenstein, *Du sollst sterben und nicht leben* [*You Shall Die and Not Live*] (Münster and Hamburg, 1993).
6. Quoted in B. Arklans, J. Dzirkalis, and J. Silabriedis, *Vini bez maskas* [*They Unmasked*] (Riga, 1966), p. 32.
7. G. Reitlinger's statements on pp. 219 and 585 that Jeckeln and a number of other generals were summarily executed is not true.
8. Kaufmann, *Churbn Lettland,* p. 67.
9. H. H. Wilhelm, *Die Einsatzgruppe A der Sicherheitspolizei und des SD 1941/42* [*Mobile Killing Unit A of the Security Police and the SD, 1941–42*] (Frankfurt am Main, 1996).
10. L. Olschwang, "Die Mörder werden noch gebraucht" ("The Murderers Are Still Needed"), *Der Spiegel* [*The Mirror*], no. 17, 1984, p. 123.
11. Miervaldis Birze, *Ari tads bija rits* [*So, Too, Was the Morning*] (Riga, 1972), p. 405.

12. Anna Pazare, *Kaps nav mems* [*The Grave Is Not Silent*] (n.p., 1962).
13. Zvonov, "Po evreiam—ogonj!" p. 133.
14. Arthur Silgailis, *The Latvian Legion* (San Jose, Calif., 1986).
15. Ibid., p. 74.
16. Quoted in J. Silabriedis and B. Arklans, *Politiskie begli bez maskas* [*Political Fugitives Unmasked*] (Riga, 1965), p. 161.
17. A. Bilmanis, *A History of Latvia* (Westport, Conn., 1951).
18. Kaufmann, *Churbn Lettland,* p. 68.

Chapter 4: Imprisonment

1. Wilhelm, "Die Einsatzgruppe A," p. 180.
2. Ezergailis, "Araja komanda," p. 120.
3. A. Berzs, *Dokumentu parbaude* [*Examination of the Documents*] (Tukums, Latvia, 1993), and N. Kabanov, "Pod znakom SS" ("Under the Sign of the SS"), *Novoe Russkoe Slovo* [*New Russian Word*], 3–4 April 1993.
4. K. Kangeris, *Baltische Emigranten und ihre "Befreiungskomitees" in Europa unterm Hakenkreuz. Okkupation und Kollaboration 1938–1945* [*Baltic Emigrants and Their "Liberation Committees" in Europe under the Swastika: Occupation and Collaboration, 1938–1945*] (Berlin and Heidelberg, 1994).
5. J. E. Kroeger, *Eine baltische Illusion* [*A Baltic Illusion*] (Lüneburg, 1974), p. 59.
6. *Mes apsudzam* [*We Accuse: Documents and Materials about the Crimes of Hitler's Occupying Forces and Latvian Bourgeois Nationalists in the Soviet Socialist Republic of Latvia, 1941–1945*] (Riga, 1965), pp. 92 and 94.

Chapter 5: The Ghetto Is Established

1. As quoted in G. Hausner, *Die Vernichtung der Juden* [*The Extermination of the Jews*] (Munich, 1979), p. 88.
2. Ibid.

Chapter 6: Daily Life in the Ghetto

1. "S. Dubnow," in *Encyclopaedia Judaica,* vol. 6, p. 262.
2. P. Vigants, "Stigas vel skaneja" ["The Strings Were Still Sounding"], in *Salaspils naves nometne* [*The Salaspils Death Camp*] (Riga, 1963).

Chapter 7: Extermination

1. D. Silbermann, *I ty eto videl* [*You Saw It Too*], ed. Cultural Center for Soviet Refugees (New York, 1989), p. 55.

Chapter 8: The Small Ghetto

1. Silbermann, *I ty eto videl.*
2. Letter from Professor Klaus J. Hermann, Concordia University, Montreal, to the author, 4 January 1991.
3. J. Wolff, *Mit Bibel und Bebel. Ein Gedenkbuch* [*With the Bible and Bebel: A Book of Commemoration*], ed. Hans Lamm (Bonn, 1981), p. 29.
4. Partial list of names of the Jews of the Small Ghetto executed in the retaliatory action of October 31, 1942 (from Kaufmann, *Churbn Lettland,* p. 209):

Amikushansky
Becker
Berlin, Mejer
Botvinkin
Cukerman
Dannemann
Eljaschewitz
Firk
Fischelsohn, A.
Fischelsohn, Ch.
Freidberg, Boris
Ginsburg, Boris (physician)
Gor, Hirsch
Gordin, Monia
Harrik
Jocin, Hirsch
Klempmann
Kramer, Bubi
Lat, Ilja
Lewi, H.
Lewi, Izrail
Lewin, Nochum
Liberman
Moisesch (teacher)
Noim Sr. (dentist)
Okun, Owsei
Orelowitz, Scholem
Ospowat

Pitel, Rafail
Polonski, Hirsch
Pomeranz brothers
Raicin, Asja
Stein, Israil
Steinbock, Sascha
Wassermann
Winnik, Ch.
Zagawalow

5. Partial list of names of the Jewish ghetto policemen shot in the Small Ghetto in the retaliatory action (from Kaufmann, *Churbn Lettland,* p. 182):

Aschmann
Bag, I.
Blankenstein, Ziga
Blumenthal (jurist)
Blumenthal, Georg
Damski, Meilach
Dubin, Simon
Freidberg
Genkin
Glaser, Moische
Goldberg, Naum
Golodec
Grikpetz
Gurewitz, Sascha
Israelowitsch
Kahn
Kölmann, David
Lewit (from Kovno)
Liwschitz, Boris
Lurie
Marianowski
Mayer (from Germany)
Mincowski
Nathan, Anatoli
Paik
Pommeranz
Safro, Senia
Schabelstock, Ch.
Schatz, Schmaja (from Kovno)
Schlomowitz
Seligsohn
Steinbock
Tankel
Ullmann

6. Kaufmann, *Churbn Lettland,* p. 183.
7. M. Vestermanis, "Der lettische Anteil an der Endlösung" ["The Latvian Contribution to the Final Solution"], in *Schatten der Vergangenheit* [*Shadows of the Past*], ed. U. Backes, R. Jesse, and R. Zitelman (Berlin, 1990), pp. 426 ff.
8. Zeugenaussage von H. Krützfeld im Prozess gegen Karl Tollkühn [Testimony of H. Krützfeld in the Trial of Karl Tollkühn], Landgericht Hamburg [State Court of Hamburg], Verfahren [case] 141 JS 534/60, p. 406.

Chapter 9: The Large German Ghetto

1. R. Andreas-Friedrich, "Das Ende einer Gemeinde" ["The End of a Community"], in *Wir haben es gesehen* [*We Saw It*], ed. G. Schoenberner (Wiesbaden, 1981), p. 285.
2. Anonymous nurse in "Die innere Front—eine Krankenschwester berichtet" ["The Inner Front: A Nurse's Report"], in *Wir haben es gesehen,* p. 313.
3. E. Kogon, *Der SS-Staat* [*The SS State*] (Munich, 1988), p. 244.
4. Alfred Winter, *Affidavit Alfred Winter, 15 October 1947,* IMT, Nuremberg Document Nr. 5448.
5. Quoted from Kogon, *Der SS-Staat,* p. 243.
6. Interrogation protocol of Viktors Arajs.
7. Cf. I. Levinson, *The Untold Story* (Johannesburg, 1958).
8. Cf. Kogon, *Der SS-Stadt.*
9. Cf. Hilberg, *Die Vernichtung der europäischen Juden.*
10. Wolff, *Mit Bibel und Bebel,* p. 29.
11. Kaufmann, *Churbn Lettland,* p. 140; Gertrude Schneider, "The Riga Ghetto 1941–1943" (Ph.D. diss., City University of New York, 1973); Wolff, *Mit Bibel und Bebel,* p. 27.
12. Schneider, "Riga Ghetto," p. 93.
13. H. Sherman, *Zwischen Tag und Dunkel* [*Between Day and Darkness*] (Frankfurt am Main, 1984), p. 77.
14. Ibid., p. 65.
15. Betty Happ, *Bortom all mänsklighet* [*Beyond All Humanity*], trans. Nils Homberg (Stockholm, 1945).

Chapter 10: The Kaiserwald Concentration Camp

1. Wolff, *Mit Bibel und Bebel,* p. 36.
2. Hannah Arendt, *Elemente und Ursprünge totaler Herrschaft* [*The Elements and Origins of Totalitarian Rule*] (Frankfurt am Main, 1975).
3. Winter, *Affidavit Alfred Winter, 15 October 1947,* p. 6.
4. Wolff, *Mit Bibel und Bebel,* p. 44.
5. Sherman, *Zwischen Tag und Dunkel,* p. 87.
6. Reitlinger, *Die Endlösung,* p. 327.

7. Kaufmann, *Churbn Lettland,* p. 347.
8. Professor L. Javorkowsky, conversation with the author, Berlin, 1994. This memory was corrected by another survivor, who remembers landing in Danzig, not Stettin.
9. M. Birze, *Ari tads bija rits* [*So, Too, Was the Morning*] (Riga, 1972).
10. Ibid.
11. Ibid.
12. Josef Katz, *Erinnerungen eines Überlebenden* (Kiel, 1988); published in English as *One Who Came Back: The Diary of a Jewish Survivor* (New York, 1973).
13. Hilberg, *Die Vernichtung der europäischen Juden,* p. 379.
14. Sherman, *Zwischen Tag und Dunkel,* p. 73.
15. Fritz Sherwitz was, according to A. Levine, a Jew from Lithuania whose real name was Elke Sirewitz and who had been brought up by Fritz Erler, a German. In Gertrude Schneider, ed., *The Unfinished Road* (New York, 1991).
16. K. D. Erdmann, "Die Zeit der Weltkriege" ["The Era of the World Wars"], in *Handbuch der Deutschen Geschichte* [*Handbook of German History*], vol. 4, ed. Bruno Gebhard (Stuttgart, 1976), p. 298.

Chapter 11: Genocide in Latvia

1. S. Zeitlin, *Dokumentalnaja istoriya evrejev Rigi* [*A Documentary History of the Jews of Riga*] ([no city,] Israel, 1989), p. 156.
2. S. Weinberg, in D. Aschoff, *In der Hölle des Ostens. Der Weinberg-Bericht* [*In the Hell of the East: The Weinberg Report*], ed. D. Aschoff. Quellen und Forschungen zur Geschichte der Stadt Münster, Neue Folge [Sources and Research on the History of the City of Münster, New Series] (Münster, 1986).
3. E. Leiser, *Leben nach dem Überleben* [*Life after Survival*] (Königstein/Ts., 1982), p. 158.
4. W. Scheffler, *Judenverfolgung im Dritten Reich 1933–1945* [*The Persecution of the Jews in the Third Reich, 1933– 1945*], Zur Politik und Zeitgeschichte 4/5 [On Politics and Modern History 4–5] (Berlin, 1966), p. 49

Chapter 12: Flight

1. On May 22, 1983, the Department for the Righteous of Yad Vashem decided to confer the Medal of the Righteous upon Arturs and Erna Krumins and their daughters as well as Elza Mieleika and Lina Pilsroze. The Medal of the Righteous was presented to Ilga Krumins in September 1995 by the Israeli ambassador to Latvia, the others being no longer alive.
2. Ilga's room had an architectural feature that could serve as a hiding place in case of emergency, for example, a house search. The wall between her room and her parents' adjacent bedroom was a fire wall about 40 centimeters [nearly 16 inches] thick, which it was very unusual to have as a dividing wall inside an apartment. Another unusual feature was the two sets of double doors connecting the two rooms, with a space between them that provided sufficient space for two men to hide. Such double doors can still be found today as entry doors to apartments in old houses. A large wardrobe stood in front of the door in the Kruminses' bedroom, and the door was visible behind it. In an emergency, we would only have had to open the door in Ilga's bedroom, slip between the two sets of double doors, and lock the door from inside. If anyone had wanted to know what was behind the locked door, the answer would have been, "The Kruminses' bedroom. But there's no point in opening the door, because behind it is a large wardrobe." A glance from the Kruminses' room would have confirmed the truth of this statement: there stood the wardrobe, and the double door could be seen behind it. Who could have suspected that it was not the same double door as the one in Ilga's room?

Chapter 13: Freedom

1. Silbermann, *I ty eto videl.*

Bibliography

Ainsztein, R. *Jewish Resistance in Nazi-Occupied Eastern Europe.* New York, 1974.

Aizsilnieks, A. *Latvijas saimniecibas vesture 1914–1945* [*A History of the Economy of Latvia, 1914–1945*]. Sandbyberg, 1968.

Altman, J. "Zhisn i sudba" ["Life and Fate"], *Literaturnaja Gaseta* [*Literary Gazette*], no. 20 (5294), 16 May 1990.

Andreas-Friedrich, R. "Die innere Front" ["The Inner Front"]. In *Wir haben es gesehen* [*We Have Seen It*], ed. G. Schoenberner. Wiesbaden, 1981.

Arendt, Hannah. *Elemente und Ursprünge totaler Herrschaft* [*The Elements and Origins of Totalitarian Rule*]. Frankfurt am Main, 1975.

Arklans, B., J. Dzirkalis, and J. Silabriedis. *Vini bez maskas* [*They Unmasked*]. Riga, 1966.

Aschoff, D., ed. *In der Hölle des Ostens. Der Weinberg-Bericht* [*In the Hell of the East: The Weinberg Report*]. Quellen und Forschungen zur Geschichte der Stadt Münster, Neue Folge [Sources and Research on the History of the City of Münster, New Series]. Münster, 1986.

Avotins, E., J. Dzirkalis, and V. Petersons. *Kas ir Daugavas vanagi?* [*Who Are the Daugava Falcons?*] Riga, 1962.

Berzs, A. *Dokumentu parbaude* [*Examination of the Documents*]. Tukums, Latvia, 1993.

Bilmanis, A. *A History of Latvia.* Westport, Conn., 1951.

Birze, Miervaldis. *Ari tads bija rits* [*So, Too, Was the Morning*]. Riga, 1972.

———. *Lai atgriestos* [*In Order to Return*]. Riga, 1984.

Bobé, M., S. Levenberg, I. Maor, and Z. Michael, eds. *The Jews in Latvia.* Tel Aviv, 1971.

Drobisch, K., R. Goguel, W. Müller, and H. Dohle. *Juden unterm Hakenkreuz* [*Jews under the Swastika*]. Frankfurt am Main, 1973.

Erdmann, K. D. "Die Zeit der Weltkriege" ["The Era of the World Wars"]. In *Handbuch der Deutschen Geschichte* [*Handbook of German History*], vol. 4, ed. B. Gebhard. Stuttgart, 1976.

Ezergailis, A. "Araja komanda" ["The Arajs Commando"]. *LPSR Zin. Ak. Vestis* [*Bulletin of the Latvian Academy of Sciences*], no. 10 (495), 1988, pp. 113–30.

Farago, L. *Martin Bormann and the Fourth Reich.* New York, 1974.

Förster, G. *Der Zweite Weltkrieg. Dokumente* [*World War II: Documents*]. Selected and introduced by O. Groehler. Berlin, 1974.

Gilbert, M. *Endlösung. Die Vertreibung und Vernichtung der Juden* [*The Final Solution: The Expulsion and Extermination of the Jews*]. Reinbek bei Hamburg, 1982.

Goral, Arie, ed. *Vernichtung im Ghetto Riga und Aufstand im Warschauer Ghetto. Eine Dokumentation* [*Extermination in the Riga Ghetto and Resistance in the Warsaw Ghetto: A Documentation*]. Hamburg, [1987].

Gordin, F. *Dienas un Nedienas* [*Days and Misfortunes*]. Stockholm, 1988.

Grinbergs, T. *Rakstu krajums 100. dzimumdienas atcerei* [*A Collection of Writings to Commemorate the Archbishop's Centenary*]. Minneapolis, 1970.

Happ, Betty. *Bortom all mänsklighet. (Övers. för tyska manuskript av Nils Homberg)* [*Beyond All Humanity*]. Translation from the German by Nils Homberg. Stockholm, 1945.

Hausner, G. *Die Vernichtung der Juden* [*The Extermination of the Jews*]. Munich, 1979.

Hehn, J. von. *Die Umsiedlung der baltischen Deutschen — das letzte Kapitel baltischdeutscher Geschichte* [*The Resettlement of the Baltic Germans: The Last Chapter of Baltic German History*]. Marburg an der Lahn, 1984.

Heinicke, H. P. *Berlins unheimliche Sehenswürdigkeiten* [*Berlin's Sinister Sights*]. Berlin, n.d.

Hilberg, Raul. *Die Vernichtung der europäischen Juden* [*The Destruction of the European Jews*]. 2d ed. Frankfurt am Main, 1990.

International Tracing Service. *Vorläufiges Verzeichnis der Konzentrationslager und deren Außenkommandos sowie andere Haftstätten unter dem Reichsführer-SS in Deutschland und deutsch besetzten Gebieten 1933–*

1945 [*An Interim List of Concentration Camps and Their External Commandos and Other Places of Confinement under the Reichsführer-SS in Germany and Areas Occupied by the Germans, 1933–1945*]. Arolsen, 1969.

Javorkowsky, L. Conversation with the author. Berlin, 1994.

Kabanov, N. "Pod znakom SS" ["Under the Sign of the SS"]. *Novoe Russkoe Slovo* [*New Russian Word*], 3–4 April 1993.

Kangeris, K. *Baltische Emigranten und ihre "Befreiungskomitees" in Europa unterm Hakenkreuz. Okkupation und Kollaboration 1938–1945* [*Baltic Emigrants and Their "Liberation Committees" in Europe under the Swastika: Occupation and Collaboration, 1938–1945*]. Bundesarchiv, Hüthig Verlagsgemeinschaft. Berlin and Heidelberg, 1994.

Katz, Josef. *Erinnerungen eines Überlebenden.* Kiel, 1988. Published in English as *One Who Came Back: The Diary of a Jewish Survivor.* New York, 1973.

Kaufmann, Max. *Churbn Lettland: Die Vernichtung der Juden Lettlands* [*The Destruction of the Jews of Lavia*]. Munich, 1947.

Kempner, Robert, M. W. *SS im Kreuzverhör* [*The SS under Cross-Examination*]. Nördlingen, 1987.

Klaus-Goldberg, Margarete. Conversation with the author. Berlin, 1994.

Klee, E., W. Dreßen, and V. Rieß. *Schöne Zeiten. Judenmord aus der Sicht der Täter und Gaffer* [*Good Times: The Murder of the Jews from the Viewpoint of the Perpetrators and Spectators*]. Frankfurt am Main, 1988.

Kogon, E. *Der SS-Staat* [*The SS State*]. Munich, 1988.

Kroeger, J. E. *Eine baltische Illusion* [*A Baltic Illusion*]. Lüneburg, 1974.

———. *So war es* [*So It Was*]. Michelstadt, 1989.

Lancmann, I. Unpublished letter to the journal *Novoe Vremja* [*New Time*] written in January 1961. Central State Archive of the Ministry of Internal Affairs of the Latvian SSR, Riga.

Leiser, E. *Leben nach dem Überleben* [*Life after Survival*]. Königstein/Ts., 1982.

Levenstein, M. *Du sollst sterben und nicht leben* [*You Shall Die and Not Live*]. Münster and Hamburg, 1993.

Levine, A. "The Jewish SS Officer." In *The Unfinished Road,* ed. Gertrude Schneider. New York, 1991.

Levinson, I. *The Untold Story.* Johannesburg, 1958.

The Lutheran Church of Latvia behind the Iron Curtain. Amsterdam, 1948.

Marnitz, H. *Nordlicht über der Düna* [*Northern Lights over the Daugava*]. Michelstadt, 1991.

Mes apsudzam [*We Accuse: Documents and Materials about the Crimes of Hitler's Occupying Forces and Latvian Bourgeois Nationalists in the Soviet Socialist Republic of Latvia, 1941–1945*]. Riga, 1965.

Michelson, M. Letter to the author. 1994.

Myllynieni, S. *Die baltische Krise 1938–1941* [*The Baltic Crisis, 1938–1941*]. Stuttgart, 1979.

———. *Die Neuordnung der baltischen Länder 1941–1944* [*The Reorganization of the Baltic Countries, 1941–1944*]. Helsinki, 1973.

Olschwang, L. "Die Mörder werden noch gebraucht" ["The Murderers Are Still Needed"]. *Der Spiegel* [*The Mirror*], no. 17, 1984, p. 123.

Rauch, G. von. *Geschichte der baltischen Staaten* [*History of the Baltic States*]. Munich, 1977.

Reitlinger, G. *Die Endlösung. Hitlers Versuch der Ausrottung der Juden Europas 1939–1945* [*The Final Solution: Hitler's Attempt to Exterminate the Jews of Europe, 1939–1945*]. Berlin, 1983.

Rückerl, A., ed. *NS-Vernichtungslager im Spiegel deutscher Strafprozesse* [*National Socialist Death Camps as Mirrored in German Criminal Trials*]. Munich, 1979.

Salzmann, E. Conversation with the author. Berlin, 1994.

Sauer, P., ed. *Dokumente über die Verfolgung der jüdischen Bürger in Baden-Württemberg durch das nationalsozialistische Regime 1933–1945* [*Documents Concerning the Persecution of Jewish Citizens in Baden-Württemberg by the National Socialist Regime, 1933–1945*], part 2. Stuttgart, 1966.

Scheffler, W. *Judenverfolgung im Dritten Reich 1933–1945* [*The Persecution of the Jews in the Third Reich, 1933–1945*]. Zur Politik und Zeitgeschichte 4/5 [On Politics and Modern History 4–5]. Berlin, 1966.

Schneider, Gertrude. "The Riga Ghetto 1941–1943." Ph.D. diss., City University of New York, 1973.

———, ed. *The Unfinished Road.* New York, 1991.

Schoenberner, G., ed. *Wir haben es gesehen: Augenzeugenberichte über Ter-*

ror und Judenverfolgung im Dritten Reich [*We Saw It: Eyewitness Reports on Terror and the Persecution of the Jews in the Third Reich*]. Wiesbaden, 1981.

Sherman, H. *Zwischen Tag und Dunkel* [*Between Day and Darkness*]. Frankfurt am Main, 1984.

Sievers, L. *Juden in Deutschland* [*Jews in Germany*]. Hamburg, 1978.

Silabriedis, J., and B. Arklans. *Politiskie begli bez maskas* [*Political Fugitives Unmasked*]. Riga, 1965.

Silbermann, D. *I ty eto videl* [*You Saw It Too*]. Edited by the Cultural Center for Soviet Refugees. New York, 1989.

Spekke, A. *History of Latvia.* Stockholm, 1951.

Tory, A. *Surviving the Holocaust.* Cambridge, Mass., 1990.

Vestermanis, M. "Der lettische Anteil an der Endlösung" ["The Latvian Contribution to the Final Solution"]. In *Schatten der Vergangenheit* [*Shadows of the Past*], ed. U. Backes, R. Jesse, and R. Zitelman, pp. 426 ff. Berlin, 1990.

Vigants, P. "Stigas vel skaneja" ["The Strings Were Still Sounding"]. In *Salaspils naves nometne* [*The Salaspils Death Camp*]. Riga, 1963.

Vogt, H. *Schuld oder Verhängnis?* [*Blame or Fate?*] Frankfurt am Main, 1962.

Wilhelm, H. H. *Die Einsatzgruppe A der Sicherheitspolizei und des SD 1941–42* [*Mobile Killing Unit A of the Security Police and the SD, 1941–42*]. Frankfurt am Main, 1996.

Winter, Alfred. *Affidavit Alfred Winter, 15 October 1947*, IMT, Nuremberg Document Nr. 5448.

Wolff, J. *Mit Bibel und Bebel. Ein Gedenkbuch* [*With the Bible and Bebel: A Book of Commemoration*]. Edited by Hans Lamm. Bonn, 1981.

Zeitlin, S. *Dokumentalnaja istoriya evrejev Rigi* [*A Documentary History of the Jews of Riga*]. [No city,] Israel, 1989.

Zweig, S. *Die Welt von gestern* [*The World of Yesterday*]. Stockholm, 1944.

Index

Jewish Lives

THOMAS TOIVI BLATT
From the Ashes of Sobibor: A Story of Survival

HERTHA FEINER
Before Deportation: Letters from a Mother to Her Daughters, January 1939–December 1942

IDA FINK
A Scrap of Time and Other Stories

LALA FISHMAN AND STEVEN WEINGARTNER
Lala's Story: A Memoir of the Holocaust

LISA FITTKO
Solidarity and Treason: Resistance and Exile, 1933–1940

PETER FURST
Don Quixote in Exile

SALOMEA GENIN
Shayndl and Salomea: From Lemberg to Berlin

RICHARD GLAZAR
Trap with a Green Fence: Survival in Treblinka

ROBERT B. GOLDMANN
Wayward Threads

HENRYK GRYNBERG
Children of Zion

INGEBORG HECHT
Invisible Walls *and* To Remember Is to Heal

DAN JACOBSON
Heshel's Kingdom

ERICH LEYENS AND LOTTE ANDOR
Years of Estrangement

RUTH LIEPMAN
Maybe Luck Isn't Just Chance

ARNOŠT LUSTIG
Children of the Holocaust
The Unloved (From the Diary of Perla S.)

LIANNA MILLU
Smoke over Birkenau

ZOFIA NAŁKOWSKA
Medallions

BERNHARD PRESS
The Murder of the Jews in Latvia, 1941–1945

ARMIN SCHMID AND RENATE SCHMID
Lost in a Labyrinth of Red Tape

WIKTORIA ŚLIWOWSKA, ED.
The Last Eyewitnesses: Children of the Holocaust Speak

ISAIAH SPIEGEL
Ghetto Kingdom: Tales of the Łódź Ghetto

ARNON TAMIR
A Journey Back: Injustice and Restitution

JIŘI WEIL
Life with a Star
Mendelssohn Is on the Roof

BOGDAN WOJDOWSKI
Bread for the Departed